SHAH MOHAMMED

Sub-Branding Playbook

Winning Strategies for Targeted Growth

Contents

1

Introduction

I n today's dynamic and competitive business environment, brands constantly seek ways to differentiate themselves, connect with their target audiences, and achieve sustainable growth. One strategy that has gained significant traction and proven to be effective is sub-branding.

Sub-branding refers to the practice of creating distinct and separate brand identities within the umbrella of a larger parent brand. It is a way for companies to extend their brand presence, target specific market segments, or differentiate their offerings to meet diverse customer needs.

Sub-branding allows companies to leverage the parent brand's reputation, resources, and equity while developing a unique identity and value proposition for a specific product, service, or market segment.

The purpose of sub-branding varies based on the company's objectives. It could target a new audience, enter a new market, address specific customer needs, or capitalise on emerging trends. Sub-brands often have their own brand name, visual identity, messaging, and positioning, which are carefully crafted to resonate with the target audience and differentiate them from the parent brand and competitors.

Successful sub-branding requires a deep understanding of the target market, consumer preferences, and competitive landscape. It involves careful market research, brand positioning, and messaging to ensure the sub-brand effectively communicates its unique value proposition and resonates with the intended audience. Consistency with the parent brand's values, reputation, and overall brand architecture is crucial to maintaining coherence and avoiding diluting brand equity.

Throughout this book, we will explore various sub-branding strategies and provide real-world examples to illustrate their effectiveness in achieving targeted growth objectives. By examining successful sub-branding initiatives, we will uncover the underlying principles, best practices, and key considerations that drive the successful implementation of sub-brands.

Sub-brand Examples

Coca-Cola and Diet Coke: Coca-Cola, a renowned beverage brand, introduced Diet Coke as a sub-brand to cater to consumers looking for a sugar-free alternative. Diet Coke has its own distinct packaging, branding, and marketing strategies while leveraging the reputation and distribution network of Coca-Cola. By creating this sub-brand, Coca-Cola was able to tap into the growing demand for healthier beverage options and target a specific audience seeking low-calorie alternatives.

Toyota and Lexus: Toyota, a leading automobile manufacturer, established the luxury sub-brand Lexus to target the premium automotive market. Lexus operates as a separate brand with its own lineup of high-end vehicles, marketing campaigns, and dealership networks. While Toyota focuses on offering reliable and affordable vehicles, Lexus positions itself as a luxury brand with superior craftsmanship, advanced technology, and exceptional customer service. Toyota successfully entered the luxury segment by creating Lexus and expanding its market reach.

The Power of Sub-brands

Sub-brands provide a framework for companies to strategically address the unique needs and preferences of specific market segments or customer niches. Here is a breakdown of how sub-brands can help businesses reach their targeted growth success:

1. Tailored Brand Experiences: Sub-brands enable companies to create tailored brand experiences for different market segments. By developing distinct sub-brands with their own positioning, personality, and visual identity, businesses can curate unique experiences that resonate deeply with specific target audiences. This customization fosters a stronger connection with customers and increases their engagement with the brand.

2. Deepened Market Penetration: Sub-brands facilitate deepened market penetration by focusing on specific market segments. Rather than adopting a one-size-fits-all approach, businesses can leverage sub-brands to penetrate niche markets more effectively. Each sub-brand is designed to appeal directly to its target segment's preferences, needs, and aspirations, thereby increasing market share and customer loyalty within those specific markets.

3. Targeted Messaging and Communication: Sub-brands allow targeted messaging and communication strategies. With distinct sub-brands, companies can tailor their messaging to resonate with each specific target audience's language, values, and interests. This customization enables more precise and compelling communication that captures the attention of the intended market segment, resulting in stronger brand awareness, recall, and engagement.

4. Product/Service Differentiation: Sub-brands enable businesses to differentiate their products or services within specific market segments. By creating sub-brands that address unique customer needs or offer specialized solutions, companies can stand out from competitors and position themselves as industry leaders within their chosen niches. This differentiation can increase customer preference and loyalty as customers recognize the value and relevance of the sub-brand's offerings.

5. Portfolio Expansion and Market Adaptation: Sub-brands provide opportunities for portfolio expansion and market adaptation. Businesses can introduce new sub-brands to enter untapped markets, expand into complementary product or service categories, or adapt to evolving customer preferences. Sub-brands allow flexibility and agility in responding to market demands, enabling businesses to capture new growth opportunities and stay ahead of the competition.

7. Risk Mitigation and Experimentation: Sub-brands offer a level of risk mitigation and experimentation for businesses. Instead of jeopardizing the reputation and equity of a single overarching brand, companies can launch sub-brands to explore new markets, test new product concepts, or target specific customer segments. Sub-brands act as separate entities that can be fine-tuned and adjusted without impacting the core brand, allowing for controlled experimentation and adaptation.

8. Expansion into New Market Segments: Sub-brands allow businesses to expand into new market segments that may have different demographics, behaviours, or preferences. By creating sub-brands that specifically target these segments, companies can effectively tap into new customer bases and unlock growth opportunities in previously untapped markets.

9. Enhanced Brand Image and Reputation: Sub-brands can enhance a company's overall brand image and reputation by showcasing its ability to cater to diverse customer needs. When customers see that a company has sub-brands dedicated to different market segments, it conveys a sense of expertise, specialization, and commitment to meeting customer expectations. This, in turn, strengthens the overall brand image and can positively impact market perception.

10. Market Segmentation Leadership: Creating sub-brands can position a company as a market leader within specific segments. Companies can establish themselves as experts and pioneers within those segments by offering specialised sub-brands that address niche market needs. This leadership status fosters customer trust and credibility and can result in increased market share and competitive advantage.

11. Brand Extension and Cross-Selling Opportunities: Sub-brands can create opportunities for brand extension and cross-selling. Once a sub-brand has gained traction and built a loyal customer base within a specific market segment, it opens doors for introducing new products or services under the same sub-brand. This facilitates cross-selling and allows the company to leverage the existing brand equity to expand its offerings.

12. Agility in Brand Positioning: Sub-brands allow businesses to adjust their brand positioning according to market dynamics. As market trends evolve or new segments emerge, companies can launch new sub-brands or reposition existing ones to capture the changing landscape. This agility allows businesses to stay relevant, adapt to customer demands, and remain competitive over time.

14. Localization and Cultural Relevance: Sub-brands can enable companies to localize their offerings and establish cultural relevance in different geographic markets. By creating sub-brands tailored to specific regions or cultures, businesses can address local preferences, customs, and sensibilities, which can enhance customer acceptance and market penetration in those areas.

15. Long-Term Growth Potential: Sub-brands contribute to long-term growth potential by allowing companies to expand their reach, diversify their customer base, and capitalize on emerging trends. By investing in sub-brands, businesses can cultivate sustainable growth strategies that extend beyond the limitations of a single brand or product line.

16. Foster Innovation and Experimentation: Sub-brands offer brands the opportunity to innovate and experiment with new products, services, and marketing approaches. By targeting different market segments, brands can explore diverse strategies, test new concepts, and gather valuable insights that can inform their overall brand strategy and drive future growth.

By strategically leveraging sub-brands, businesses can effectively navigate the complexities of diverse markets, connect with specific target audiences, and achieve sustainable growth in today's competitive landscape.

Putting Users First: A Key Factor in Sub-Branding Decisions

Adopting a user-centric perspective rather than a product- or company-centred approach is crucial when making sub-branding decisions. Failing to consider the needs, preferences, and perceptions of your target audience can result in marketing myopia and hinder the success of your sub-branding efforts.

1. **Understanding User Needs:** User-centric thinking places the focus on understanding the specific needs and desires of your target audience. By conducting thorough market research, analyzing consumer behaviour, and engaging in customer feedback, you can gain valuable insights into what drives your users and how your brand can fulfil their expectations. This understanding forms the foundation for developing a sub-brand that effectively targets and resonates with your intended users.

2. **Tailoring Sub-Brands to User Segments:** Each market segment or user group may have distinct preferences, aspirations, and pain points. By adopting a user-centric approach, you can identify these segments and create sub-brands that specifically cater to their unique needs. This level of customization allows you to craft compelling value propositions, tailored messaging, and differentiated experiences that resonate with your target users, ultimately increasing their engagement and loyalty.

3. **Avoiding Marketing Myopia:** Product-centered or company-centred thinking often leads to marketing myopia, where organizations become too internally focused and fail to recognize evolving customer demands. By solely considering your products or company identity, you may overlook the changing dynamics of the market, emerging trends, or evolving user preferences. User-centric thinking helps you stay attuned to the needs of your audience, ensuring that your sub-brand remains relevant, competitive, and aligned with your users' expectations.

4. **Creating Meaningful Connections:** Sub-brands that are developed with a user-centric mindset have a greater potential to create meaningful connections with consumers. By addressing their pain points, aspira-

tions, and desires, you can position your sub-brand as a solution that resonates on an emotional level. Building these emotional connections enhances brand loyalty, advocacy, and long-term customer relationships, ultimately driving the success of your sub-brand and contributing to overall brand growth.

5. **Driving Customer-Centric Innovation:** User-centric thinking encourages continuous innovation driven by customer insights. By actively engaging with your target audience, soliciting feedback, and involving them in the co-creation process, you can uncover new opportunities for growth, refine your sub-brand offerings, and deliver exceptional customer experiences. This iterative approach ensures that your sub-brand remains responsive to evolving user needs and preferences, maintaining its relevance and competitive edge in the market.

"Sub-branding decisions should always be driven by what your customers need, not by what your brand or company wants. Putting the customer at the centre of your sub-branding strategy ensures that you deliver the value, relevance, and experiences that resonate with their unique needs and desires."

Ultimately, putting the user at the centre of your sub-branding strategy enables you to build strong, long-lasting relationships and establish a competitive advantage in the marketplace.

Challenges

While sub-branding can bring numerous benefits, there are also several challenges associated with this strategy that businesses should be aware of:

1. Brand Dilution: Introducing multiple sub-brands within a brand portfolio can potentially dilute the overall brand equity and messaging. Customers may perceive the brand as fragmented or lacking a clear identity if not managed carefully. Maintaining consistency across sub-

brands while differentiating them enough to appeal to specific segments is a delicate balancing act.

2. Cannibalization: Sub-brands run the risk of cannibalizing sales from existing products/services within the brand portfolio. If customers perceive the sub-brand as a substitute for an established offering, it can lead to internal competition and decreased overall sales. Effective market research and strategic positioning are necessary to ensure that sub-brands complement existing offerings rather than compete with them.

3. Operational Complexity: Managing multiple sub-brands can increase operational complexity. Each sub-brand requires its own marketing strategies, messaging, product development, and customer support. The resources and efforts needed to maintain and promote multiple sub-brands should be carefully allocated to avoid overstretching the organization's capabilities.

4. Consumer Perception and Confusion: While sub-brands aim to provide clarity, there is a risk of confusing consumers if the sub-brands are not distinct or clearly differentiated. Customers may struggle to understand the unique value proposition of each sub-brand or the relationship between the sub-brand and the parent brand. Effective branding and communication strategies are essential to address this challenge.

5. Resource Allocation: Launching and maintaining sub-brands requires additional investments in marketing, branding, product development, and customer support. Businesses must carefully evaluate the financial implications and allocate resources accordingly to ensure the success of both the sub-brands and the core brand. Limited resources can pose a challenge when trying to balance the growth of sub-brands while sustaining the overall brand's strength.

6. Brand Reputation Management: If a sub-brand encounters issues or receives negative feedback, it can potentially impact the reputation of the parent brand. Close monitoring and swift action are necessary to address any reputational risks and ensure that the sub-brands maintain the desired quality and customer experience.

By acknowledging and addressing these challenges, businesses can develop effective strategies to mitigate risks and maximize the benefits of sub-branding.

Overview of the book

The book "Sub-Branding Playbook: Winning Strategies for Targeted Growth" is a valuable resource that explores sub-branding and its role in achieving targeted growth and market success. It introduces the concept of sub-branding as a powerful tool in brand strategy, allowing companies to segment markets, target specific customer groups, and expand their brand's reach. The book emphasizes the importance of clarity and alignment in sub-branding strategies, ensuring that sub-brands align with the overall brand positioning and value proposition. The book provides insights into successful sub-branding initiatives through real-world case studies, offering practical, actionable strategies for leveraging sub-brands to achieve targeted growth. By examining the considerations and criteria for developing sub-brands, readers can understand how sub-brands contribute to brand differentiation, customer targeting, and market expansion. Overall, the "Sub-Branding Playbook" empowers readers to develop and implement effective sub-branding strategies that resonate with their target audiences and drive long-term business success.

Target Readers

The book "Sub-Branding Playbook: Winning Strategies for Targeted Growth" is designed to cater to a diverse range of professionals who are interested in leveraging sub-brands as a strategic tool to achieve targeted growth. The primary target audience for the book includes:

1. **Entrepreneurs:** Entrepreneurs who are starting their own businesses or

looking to expand their existing ventures can benefit from the book's insights. It provides them with a framework for developing sub-branding strategies that effectively target specific market segments, differentiate their offerings, and drive growth.

2. **Marketers:** Marketing professionals responsible for developing brand strategies, launching new products or services, and reaching specific customer segments will find the book valuable. It equips them with a deeper understanding of sub-branding's potential and provides actionable strategies to enhance their marketing efforts.

3. **Brand Managers:** Brand managers seeking to strengthen and expand their brand portfolio will gain practical insights from the book. It guides them in developing and managing sub-brands that complement their core brand, address different market segments, and maximize brand equity.

4. **Product Managers:** Product managers who are responsible for launching and positioning new products or services within an organization can leverage the book's strategies. It helps them explore sub-branding to effectively target specific customer needs, enhance product differentiation, and drive growth in their respective product categories.

The book caters to both seasoned professionals and those new to the concept of sub-branding, offering unique benefits to each group.

* * *

2

Sub-brand Development and Launch Process

A sub-brand's development and launch process involves strategic planning, careful analysis, and effective execution to successfully introduce a new product or service under an existing brand portfolio. While the specific steps may vary depending on the brand's strategy and objectives, there are common elements involved in the process. This chapter provides a general guide to understanding the key steps and considerations in developing and launching a sub-brand.

Key steps in developing and launching a sub-brand—

- Identify Market Opportunities
- Analyze Brand Fit
- Define Sub-brand's Value Propositions
- Brand Architecture Fit
- Launching and Managing the Sub-brand
- Integrated Marketing Communication
- Monitoring and Adaptation

Note 01: *It is important to acknowledge that certain sub-brand development and launch topics require more in-depth discussion and exploration. This book primarily focuses on presenting various sub-branding strategies and will therefore provide only a brief explanation of the different steps involved in the process. However, it is important to recognize that areas such as Brand Architecture and Brand Fit are extensive subjects that merit further study. Readers are encouraged to explore additional resources available in the market to gain a more comprehensive understanding of these critical aspects, particularly by delving into other books specifically dedicated to Brand Architecture. It's also worth noting that the specific steps involved in the sub-brand development and launch process may vary depending on each case's branding strategy, target customer segment, market dynamics, and brand architecture. The framework provided in this book serves as a general guide that can be adapted and customized to suit the unique needs and circumstances of a brand and its target market.*

01 Identify Market Opportunities

Identifying market opportunities is a crucial first step in conceptualizing, developing, and implementing a sub-branding strategy for product/service expansion. It involves conducting thorough market research to gain insights into customer needs, preferences, and untapped segments.

Here are some specific steps one can take to identify market opportunities for sub-branding:

1. Conduct Market Research: Market research is the foundation of identifying market opportunities. It involves gathering data and insights about the target market, competition, trends, and customer behaviour. One can use several methods to conduct market research, such as surveys, interviews, focus groups, observational research, and analyzing existing market data.

2. Define Your Target Audience: Clearly defining your target audience is essential to identify market opportunities. Understand the demographic,

psychographic, and behavioural characteristics of your potential customers. This information helps you segment the market and identify
specific groups that have unmet needs or preferences.

3. Analyze Customer Needs: Analyzing customer needs is crucial to identify gaps in the market. Look for pain points, challenges, or unmet
   desires that customers may have within your industry. Conduct surveys,
   observational research, or interviews to understand their preferences,
   expectations, and areas where existing products/services fall short.

4. Monitor Industry Trends: Stay updated on the latest industry trends,
   technological advancements, and emerging customer demands. Trends
   can open up new market opportunities and highlight areas where existing
   brands are not adequately addressing customer needs. Follow industry
   publications, attend conferences, and engage with thought leaders to
   gain insights into the evolving landscape.

5. Evaluate Competitors: Analyze your competitors' offerings, strengths,
   weaknesses, and market positioning. Identify areas where competitors
   may overlook certain customer segments or fail to meet specific needs.
   This allows you to spot potential gaps in the market that can be leveraged
   for your sub-branding strategy.

6. Assess Market Size and Growth Potential: Understand the size and growth
   potential of your target market segments. Evaluate factors such as market
   size, growth rate, market share, and competitive intensity. This analysis
   helps you prioritize the most attractive opportunities for your sub-brand
   expansion.

7. Seek Customer Feedback: Engage directly with your existing customers
   and seek their feedback on your current offerings. Ask for suggestions,
   identify areas of improvement, and explore potential new product/service
   ideas. Customer feedback can provide valuable insights into unmet needs
   and guide your sub-branding strategy.

8. Analyze External Factors: Consider external factors that may impact
   the market and create opportunities. These factors include regulatory
   changes, cultural shifts, technological advancements, and emerging
   social trends. Stay alert to these external influences that can shape

consumer behaviour and uncover new market opportunities.

By following these steps and conducting comprehensive market research, you can identify market opportunities that align with your business objectives. This information is a foundation for developing a sub-branding strategy that effectively targets specific market segments and addresses unmet customer needs. Remember to continuously monitor the market landscape to stay agile and adapt your sub-branding strategy as market dynamics evolve.

Example 01: Apple Watch

Apple, renowned for its astute market approach, demonstrated its prowess by identifying a lucrative opportunity in the burgeoning wearable technology market. This led to the development of the Apple Watch, a device that seamlessly combined connectivity, health tracking, and productivity features while maintaining the brand's distinctive style and functionality.

In the early 2010s, Apple conducted extensive research on the wearable technology landscape and recognized the increasing demand for devices that offered convenience, personalization, and fashionable design. They observed that existing options fell short of meeting these criteria, giving Apple a chance to make a significant impact.

This research provided valuable insights into potential customers' needs, behaviours, and desires. With this knowledge, Apple honed in on the key features crucial to consumers, such as robust fitness tracking capabilities, seamless notifications, and integrated mobile payment functionality.

Apple's research not only informed the development of the Apple Watch's features but also played a pivotal role in shaping its brand identity. The company aimed to position the Apple Watch as a premium product, aligning it with the core values of the Apple brand—simplicity, elegance, and innovation. This strategic approach allowed the Apple Watch to differentiate itself from competitors and resonate with consumers seeking a device that seamlessly blended style and functionality.

With a clear understanding of the market landscape and consumer needs, Apple conceptualized and developed the Apple Watch as a dedicated sub-brand within its portfolio, tailored specifically to the wearable technology segment. The seamless integration of the Apple Watch with other Apple devices further solidified its position within the brand ecosystem, appealing to existing Apple users while also attracting new customers.

The Apple Watch has emerged as a resounding success, capturing a substantial market share and effectively addressing the needs of consumers in search of a convenient and feature-rich wearable device. This achievement can be attributed to Apple's meticulous research, which guided the device's development and ensured its alignment with consumer expectations.

Example 02: Nike+

Nike, a renowned athletic footwear and apparel brand, has consistently demonstrated its ability to identify market opportunities and develop innovative products that resonate with consumers. One notable example is the development of the Nike+ sub-brand, which emerged from a comprehensive understanding of customer needs and behaviours.

Nike recognized the growing interest among consumers in tracking their fitness activities and performance. They identified an opportunity to leverage technology and create a product to enhance the athletic experience. Nike conducted extensive research to gain deeper insights into customer preferences and behaviours, including consumer surveys, interviews, and data analysis.

Through their research, Nike discovered that many customers sought ways to monitor their workouts, track their progress, and set fitness goals. Additionally, they found that individuals increasingly use technology, particularly smartphones, as an integral part of their fitness routines.

Armed with these insights, Nike developed the Nike+ sub-brand, which combined physical products with digital technology to provide a comprehensive fitness tracking and training experience. The centrepiece of the Nike+ sub-brand was the Nike+ sensor, a small device that could be inserted into specially designed Nike shoes to track various metrics such as distance, speed, and calories burned. This sensor is connected wirelessly to smartphones or other Nike+ devices, allowing users to track and analyze their performance in real time.

Nike+ also included a digital platform, the Nike+ app, where users could set fitness goals, track their progress, and compete with friends. This app provided personalized coaching, training programs, and a community of like-minded individuals, fostering user engagement and motivation.

By leveraging technology and integrating it seamlessly into its products and services, Nike created a sub-brand that tapped into its target market's evolving needs and behaviours. The Nike+ sub-brand aligned with Nike's overarching brand identity of empowering athletes and providing innovative solutions.

Nike+ successfully capitalized on the market opportunity by offering a unique value proposition: a holistic fitness tracking and training ecosystem that combined physical products with digital capabilities. This integration allowed Nike to establish a deeper connection with their customers, enhance their overall experience, and strengthen brand loyalty.

02 Analyze Brand Fit

Brand fit refers to the degree of alignment and compatibility between a sub-brand and its parent brand. It involves assessing how well the sub-brand aligns with the parent brand's core values, positioning, and target audience.

When introducing a sub-brand, it is essential to consider whether the new brand's identity, values, and offerings are consistent with the existing brand's overall image and reputation.

Importance of Aligning Brand Fit:

1. Consistency and Coherence: Aligning the new product/service with the

existing brand's core values, positioning, and target audience ensures consistency and coherence in the brand's messaging, image, and overall identity. It helps create a seamless brand experience for customers and strengthens brand recognition.

2. Reinforce Brand Identity: A strong brand identity is built on the core values of the parent brand and clear positioning. By aligning the new product/service with these elements, the sub-brand reinforces the brand's identity and what the brand stands for in the minds of consumers.

3. Enhanced Customer Trust: When a sub-brand aligns with the existing brand's values and resonates with the target audience, it enhances customer trust. Customers are more likely to trust and engage with a sub-brand that they perceive as an extension of a brand they already trust and value.

How to Analyze Brand Fit:

1. Define Brand Values and Positioning: Clearly articulate the core values and positioning of the existing brand(parent brand). Identify the key attributes, benefits, and promises associated with the brand. This provides a foundation for evaluating the fit of the new product/service.

2. Evaluate Product/Service Alignment: Assess how well the new product/service aligns with the existing brand's core values and positioning. Examine factors such as product attributes, features, benefits, pricing, packaging, and communication strategies. Ensure they align with the overall brand identity and resonate with the target audience.

3. Conduct Customer Research: Gather insights from the target audience to gauge their perception of the existing brand and their expectations for the new product/service. Conduct surveys, interviews, or focus groups to understand their preferences, needs, and perceptions. This research helps ensure the sub-brand meets customer expectations and aligns with their preferences.

4. Internal Alignment: Ensure internal alignment and consensus among

key stakeholders involved in the sub-branding process. Evaluate if the new product/service aligns with the brand's vision, mission, and strategic goals. Engage in cross-functional discussions and seek input from different departments to ensure buy-in and alignment.

By rigorously evaluating brand fit, brands can ensure that the new product/service aligns seamlessly with the existing brand's core values, positioning, and target audience. This alignment enhances brand coherence, customer trust, and the overall success of the sub-branding strategy.

Potential Risks of Introducing a Sub-Brand:

1. Brand Dilution: Introducing a sub-brand that does not align with the existing brand's core values or target audience can dilute the brand's equity and confuse customers. It may lead to a loss of brand loyalty and decreased customer trust.
2. Cannibalization: Introducing a sub-brand that competes directly with existing products/services within the brand portfolio can lead to cannibalization, where sales and market share are diverted internally rather than capturing new customers or markets.
3. Overextension: If a brand introduces too many sub-brands, it can lead to overextension, where the brand becomes fragmented, loses focus, and struggles to maintain consistent brand identity and positioning.

By carefully analyzing brand fit, brands can mitigate these risks and ensure a successful sub-branding strategy that aligns with the existing brand's values, resonates with the target audience, and effectively leverages the brand's equity and reputation.

Example 01: Apple Watch

Apple's introduction of the Apple Watch exemplifies its strategic decision to maintain brand fit during product expansion. Despite entering a new product category, Apple leveraged its strong brand identity and commitment to innovation to ensure seamless integration of the Apple Watch within its existing brand ecosystem.

Here are some of the ways in which the Apple Watch achieves brand fit with Apple:

1. Core Values and Identity: The Apple brand is known for its focus on innovation, design excellence, and user experience. The Apple Watch aligns with these core values by introducing groundbreaking features, a sleek design, and an intuitive user interface. Both the Apple brand and the Apple Watch emphasize simplicity, elegance, and cutting-edge technology, ensuring a strong alignment in terms of brand identity.

2. Positioning: The Apple Watch's positioning complements the overall brand strategy of Apple. It targets a specific market segment interested in wearable technology and aims to provide a seamless extension of the Apple ecosystem. The Apple Watch's positioning as a premium smartwatch integrates with other Apple devices, leveraging the brand's reputation for quality, reliability, and integration.

3. Target Audience: The Apple Watch caters to tech-savvy individuals who value both functionality and style. It appeals to Apple's existing customer base, including iPhone and Mac users, who seek a convenient and feature-rich wearable device that seamlessly integrates with their Apple ecosystem. The target audience for the Apple Watch aligns with the broader target audience of the Apple brand.

4. Design: The Apple Watch is designed in the same minimalist style as other Apple products. It has a sleek, futuristic look that is consistent with Apple's brand identity. The Apple Watch inherited the premium build and attention to detail. This brand consistency created a sense of

familiarity and trust among Apple's existing customer base, who were already accustomed to Apple's commitment to high-quality products.

5. Seamless Integration: Apple strategically integrated the Apple Watch with their existing product lineup and ecosystem. The seamless integration with iPhones, Macs, and other Apple devices allowed users to easily connect and sync their devices, enhancing the overall user experience.

6. Brand Equity and Reputation: Apple has built a strong brand equity and reputation over the years, known for its innovation, user-friendly products, and exceptional customer experience. The introduction of the Apple Watch enhances the brand's equity by expanding into the growing wearable technology market. The reputation for quality and customer satisfaction associated with Apple extends to the Apple Watch, ensuring a positive brand fit.

7. Visual Identity and Communication: The visual identity of the Apple Watch, including the iconic Apple logo and minimalist design, maintains consistency with the overall Apple brand. The communication and marketing efforts for the Apple Watch align with Apple's distinctive advertising style, emphasizing product features, user experience, and lifestyle benefits.

By aligning the new product with its existing brand values, design principles, and target audience, Apple effectively leveraged their strong brand identity to create a desirable and aspirational product within the wearable technology market.

Example 02: Coca-Cola Zero

Recognizing the growing consumer demand for low-calorie and sugar-free options, Coca-Cola strategically created a sub-brand Coca-Cola Zero that aligned with its core brand values while addressing specific consumer preferences.

Coca-Cola Zero was positioned as a beverage that offered the same great taste as the original Coca-Cola but with zero sugar. This positioning allowed Coca-Cola to cater to health-conscious consumers without compromising on flavour. By aligning the taste profile of Coca-Cola Zero with the original Coca-Cola, Coca-Cola leveraged its strong brand heritage and association with refreshing beverages, ensuring that consumers could easily recognize the connection and trust the quality of the new product.

Here are some of the ways in which Coca-Cola Zero achieves brand fit with Coca-Cola:

1. Taste and Flavor: Coca-Cola Zero was developed as a sugar-free alternative to Coca-Cola, aiming to provide a similar taste experience without calories. The taste and flavour of Coca-Cola Zero closely resemble the original Coca-Cola, ensuring consistency with the parent brand's iconic taste and satisfying consumers who prefer a sugar-free option.

2. Brand Identity and Values: Coca-Cola Zero aligns with Coca-Cola's brand identity and values. Both brands emphasize enjoyment, refreshment, and happiness. Coca-Cola Zero carries forward Coca-Cola's commitment to delivering positive experiences and indulgence, catering to consumers who want to enjoy the taste of Coca-Cola while managing their sugar intake.

3. Visual Identity: The visual identity of Coca-Cola Zero maintains consistency with Coca-Cola's branding elements. It features the familiar red and black colour scheme, the iconic Coca-Cola logo, and a similar packaging design. This visual continuity helps consumers associate Coca-Cola Zero with the parent brand and recognize it as part of the Coca-Cola family.

4. Marketing and Communication: Coca-Cola Zero's marketing and communication efforts align with Coca-Cola's overall advertising strategies. They focus on the brand's core values, such as sharing moments of happiness and connecting with others. Coca-Cola Zero campaigns often emphasize the taste and zero-calorie aspect, appealing to health-conscious consumers who still want to enjoy the Coca-Cola experience.

5. Brand Equity: Coca-Cola Zero leverages the strong brand equity of Coca-Cola. The parent brand's reputation for quality, taste, and global recognition contributes to the credibility and trustworthiness of Coca-Cola Zero. Consumers are more likely to try and trust a sub-brand that carries the name and legacy of a well-established parent brand.

6. Market Segmentation: Coca-Cola Zero targets a specific market segment—consumers who desire the taste of Coca-Cola but prefer a sugar-free option. By addressing this segment's needs and preferences, Coca-Cola Zero expands the brand's reach and attracts a broader customer base without diluting the overall Coca-Cola brand.

7. Product Portfolio: Coca-Cola Zero enhances Coca-Cola's product portfolio by offering a choice for consumers seeking a zero-sugar beverage. This diversification allows Coca-Cola to cater to a wider range of consumer preferences and lifestyles while maintaining a cohesive brand identity.

Coca-Cola's strategic decision to maintain brand fit during the introduction of Coca-Cola Zero showcases the importance of aligning new products with core brand values, maintaining visual consistency, and delivering on consumer expectations. This approach ensures that consumers can trust and relate to the sub-brand, ultimately contributing to the success of product/service expansion within the existing brand portfolio.

03 Defining the Sub-Brand's Value Proposition

In the process of developing a sub-brand strategy, one crucial step is defining the sub-brand's value proposition. The value proposition is a concise statement that articulates the unique benefits and differentiation of the new product or service under the sub-brand.

Crafting a compelling value proposition involves considering various elements. First, it is essential to identify the factors that set the sub-brand apart from competitors and the parent brand. This could be in terms of features, design, quality, or functionalities that address specific customer needs.

Additionally, understanding the target audience is vital. Defining the target audience's demographics, psychographics, and behaviour helps tailor the value proposition to their specific needs and preferences.

The value proposition should clearly communicate the unique benefits that the sub-brand offers. These benefits should solve a problem or fulfil a particular need for customers, demonstrating the value they will receive by choosing the sub-brand.

It is crucial to ensure that the sub-brand's value proposition aligns with the overall brand positioning and values of the parent brand. Consistency between the sub-brand and the parent brand helps build customer trust and familiarity.

By developing a compelling value proposition, the sub-brand establishes a clear and appealing message that differentiates itself from competitors and resonates with the target audience. This enables customers to understand the unique benefits and value that the sub-brand provides, ultimately driving their engagement and preference for the sub-brand over alternatives.

For example, if a sportswear brand is launching a sub-brand targeting eco-conscious consumers, the value proposition could focus on sustainability, using recycled materials, and reducing environmental impact. The sub-brand's value proposition might be: "Our eco-sportswear sub-brand provides high-performance athletic wear crafted from recycled materials, helping you stay fit while reducing your carbon footprint."

Example 01: Nike Jordan

Nike's Jordan Brand is a sub-brand that has successfully developed a strong value proposition by strategically leveraging the elements of sports, style, and the iconic legacy of Michael Jordan.

The development of the Jordan Brand's value proposition involved several key steps. Firstly, Nike recognized the unique attributes associated with Michael Jordan, such as his unparalleled on-court performance, his charisma, and his impact on popular culture. These attributes formed the basis for differentiating the Jordan Brand from other athletic footwear brands in the market.

Secondly, Nike conducted in-depth market research to understand its target audience's preferences, aspirations, and emotional connections, particularly basketball fans and sneaker enthusiasts. Insights revealed that consumers were not only seeking high-performance athletic shoes but also desired a sense of exclusivity and the opportunity to connect with Michael Jordan's legacy.

The value proposition of the Jordan Brand was designed to address these consumer desires. It emphasized premium performance, showcasing cutting-edge technology and innovative design in each product release. By continuously pushing the boundaries of athletic footwear technology, the Jordan Brand positioned itself as a leader in the industry, delivering an exceptional performance that resonates with athletes and fans alike.

In addition to performance, the Jordan Brand recognized the significance of style and fashion in its target audience's lives. Nike integrated elements of streetwear and fashion into the design of Jordan Brand products, making them desirable beyond the basketball court. This approach allowed the brand to tap into the broader sneaker culture and attract consumers who valued both athletic performance and style.

Furthermore, Nike carefully curated the brand's image, utilizing strategic marketing campaigns and partnerships to build an aura of exclusivity and authenticity. Limited edition releases, collaborations with renowned designers, and celebrity endorsements created a sense of rarity and desirability among consumers, further strengthening the value proposition.

Nike's Jordan Brand developed a strong value proposition by capitalizing on the intersection of sports, style, and the iconic legacy of Michael Jordan. Through meticulous research, the brand identified the desires and aspirations of its target audience, crafting a value proposition that offers not only high-performance athletic footwear but also a unique and aspirational experience.

The Nike Jordan value proposition combines high-performance athletic footwear, authenticity, exclusivity, style, and cultural influence to create a unique and aspirational brand experience for basketball enthusiasts and sneaker collectors worldwide.

Example 02: Dove's Men+Care

Dove Men+Care, a sub-brand of Dove, was created to cater to male consumers' distinct needs and preferences in the grooming industry. Recognizing that men often have different skincare and hygiene requirements compared to women, Dove conducted extensive market research to understand men's grooming habits and desires. The findings revealed that men often felt excluded or overlooked in an industry predominantly targeted towards women.

Based on these insights, Dove Men+Care developed a value proposition that revolves around the concept of care. The brand acknowledged that men desire products that not only nurture their skin but also promote a sense of confidence and masculinity. Emphasizing simplicity and effectiveness, Dove Men+Care offers a range of specifically formulated products addressing men's skincare concerns, such as facial cleansing, shaving, and body care. These products are designed to be easy to use, seamlessly fitting into men's grooming routines.

Beyond addressing grooming concerns, Dove Men+Care places a strong focus on promoting self-care and emotional well-being. The brand's messaging encourages men to prioritize their physical health and mental and emotional well-being. Through impactful marketing campaigns, Dove Men+Care highlights the significance of self-confidence, healthy relationships, and positive masculinity, resonating with male consumers who value holistic well-being.

By addressing men's grooming concerns and promoting a sense of care, simplicity, and emotional well-being, Dove's Men+Care sub-brand has successfully differentiated itself in the market and created a compelling value proposition that resonates with male consumers.

Dove Men+Care offers a range of grooming products specifically designed for men, providing effective solutions that nurture the skin while promoting self-care and emotional well-being, catering to male consumers' unique needs and desires.

04 Brand Architecture

Brand architecture is the way that a company organizes its brands and sub-brands. It defines the relationships between the brands and how they are communicated to consumers.

Brand architecture is important for several reasons. It can help to:

- **Create a clear and consistent brand identity.** When a company has a well-defined brand architecture, it is easier for consumers to understand the different brands and what they stand for. This can lead to stronger brand loyalty and customer satisfaction.
- **Differentiate between different product lines.** Brand architecture can help a company differentiate between different product lines, even under the same parent brand. This can be helpful for companies that want to target different segments of the market with different products.
- **Expand into new markets.** Brand architecture can help a company expand into new markets by creating sub-brands tailored to the specific needs of those markets. This can help the company avoid diluting its core brand's equity.

When making sub-brand decisions, considering the brand architecture is essential to ensure alignment and coherence within the overall brand portfolio. The brand architecture model chosen will influence how the sub-brand is positioned and connected to the parent brand.

Here are some considerations when making sub-brand decisions within the brand architecture:

1. Clarity of Brand Relationships: Evaluate how the sub-brand will relate to the parent brand and other brands within the portfolio. Determine

the level of connection and association desired. Will the sub-brand carry the parent brand's name or logo? Will it have a distinct visual identity or messaging? Ensure that the brand relationship is clear and understandable to customers.

2. Consistency in Brand Expression: Maintain consistency in brand expression across the parent brand and sub-brand. The sub-brand should align with the parent brand's core values, brand promise, and visual identity. Consistency ensures that customers recognize the connection between the brands and builds trust and credibility.

3. Consumer Perception: Consider how consumers perceive the parent brand and how the introduction of a sub-brand might impact their perceptions. Will the sub-brand enhance or dilute the parent brand's equity? Ensure that the sub-brand aligns with the parent brand's positioning and resonates with the target audience.

4. Brand Extension Opportunities: Assess the potential for brand extensions within the sub-brand. Will the sub-brand have the flexibility to introduce new products or services? Consider the scalability and adaptability of the sub-brand to accommodate future growth and diversification.

5. Competitive Landscape: Analyze the competitive landscape and market trends to determine the optimal brand architecture for sub-branding. Evaluate how competitors structure their brand portfolios and the impact it has on customer perceptions and market positioning.

6. Risk Assessment: Understand the potential risks associated with introducing a sub-brand versus leveraging the existing brand. Evaluate the potential for confusion, cannibalization, or dilution of brand equity. Conduct thorough market research and consumer testing to gauge the viability and acceptance of the sub-brand.

By carefully considering the brand architecture, companies can make informed decisions about introducing sub-brands that align with their overall brand strategy, enhance the brand portfolio, and effectively target specific market segments.

Example 01: Unilever

Unilever is a multinational consumer goods company with a diverse portfolio of brands. They employ a hybrid brand architecture model that incorporates both individual brands and endorsed brands. For example, within their personal care category, Unilever has sub-brands like Dove, Axe, and Sunsilk, each with its own distinct identity and target audience. These individual brands operate independently and have their own brand positioning. However, they are also endorsed by the overarching Unilever brand, which provides credibility and reassurance to consumers. Unilever's brand architecture approach allows for brand differentiation while leveraging the strength of the parent brand.

Let's delve into a specific sub-brand decision made by Unilever with respect to its brand architecture requirements:

One example of a sub-brand decision made by Unilever is the creation of the Dove Men+Care sub-brand. Unilever recognized the need to cater specifically to the male grooming segment, which required a different positioning and messaging than their existing Dove brand.

To address this opportunity, Unilever decided to introduce Men+Care as a sub-brand under the Dove umbrella. This sub-brand decision allowed them to leverage the equity and recognition of the Dove brand while targeting a specific demographic—men.

In terms of brand architecture, Unilever adopted an endorsed brand model for Dove Men+Care. While it operates as an individual sub-brand, it carries the endorsement of the overarching Dove brand. This endorsement provides credibility and reassurance to consumers, as they can trust that the same values of care and quality associated with Dove are extended to Dove Men+Care.

By using the endorsed brand approach, Unilever ensured that Dove Men+Care had its own distinct identity, packaging, and communication tailored to men's specific grooming needs. However, the endorsement from the Dove brand also helped establish immediate brand recognition and trust among consumers.

This strategic sub-brand decision allowed Unilever to capture a specific market segment while maintaining consistency and clarity within its brand architecture. It showcases how brand architecture considerations play a vital role in making sub-brand decisions to ensure effective communication, differentiation, and customer loyalty.

Example 02: General Electric (GE)

GE is a conglomerate operating in various industries, including aviation, healthcare, and energy. GE employs a sub-brand strategy within its brand architecture.

One example of a sub-brand decision made by GE is its healthcare division, which includes sub-brands such as GE Healthcare and GE Life Sciences. The sub-brand decision aligns with GE's brand architecture strategy, which emphasizes brand coherence and leveraging the reputation of the parent brand.

By incorporating the GE name into the sub-brands, GE Healthcare and GE Life Sciences, the company establishes a clear connection to the parent brand and capitalizes on its reputation for innovation, reliability, and technological expertise. This brand architecture decision helps build immediate recognition and trust among customers.

GE Healthcare, for instance, operates as a distinct sub-brand within the healthcare sector. It focuses on providing advanced medical imaging, diagnostics, and healthcare IT solutions. By carrying the GE name, GE Healthcare benefits from the parent brand's established track record and market presence, which adds credibility and assurance to its products and services.

Similarly, GE Life Sciences operates as another sub-brand, specializing in the development and production of bioprocessing technologies and solutions. By associating the GE name with this sub-brand, GE Life Sciences taps into the reputation of GE in the broader industrial and technological landscape, positioning itself as a reliable and innovative provider within the life sciences industry.

The sub-brand decision made by GE aligns with its brand architecture requirements by maintaining consistency and coherence across its diverse range of products and services. It allows GE to leverage the overall brand equity and reputation of GE while providing focused offerings within specific industry sectors.

By strategically incorporating the GE name into their sub-brands, GE ensures that customers recognize the connection between the sub-brands and the parent brand, facilitating trust and fostering brand loyalty. This approach strengthens the overall brand perception and enables GE to effectively communicate its commitment to quality, innovation, and technological advancements in various sectors.

05 Launching and Managing The Sub Brand

Launching and managing a sub-brand involves a series of strategic decisions and actions to establish and nurture the new brand within the broader brand portfolio. Let's delve into the process in detail:

1. Brand Positioning: The first step in launching a sub-brand is defining its unique market positioning. This involves identifying the target audience, understanding their needs and preferences, and determining how the sub-brand will differentiate itself from competitors and the parent brand. The positioning should align with the overall brand strategy and complement the existing brand portfolio.
2. Brand Identity: Developing a distinct brand identity for the sub-brand is crucial. This includes creating a compelling brand name, designing a visually appealing logo and brand elements, and defining the brand's tone of voice and personality. The sub-brand's identity should be consistent with the parent brand's overarching brand identity while having its own unique attributes that resonate with the target audience.
3. Communication Strategy: Crafting a targeted communication strategy is essential to effectively launch and promote the sub-brand. This involves determining the key messages, channels, and touchpoints that will be

used to reach and engage the target audience. The communication strategy should emphasize the sub-brand's value proposition, highlight its differentiation, and reinforce its connection to the parent brand when relevant.

4. Integration with the Parent Brand: Ensuring a seamless integration between the sub-brand and the parent brand is vital. The sub-brand should be clearly connected to the parent brand in terms of visual identity, brand voice, and values. This connection helps leverage the parent brand's equity, credibility, and customer trust while establishing a distinct identity for the sub-brand.

5. Distribution and Channel Strategy: Determining the appropriate distribution channels and retail strategies for the sub-brand is crucial for its success. This involves considering whether the sub-brand will be sold through existing distribution networks or require a separate channel strategy. Aligning the distribution approach with the target audience's preferences and behaviours is key to maximising the sub-brand's reach and accessibility.

6. Monitoring and Adaptation: Once the sub-brand is launched, ongoing monitoring and adaptation are necessary. Regularly assessing the sub-brand's performance, customer feedback, and market dynamics helps identify areas of improvement and opportunities for growth. This enables timely adjustments to marketing strategies, product offerings, and brand positioning to ensure the sub-brand remains relevant and competitive.

7. Brand Governance: Establishing brand governance processes and guidelines ensures consistent brand management across the sub-brand and the parent brand. This involves setting clear guidelines for brand usage, visual identity, messaging, and brand voice. Brand governance ensures brand consistency, strengthens brand equity, and protects the sub-brand's integrity within the broader brand portfolio.

Launching and managing a sub-brand requires a strategic approach, attention to detail, and a deep understanding of the target audience, market dynamics, and brand architecture. By carefully planning and executing these steps, businesses can successfully introduce and nurture a sub-brand that contributes to their overall brand growth, market expansion, and customer engagement.

Example 01: Nestlé's Nespresso

Nestlé, a multinational food and beverage company, successfully launched and managed the sub-brand Nespresso. Nespresso is a premium coffee brand that offers a range of single-serve coffee machines and capsules. Here's how they approached the launch and management of the sub-brand:

Brand Positioning: Nespresso positions itself as a premium coffee brand that offers high-quality, gourmet coffee experiences at home or in professional settings. It emphasizes the convenience, exceptional taste, and customization options of its coffee capsules and machines. By positioning itself as a luxury coffee brand, Nespresso targets discerning coffee enthusiasts who appreciate a premium coffee experience. This positioning differentiated Nespresso from the mainstream Nestle coffee brands, such as Nescafé, which targeted a broader consumer segment.

Brand Identity: Nespresso has a distinct brand identity that embodies elegance, sophistication, and innovation. Its sleek and modern design elements are present in coffee machines, packaging, and retail spaces, creating an exclusive and luxurious atmosphere. This visual identity consistently conveys Nespresso's commitment to delivering exceptional coffee moments.

As a premium brand, Nespresso sets itself apart from Nestlé's broader portfolio of mass-market products. By emphasizing its premium nature, Nespresso establishes a unique identity centered around luxury and sophistication.

While Nespresso has its own design language, it maintains consistency by incorporating elements of Nestlé's brand colors and logo. This ensures visual coherence within the Nestlé family while still differentiating Nespresso as a distinctive sub-brand.

Nespresso upholds Nestlé's high-quality standards by sourcing premium coffee beans and maintaining product excellence. This consistency in quality reinforces the overall brand reputation and consumer trust associated with Nestlé.

Although Nespresso has its own brand identity, it aligns with Nestlé's core corporate values, including consumer-centricity, innovation, and ethical business practices. These shared values contribute to the overall coherence and integrity of the Nestlé brand as a whole.

Value Proposition: Nespresso's value proposition revolves around the promise of delivering the perfect cup of coffee with convenience and consistency. The brand offers a wide variety of coffee blends and flavours, allowing customers to customize their coffee experience. Nespresso also emphasizes sustainability through its recycling program, further enhancing its value proposition.

Brand Fit: Nestlé Nespresso demonstrates a strong brand fit with its parent brand, Nestlé. Let's examine the aspects of brand fit between Nespresso and Nestlé:

1. Product Category: Nespresso fits within the broader Nestlé brand portfolio as both brands operate in the food and beverage industry. While Nestlé offers a wide range of food and beverage products, Nespresso specializes in premium coffee experiences.
2. Quality Standards: Nestlé is known for its commitment to high-quality products and rigorous quality control processes. Nespresso upholds the same standards by sourcing premium coffee beans and ensuring that its coffee capsules and machines meet strict quality criteria. This shared commitment to quality establishes brand coherence and reinforces Nestlé's reputation.
3. Sustainability: Nestlé has a strong focus on sustainability and environmental responsibility. Nespresso aligns with this ethos by implementing sustainable practices throughout its supply chain, including responsible

sourcing of coffee beans and recycling programs for its coffee capsules. The shared emphasis on sustainability enhances the brand fit between Nespresso and Nestlé.

4. Brand Reputation and Trust: Nestlé is a globally recognized brand with a long-standing reputation for reliability, trustworthiness, and consumer satisfaction. Nespresso benefits from this positive brand perception and leverages Nestlé's reputation to enhance its own credibility in the coffee market. The association with Nestlé strengthens consumer trust in Nespresso products.

5. Distribution and Global Presence: Nestlé has an extensive distribution network and a global presence. Nespresso leverages Nestlé's distribution channels and partnerships to reach a wider audience, expanding its market reach and accessibility. This integration with Nestlé's distribution capabilities enhances the brand fit and facilitates Nespresso's growth.

6. Research and Development: Nestlé invests heavily in research and development to drive innovation in the food and beverage industry. Nespresso benefits from Nestlé's expertise and resources in this area, enabling the sub-brand to continuously improve its coffee machines, capsules, and brewing techniques. The collaboration in research and development strengthens the brand fit between Nespresso and Nestlé.

Brand Architecture: Within the Nestlé brand architecture, Nespresso holds a distinct position as a specialist coffee brand. It complements Nestlé's broader range of food and beverage products by specifically targeting consumers seeking premium coffee experiences. This allows Nestlé to cater to different customer preferences and expand its presence in the coffee industry.

The relationship between Nespresso and other Nestlé brands is complementary, enabling cross-promotion and resource sharing. However, each brand maintains its unique positioning and identity. This approach ensures that Nespresso can benefit from the reputation and resources of the parent brand while preserving its own distinct brand identity.

Distribution Channel Strategy: Nespresso initially established itself through a direct-to-consumer model with its boutiques and online platform. It strategically limited access to its coffee capsules and machines to maintain exclusivity. Over time, Nespresso expanded its distribution channels by partnering with select retail outlets and establishing a presence in high-end hotels, restaurants, and offices.

Monitoring and Adaptation: Nespresso continually monitors market trends, customer feedback, and industry developments to adapt its offerings and strategies. The brand regularly introduces limited edition coffee blends, collaborates with renowned coffee experts, and innovates its machines to stay ahead in the competitive market.

Brand Governance: Nestlé ensures proper brand governance by maintaining quality standards, adhering to sustainability practices, and protecting the Nespresso brand's reputation. This includes ensuring the ethical sourcing of coffee beans, providing recycling initiatives for coffee capsules, and delivering consistent product quality.

Through a well-executed brand positioning, identity, value proposition, brand fit, architecture fit, communication strategy, integration with the parent brand, distribution channel strategy, monitoring and adaptation, and brand governance, Nestlé Nespresso has successfully established itself as a premium sub-brand within the Nestlé brand portfolio. It has become synonymous with luxury coffee experiences, catering to a specific segment of coffee enthusiasts while upholding the values and standards of the parent brand.

Example 02: Samsung Galaxy

Samsung, a global technology conglomerate, launched the sub-brand Samsung Galaxy for its line of smartphones and tablets. Here's an overview of their sub-brand launch and management strategy:

Brand Positioning: Samsung Galaxy's brand positioning is focused on offering innovative and high-performance mobile devices to meet the needs of tech-savvy consumers. It positions itself as a premium and cutting-edge brand within the smartphone market, emphasizing advanced features, sleek design, and user-friendly interfaces.

Value Proposition: The Samsung Galaxy sub-brand offers consumers cutting-edge technology, premium design, and a seamless user experience. Whether you're looking for a flagship smartphone or a specialized device like the Galaxy Note series, Samsung Galaxy delivers a premium value proposition that combines superior performance, stylish aesthetics, and a comprehensive ecosystem of interconnected products and services.

Brand Identity: Samsung Galaxy's brand identity is built upon several key elements that distinguish it in the mobile industry. First and foremost is its technological advancement, as Samsung Galaxy is renowned for its constant innovation and the introduction of new features, technologies, and capabilities in its devices. This commitment to pushing boundaries has established Samsung Galaxy as a leader in the field.

Another crucial aspect of the brand identity is its premium design. Samsung Galaxy devices are characterized by their sleek and visually appealing aesthetics. The brand focuses on clean lines, high-quality materials, and meticulous attention to detail, resulting in products that exude sophistication and modernity.

Samsung Galaxy also prioritizes providing a user-centric experience. The brand's user interface (UI) and user experience (UX) design are tailored to be intuitive, simple to use, and highly customizable. This emphasis on a seamless and personalized user experience ensures that consumers can effortlessly navigate and personalize their devices according to their preferences.

The brand's ecosystem is another integral element of Samsung Galaxy's identity. It is part of a larger interconnected ecosystem that includes wearables, smart home devices, and software applications. This integration allows users to seamlessly connect and synchronize their Samsung devices, creating a cohesive and interconnected experience across multiple product categories.

Trust and reliability are fundamental pillars of the Samsung Galaxy brand. The brand is committed to quality control, rigorous testing, and exceptional customer support, all of which contribute to its reputation for delivering reliable and high-quality devices. This dedication builds trust among consumers, establishing Samsung Galaxy as a dependable choice.

Finally, Samsung Galaxy positions itself as an innovation leader in the industry. By consistently introducing groundbreaking features and advancements, such as cutting-edge camera capabilities and enhanced display technologies, the brand solidifies its reputation as an industry innovator and reinforces its leadership position in driving technological progress.

Brand Fit: Samsung Galaxy focuses on delivering high-end smartphones and devices with innovative features, premium design, and superior user experiences, aligning well with Samsung's positioning as a provider of technologically advanced products.

The target audience for Samsung Galaxy consists of tech-savvy consumers who value innovation, performance, and a premium user experience. This target audience overlaps with Samsung's broader customer base, as both brands cater to individuals seeking the latest technological advancements and high-quality products.

Maintaining visual consistency is crucial in brand fit, and Samsung Galaxy achieves this by incorporating the Samsung logo and brand colours in its marketing materials and product designs. This visual alignment reinforces the connection between the sub-brand and the parent brand, enhancing brand recognition and creating a cohesive brand identity within the Samsung brand portfolio.

Brand Architecture Fit: Samsung Galaxy is a sub-brand of Samsung that focuses on mobile devices. It maintains a close alignment with the parent brand while carving out its own unique positioning and identity.

Samsung Galaxy benefits from the brand equity, reputation, and resources of the Samsung master brand. This integration allows Samsung Galaxy to benefit from the overall brand recognition and trust associated with the Samsung name.

At the same time, Samsung Galaxy has its own distinct brand identity, value proposition, and target audience. It complements the Samsung brand by offering a specialized range of mobile devices that cater to consumers seeking cutting-edge technology, premium design, and a seamless user experience.

Samsung Galaxy sub-brand strategically differentiates itself within the Samsung brand portfolio by targeting specific market segments. For example, the Galaxy Note series focuses on productivity and creativity, appealing to professionals and power users, while the Galaxy S series targets a broader audience with flagship devices. This segmentation allows Samsung to address different customer needs and preferences effectively.

Communication and Marketing Strategy: The key elements of Samsung Galaxy's communication and marketing strategy include:

1. Integrated Marketing Campaigns: Samsung Galaxy employs integrated marketing campaigns that span various channels, including television, digital platforms, social media, and print media. These campaigns showcase the brand's technological advancements, product features, and unique experiences offered by Samsung Galaxy devices.

2. Emotional Branding: Samsung Galaxy leverages emotional branding to create a connection with consumers. The brand often focuses on storytelling, highlighting how its products can enhance and enrich people's lives, showcasing the emotional aspects of technology and its impact on personal experiences.

3. Influencer Partnerships: Samsung Galaxy collaborates with influencers and key opinion leaders in the technology and entertainment industries. By partnering with these influencers, the brand extends its reach and credibility, reaching a wider audience and tapping into niche communities.

4. Product Launch Events: Samsung Galaxy organizes high-profile product launch events to generate excitement and anticipation. These events

serve as platforms to unveil new devices, demonstrate their features, and create buzz around the brand. Product launch events are often accompanied by media coverage and press releases to generate maximum exposure.

5. Digital Marketing and Social Media: Samsung Galaxy leverages digital marketing and social media platforms to engage with its target audience. It actively maintains a strong presence on platforms like Instagram, Twitter, and YouTube, sharing product updates, user-generated content, and interactive campaigns to foster community engagement and build brand loyalty.

6. Retail Partnerships and In-Store Experience: Samsung Galaxy collaborates with retail partners to provide immersive and interactive in-store experiences. The brand ensures that customers can explore and experience its devices firsthand, encouraging them to make informed purchase decisions.

7. Customer Support and Engagement: Samsung Galaxy places a strong emphasis on customer support and engagement. The brand offers dedicated customer support channels, online forums, and social media platforms where customers can seek assistance, share feedback, and engage in conversations about their Samsung Galaxy devices.

Distribution and Channel Strategy: Samsung Galaxy utilizes a multi-channel distribution strategy to reach a wide range of customers. This includes partnerships with mobile network carriers, online retailers, and brick-and-mortar stores, ensuring broad availability and accessibility of Galaxy devices.

Monitoring and Adaptation: Samsung Galaxy continuously monitors market trends, customer feedback, and the competitive landscape to adapt its strategies and offerings accordingly. This allows the brand to stay agile, address evolving customer needs, and maintain a competitive edge in the dynamic smartphone market.

Brand Governance: Samsung Galaxy operates under the brand governance framework established by Samsung to ensure consistent brand standards, messaging, and quality across all products and touchpoints. This governance structure helps maintain brand integrity and coherence within the overall brand portfolio.

These examples illustrate how strategic decisions and actions were crucial in successfully launching and managing sub-brands within the broader brand portfolios of Nestlé and Samsung. By carefully considering brand positioning, identity, communication, integration, distribution, and adaptation, these companies achieved market success and customer engagement with their sub-brands.

06 Integrated Marketing Communications

Developing a comprehensive marketing communications plan is crucial for a successful sub-brand launch as it allows the brand to effectively reach and engage its target audience, create brand awareness, and convey the unique value proposition of the sub-brand. Here's an overview of how to develop a comprehensive marketing communications plan for a sub-brand launch:

1. Define Objectives: Start by clearly defining the marketing objectives for the sub-brand launch. These objectives could include increasing brand awareness, generating leads, driving sales, or positioning the sub-brand in a specific market segment.

2. Identify Target Audience: Conduct market research to identify the target audience for the sub-brand. Understand their demographics, psychographics, behaviours, and preferences to tailor the marketing communications efforts accordingly.

3. Craft Key Messages: Develop key messages that effectively communicate the unique value proposition of the sub-brand. These messages should align with the brand's positioning, differentiation, and target audience's needs and desires.

4. Select Communication Channels: Identify the most suitable communication channels to reach the target audience. This can include a combination of traditional channels such as print, TV, radio, and outdoor advertising, as well as digital channels like social media, email marketing, content marketing, and influencer partnerships.

5. Develop Creative Assets: Create compelling and consistent creative assets that reflect the sub-brand's positioning and resonate with the target audience. This includes visual elements such as logos, branding guidelines, website design, packaging, and advertising materials.

6. Plan Media Strategy: Determine the media channels, placements, and scheduling to maximize the reach and impact of marketing communications efforts. Consider the budget, the target audience's media consumption habits, and the most effective media outlets for reaching them.

7. Implement Public Relations Activities: Leverage public relations strategies to generate media coverage, create buzz, and enhance the brand's credibility. This can include press releases, media events, influencer collaborations, and strategic partnerships.

8. Monitor and Measure: Set up metrics and tracking mechanisms to monitor the effectiveness of the marketing communications plan. Analyze data, such as website traffic, social media engagement, lead generation, and sales, to assess the impact of the communications efforts and make necessary adjustments.

Throughout the process, ensure consistency in messaging, branding, and visual identity across all communication channels to establish a strong and unified brand presence. Regularly evaluate the performance of the marketing communications plan and make refinements based on the feedback and insights gathered.

By developing a comprehensive marketing communications plan, a sub-brand can effectively introduce itself to the market, create awareness, and generate excitement among the target audience, leading to a successful launch and long-term brand growth.

Example 01: Red Bull's "Stratos" Campaign

Red Bull, an energy drink company, launched an integrated marketing communications campaign for its sub-brand, Red Bull Stratos. The campaign aimed to generate brand buzz and showcase the brand's association with extreme sports and adrenaline-pumping experiences.

Here's an overview of the campaign:

About the Campaign: Red Bull Stratos was a project that involved Austrian skydiver Felix Baumgartner jumping from a balloon in the stratosphere, the second layer of Earth's atmosphere. The project was sponsored by Red Bull and was designed to break several world records, including the highest freefall jump and the first manned balloon flight to the stratosphere.

The jump took place on October 14, 2012, from a balloon that had taken Baumgartner to an altitude of 39,045 meters (128,100 feet). Baumgartner fell for 4 minutes and 20 seconds before opening his parachute and landing safely on the ground. He reached a top speed of 1,357.64 kilometres per hour (843.6 miles per hour), breaking the sound barrier during his freefall.

Key Messages: The key messages of the campaign focused on pushing boundaries, challenging limits, and achieving the extraordinary. It positioned Red Bull Stratos as a brand that embodies daring and adventure.

- **Red Bull gives you the wings to achieve great things.** This message was communicated through the image of Felix Baumgartner breaking the sound barrier and reaching the edge of space. It was also communicated through the use of the hashtag #RedBullWings, which was used on social media.
- **Red Bull is a brand that is associated with adventure, excitement, and pushing the limits.** This message was communicated through the nature of the stunt itself, as well as through the use of imagery and language that evoked these emotions.

- **Red Bull is a brand that is committed to innovation and pushing the boundaries of what is possible.** This message was communicated through the fact that the Stratos jump was a world record-breaking event. The Red Bull Stratos project was a major undertaking that required years of planning and preparation. The balloon that took Baumgartner to the stratosphere was the largest ever built, and the parachute that he used was specially designed to withstand the high speeds that he reached during his freefall. The project also involved a team of scientists and engineers who were responsible for ensuring that the jump was safe. The Red Bull Stratos project was a groundbreaking achievement that pushed the boundaries of human potential.

Communication Channels: Red Bull utilized a wide range of communication channels to reach its target audience. This included traditional advertising (TV, print, outdoor), digital platforms (website, social media), and public relations activities.

- **Website:** Red Bull created a dedicated website for the campaign, which featured live streaming of the jump, as well as behind-the-scenes footage and interviews. The website also had a strong social media presence, with over 1 million followers on Facebook and Twitter.
- **TV:** The jump was broadcast live on TV in over 50 countries. Red Bull also produced a documentary about the campaign, which was shown on TV and in cinemas.
- **Print:** Red Bull ran print ads in major newspapers and magazines around the world. These ads featured images of Felix Baumgartner in his spacesuit, as well as quotes from him about the jump.
- **Outdoor:** Red Bull plastered billboards, and bus stops with images of Baumgartner and the campaign logo. They also created a series of experiential marketing events where people could try out skydiving simulators and learn more about the campaign.

Content Creation: Red Bull created compelling content that documented the entire Stratos project, from planning to execution. Here are some specific examples of how content was created for the campaign:

- **Live streaming:** The jump was live-streamed on the Red Bull website and on social media. This allowed people to follow the event in real-time and get a sense of the excitement and danger involved.
- **Behind-the-scenes footage:** Red Bull released behind-the-scenes footage of the jump, which gave people a glimpse into the training and preparation that went into the event. This footage helped to build excitement for the jump and made it more relatable to the audience.
- **Interviews:** Red Bull conducted interviews with Felix Baumgartner and other members of the team, which gave people a chance to learn more about the jump and the people involved. These interviews helped to build credibility for the campaign and make it more believable.
- **Blog posts:** Red Bull published blog posts about the jump, which provided more in-depth information about the event. These blog posts helped to educate the audience about the science behind the jump and the challenges that Baumgartner faced.
- **Social media:** Red Bull used social media to promote the campaign and engage with the audience. They created hashtags for the campaign, such as #RedBullStratos and #RedBullWings, and they encouraged people to use these hashtags to share their thoughts and reactions to the event. This helped to create a sense of community around the campaign and made it more shareable.

Event Sponsorship: Red Bull leveraged its sub-brand to sponsor and promote extreme sports events and activities. This included partnerships with athletes and teams, as well as organizing and supporting adrenaline-fueled events that aligned with the brand's image.

Experiential Marketing: Red Bull engaged in experiential marketing to give consumers a taste of the brand's adventurous spirit. They organized stunts, demonstrations, and interactive experiences at various locations, allowing people to experience the brand's energy and excitement firsthand.

Social Media Engagement: Red Bull heavily utilized social media platforms to engage with its target audience. They encouraged user-generated content, conducting contests and giveaways, and shared captivating content related to extreme sports, adventure, and the Red Bull Stratos campaign.

The integrated marketing communications campaign for Red Bull Stratos successfully created a buzz around the sub-brand, generated widespread media coverage, and positioned Red Bull as a brand associated with adrenaline and extreme experiences.

Example 02: Apple's "Shot on iPhone" Campaign

Apple, a technology company, launched the "Shot on iPhone" campaign to promote the camera capabilities of its iPhone sub-brand. The campaign aimed to showcase the exceptional photography and video quality that could be achieved using an iPhone. Here's how the integrated marketing communications campaign was executed:

1. User-Generated Content: Apple encouraged users to submit their best photos and videos taken with an iPhone for a chance to be featured in the campaign. This approach allowed Apple to tap into the creativity and passion of its user base and showcase the real-world capabilities of the iPhone's camera.
2. Social Media Engagement: Apple leveraged social media platforms, particularly Instagram, to share stunning user-generated content. They utilized hashtags, engaged with followers, and created a sense of community around the campaign.
3. Outdoor Advertising: Apple showcased the captivating images captured with an iPhone on billboards, transit ads, and other outdoor advertising spaces. These visually striking images caught passersby's attention and

demonstrated the iPhone camera's power in real-world scenarios.

4. Online and Print Advertising: Apple incorporated user-generated content into their online and print advertising campaigns. They featured the stunning visuals in digital ads, magazine spreads, and on their website, reinforcing the message that the iPhone can capture professional-quality photos and videos.

5. Retail stores: Apple showcased user-generated content in their retail stores. They have dedicated displays where people can see photos taken on the iPhone. This helped show off the iPhone's camera capabilities to people considering buying an iPhone.

6. Events: Apple hosted events to showcase the "Shot on iPhone" campaign. They have held photo exhibitions and contests where people can share their photos. This helps to engage people with the campaign and show off the iPhone's camera capabilities.

7. Television Commercials: Apple aired television commercials that high-lighted the beautiful imagery captured with an iPhone. These commercials showcased different scenes, subjects, and creative techniques to demonstrate the versatility and quality of the iPhone camera.

8. Influencer Partnerships: Apple collaborated with influential photographers and content creators to further amplify the campaign. These partnerships helped reach a wider audience and provided credibility to the messaging.

9. Brand Partnerships: Apple has partnered with other brands to promote the "Shot on iPhone" campaign. For example, they have partnered with National Geographic to create a series of short films shot on the iPhone. This helps to reach a wider audience and show off the iPhone's camera capabilities in a new way.

Key Messages: The "Shot on iPhone" campaign by Apple aimed to showcase the capabilities of the iPhone camera and emphasize the power of creativity in capturing moments. The key messages conveyed through this campaign include:

1. Empowering Creativity: The campaign positioned the iPhone as a tool that enables users to unleash their creativity and capture stunning photographs and videos.

2. Everyday Moments, Extraordinary Results: By featuring everyday moments captured by iPhone users, the campaign highlighted how the iPhone can transform ordinary moments into extraordinary visual stories.

3. High-Quality Imaging: The campaign emphasized the iPhone camera's exceptional image quality and advanced features, showcasing the ability to capture professional-looking photos and videos with a smartphone.

4. User-Generated Content: The campaign tapped into the power of user-generated content, highlighting iPhone users' talents and unique perspectives worldwide.

5. Accessibility and Simplicity: The campaign showcased that capturing stunning photos and videos is not limited to professional photographers but can be achieved by anyone with an iPhone, making high-quality imaging accessible to a wide range of users.

6. Community and Connection: By featuring user-generated content, the campaign fostered a sense of community and connection among iPhone users who share their visual stories.

7. Innovation and Technological Advancements: The campaign positioned Apple as an innovative brand that continuously pushes the boundaries of technology, delivering cutting-edge camera capabilities in their iPhones.

In summary, the "Shot on iPhone" campaign successfully showcased the iPhone's camera capabilities through real user-generated content, engaged with the audience through social media, and leveraged various advertising channels to create widespread awareness and admiration for the sub-brand.

07 Monitoring and Adaptation

Monitoring and adaptation are crucial aspects of managing a sub-brand after its launch. It involves consistently tracking the sub-brand's performance, gathering feedback from customers and stakeholders, and making necessary adjustments to ensure its success. Here's why monitoring and adaptation are important and some key metrics to track:

1. Performance Evaluation: Monitoring allows you to evaluate the performance of the sub-brand against pre-defined goals and objectives. It helps you assess its market position, sales growth, profitability, and success in reaching the target audience. Regularly monitoring performance can identify areas of improvement or potential challenges.

2. Customer Satisfaction: Tracking customer satisfaction is essential for understanding how well the sub-brand meets customer expectations. Surveys, feedback mechanisms, and customer reviews can provide valuable insights into customer sentiment, their perception of the sub-brand, and areas where improvements can be made.

3. Sales Growth: Monitoring sales growth is a vital metric to track the sub-brand's commercial success. By analyzing sales data and trends, you can assess whether the sub-brand is generating the desired revenue and market share. This information can help identify potential areas for expansion or adjustments to marketing and sales strategies.

4. Brand Awareness and Perception: Brand awareness is another key metric to track to understand the visibility and recognition of the sub-brand in the market. Monitoring brand awareness metrics, such as aided and unaided brand recall, can help assess the effectiveness of marketing and communication efforts. Additionally, tracking brand perception metrics, such as brand reputation and brand associations, provides insights into how its target audience perceives the sub-brand.

5. Competitor Analysis: Monitoring the activities and performance of competitors is important to stay informed about the market landscape. By analyzing competitor strategies, product launches, and customer

48

responses, you can identify potential threats or opportunities for differentiation and adaptation.

6. Feedback and Reviews: Actively collecting and analyzing customer feedback, reviews, and social media conversations provides valuable insights into customer preferences, satisfaction, and potential areas for improvement. This feedback can guide product development, marketing campaigns, and overall brand management.

By monitoring and adapting based on the above metrics, brands can stay responsive to market dynamics, customer needs, and emerging trends. This iterative process allows for continuous improvement and optimization of the sub-brand's performance, ensuring its long-term success in the market.

Example 01: Amazon Echo

The Amazon Echo, introduced in 2014, is a smart speaker powered by the virtual assistant Alexa. It was a pioneering product in the market, combining voice recognition technology with various functionalities such as playing music, providing information, and controlling smart home devices.

After the launch of the Amazon Echo, Amazon actively monitored customer feedback and market trends to assess the sub-brand's performance and identify areas for improvement. This monitoring and adaptation process played a crucial role in the evolution and success of the Amazon Echo sub-brand. Here are some key aspects of how Amazon monitored and adapted the Echo:

1. Monitoring Performance: Amazon continuously tracks sales growth and market share of the Echo devices. They also monitor usage data, such as the number of voice commands processed, device interactions, and engagement metrics. This helps them understand their sub-brand's adoption rate, usage patterns, and overall performance.

2. Gathering Customer Feedback: Amazon actively encourages customers to

provide feedback through online reviews, ratings, and customer surveys. They also leverage their customer service channels to gather direct feedback on product experiences and suggestions for improvement. They actively listened to user experiences and gathered feedback to enhance the device's performance, user interface, and overall functionality. This continuous feedback loop allowed them to identify pain points and address them through software updates and product improvements.

3. Market Trends: Amazon closely monitored the evolving market trends and competitors' offerings in the smart speaker and virtual assistant space. They analyzed consumer preferences, emerging technologies, and market dynamics to stay ahead of the curve and ensure the Amazon Echo remained relevant and competitive. This allowed them to introduce new features and capabilities to meet changing customer expectations and outperform competing products.

4. Adaptation and Refinement: Based on the data and feedback, Amazon has made several adaptations to the Echo sub-brand. They have introduced new features, expanded compatibility with third-party devices and services, and enhanced the voice recognition capabilities of their products. Amazon also regularly releases software updates to address bugs, introduce new functionalities, and enhance user experiences. These adaptations are aimed at better meeting customer expectations and maintaining a competitive edge in the smart speaker market.

5. Iterative Development: Amazon embraced an iterative approach to product development and updates for the Amazon Echo. They released regular software updates and introduced new features based on customer needs and technological advancements. This iterative development process enabled them to continually enhance the sub-brand's capabilities, fix bugs, and deliver a better user experience over time.

6. Expansion of Ecosystem: Amazon recognized the importance of expanding the Echo ecosystem by integrating it with other smart home devices and third-party services. They actively collaborated with external developers and partners to create a diverse range of skills and capabilities for Alexa, the virtual assistant powering the Echo. This expansion helped

position the Echo as a central hub for smart home automation and increased its value proposition to consumers.

7. Continuous Innovation: Amazon demonstrated a commitment to continuous innovation with the Echo sub-brand. They introduced new Echo device models with enhanced features and capabilities, such as improved audio quality, built-in screens, and compatibility with other smart devices. This ongoing innovation ensured that the Echo remained at the forefront of the market and sustained customer interest.

By actively listening to customer feedback, monitoring market trends, iterating on product development, expanding the ecosystem, leveraging customer data, and continuously innovating, Amazon was able to refine and enhance the Echo sub-brand over time.

Conclusion

Developing and launching a sub-brand requires a thoughtful and strategic approach to ensure its success in the market. This chapter has provided an overview of the key steps involved in the process, including identifying opportunities, analyzing brand fit, defining the sub-brand's value proposition, considering brand architecture, launching and managing the sub-brand, implementing integrated marketing communications, and monitoring and adapting the sub-brand strategy.

While the specific details may vary depending on the brand's unique circumstances, this chapter has provided a general framework to guide the development and launch of a sub-brand. By following these steps and considering the various factors involved, brands can effectively introduce new products or services under their existing brand portfolio, cater to specific market segments, and drive growth and success in the competitive marketplace.

It is important for brands to continuously monitor the performance of the sub-brand, gather customer feedback, and analyze data to make informed decisions and adapt the strategy as needed. By staying agile and responsive, brands can ensure the sub-brands' long-term viability and their ability to meet the evolving needs and preferences of their target audience.

* * *

In the subsequent chapters, we will delve into various sub-brand strategies employed by brands to achieve specific goals and objectives. These strategies include targeting specific market segments, expanding product or service offerings through sub-brands, entering new geographic markets with sub-brands, implementing sub-brands for lifestyle branding, and more.

By exploring these strategies in detail, readers will gain insights into how brands effectively leverage sub-brands to cater to diverse customer needs, expand their market reach, and strengthen their brand presence. Each chapter will provide practical examples and valuable lessons to help readers understand the nuances of each sub-brand strategy and apply them strategically in their own brand management efforts.

3

Demographic Segmentation

D emographic segmentation involves dividing a market into distinct groups based on demographic factors such as age, gender, income, education, and lifestyle. By analyzing these characteristics, brands can gain valuable insights into their target market and tailor their marketing efforts accordingly.

Brands need demographic segmentation for several reasons. Firstly, it allows them to understand their customers on a deeper level. By studying demographic data, brands can identify commonalities within specific groups, such as the preferences and purchasing behaviours of different age groups or income levels. This knowledge enables brands to create more targeted and effective marketing strategies that resonate with their intended audience.

Furthermore, demographic segmentation helps brands to identify untapped opportunities in the market. By recognizing the unique needs and desires of different demographic segments, brands can develop specialized products or services that cater specifically to those groups. This targeted approach increases the chances of success by aligning offerings with the specific demands of each segment.

While demographic segmentation is valuable, brands sometimes face the challenge of catering to multiple segments within their target market. This is where sub-brands come into play.

Using sub-brands allows brands to craft tailored strategies for each segment. With their own unique positioning, personality, and value proposition, sub-brands can effectively cater to the specific needs and preferences of different groups. This approach creates a stronger connection with customers as they feel that the brand truly understands and caters to their individual requirements.

Moreover, sub-brands help brands avoid diluting their main brand image. By creating separate identities for different segments, brands can maintain consistency and clarity in their messaging. Customers can easily associate each sub-brand with the specific demographic it targets, fostering brand loyalty and trust.

Demographic Variables

Demographic segmentation means dividing the market based on variables such as age, gender, income, occupation, education, family size, and more. It allows brands to categorize consumers into homogeneous groups with similar demographic characteristics and tailor their sub-brands to meet each segment's specific needs and preferences.

Various Demographic Variables:

1. Age: Age-based segmentation divides consumers into different age groups, such as children, teenagers, young adults, middle-aged, or seniors. Age is a fundamental demographic variable that influences consumer behaviours, preferences, and consumption patterns. Sub-brands can be designed to specifically target the unique needs and interests of each age group.

2. Gender: Gender-based segmentation categorizes consumers as male or female. It recognizes the differences in attitudes, preferences, and buying behaviours between genders. Brands may develop sub-brands that are tailored to cater to the specific needs, desires, and aspirations of

each gender.

3. Income: Income-based segmentation divides consumers into different income brackets, such as low-income, middle-income, or high-income groups. Income is a critical variable that affects consumers' purchasing power and spending habits. Sub-brands can be created to offer products or services that align with different income segments' affordability and lifestyle expectations.

4. Occupation: Occupation-based segmentation categorizes consumers based on their job or profession. Different occupations may have unique needs, preferences, or requirements, making occupation a relevant variable for sub-branding. Brands can create sub-brands that cater to specific occupational groups, providing tailored solutions or products.

5. Education: Education-based segmentation considers consumers' educational backgrounds, such as high school, college graduates, or postgraduate degrees. Education level often correlates with knowledge, interests, and preferences. Sub-brands can be developed to target segments with specific educational backgrounds and provide products or services that align with their intellectual or cultural interests.

By understanding and leveraging various demographic variables, brands can create sub-brands that effectively address specific demographic segments' distinct needs, desires, and behaviours.

Example 01: Pampers Easy Ups

One example of a sub-brand that targets a specific demographic market segment is Pampers Easy Ups, a product line by the well-known baby care brand Pampers. Pampers Easy Ups is designed specifically for toddlers who are transitioning from diapers to underwear.

Demographic Market Segment: The target demographic for Pampers Easy Ups is parents or caregivers of toddlers who are in the process of potty training.

This segment typically includes children between the ages of 1 and 3 years. Pampers recognized the need for a product that caters to this specific stage of a child's development as parents seek more convenient and comfortable alternatives to traditional diapers.

Product Features and Benefits: Pampers Easy Ups offer a range of features and benefits specifically tailored to meet the needs and preferences of toddlers during the potty training stage. Firstly, their design resembles real underwear, with elastic waistbands and leg cuffs that provide a comfortable and secure fit. This design allows toddlers to easily pull them up and down, promoting independence and a sense of accomplishment.

Secondly, despite their underwear-like appearance, Pampers Easy Ups maintain the absorbency and leak protection of traditional diapers. This gives parents peace of mind and reduces the likelihood of accidents and messes during the potty training process.

Additionally, Pampers Easy Ups feature colourful designs and popular characters from children's shows and movies. These engaging designs not only make the training pants visually appealing but also add an element of fun and excitement to the potty training experience.

Furthermore, Pampers Easy Ups are designed for easy changes, incorporating tear-away sides that allow parents to remove them quickly, even in the event of accidents. This convenience ensures that parents can handle any accidents with minimal fuss and disruption.

Brand Fit: Pampers Easy Up aligns well with its parent brand, Pampers, in several key ways. Firstly, Pampers has established itself as a trusted and reputable brand in the baby care industry. This reputation and trust carry over to the Easy Up sub-brand, as parents already rely on Pampers for high-quality and reliable baby care products. This makes them more likely to choose Pampers Easy Up for their toddlers during the potty training stage.

Secondly, Pampers has extensive expertise in developing diapers and other baby care products that meet the specific needs of infants and toddlers. With Pampers Easy Up, the brand leverages its knowledge and experience to create training pants that offer the right balance of absorbency, fit, and comfort for toddlers during their potty training journey. This ensures that parents can rely on Pampers Easy Up for effective and convenient solutions.

Thirdly, Pampers Easy Up maintains a consistent brand identity and messaging that aligns with the parent brand. By incorporating the Pampers logo, visual elements, and brand voice, the sub-brand creates a recognizable and cohesive experience for consumers. This brand consistency strengthens the association between Pampers Easy Up and the overall brand values of Pampers, reinforcing the trust and familiarity that parents have with the brand.

Moreover, Pampers Easy Up benefits from the parent brand's extensive distribution channels. The sub-brand can leverage Pampers' existing partnerships with retailers and online platforms, ensuring wide availability and accessibility to its target audience. This makes it easier for parents to find and purchase Pampers Easy Up training pants, further solidifying the sub-brand's position in the market. Shorten it slightly

Brand Portfolio Architecture: Pampers Easy Up plays a vital role within the Pampers brand portfolio by targeting the specific market segment of toddlers transitioning from diapers to underwear. This strategic focus allows Pampers to provide comprehensive coverage of baby care needs, catering to newborns, infants, and toddlers, ensuring that parents can rely on the brand throughout their child's development.

While Pampers offers a range of products for infants, Pampers Easy Up stands out by providing tailored solutions for parents and toddlers during the potty training phase. This specialization enables the sub-brand to capture a unique market segment and effectively meet the specific needs of parents and toddlers during this important transition.

To maintain consistency and strengthen the connection with the parent brand, Pampers Easy Up incorporates the recognizable Pampers logo and design elements. This cohesive and consistent brand experience enhances brand recognition, fosters loyalty among consumers, and reinforces the association between Pampers Easy Up and the broader Pampers brand.

Another advantage of Pampers Easy Up is its ability to leverage the established distribution channels of the parent brand. By utilizing Pampers' strong presence in retail stores, online platforms, and other sales channels, the sub-brand ensures wide availability and accessibility to its target demographic. This extensive distribution network plays a crucial role in expanding the sub-brand's reach and reinforcing its position within the competitive baby care market.

Communication and Marketing Strategies: To capture the attention of parents, Pampers utilizes targeted advertising campaigns that focus on the challenges and joys of potty training. These campaigns are strategically placed on platforms that reach parents, such as television, parenting magazines, and online parenting communities. Pampers creates a connection with its target audience by addressing the specific concerns and experiences related to potty training.

Collaborating with parenting influencers and bloggers specialising in child development and potty training is another effective strategy Pampers employs. These partnerships provide opportunities to raise awareness of Pampers Easy Ups and offer trusted recommendations from influencers who have expertise in this area. This influencer-driven approach helps build credibility and trust among parents within the target demographic.

Pampers also offers educational resources and guides for parents, providing valuable information and tips on potty training. By offering these resources online, Pampers supports parents in navigating this developmental stage while highlighting the benefits of using Pampers Easy Ups. This educational content establishes Pampers as a helpful and knowledgeable resource for parents during the potty training journey.

In addition, Pampers strategically places Easy Ups displays in stores, particularly in the baby care aisle. These displays attract attention and inform parents about the availability and benefits of Pampers Easy Ups. By placing the product in a prominent location, Pampers increases visibility and encourages parents to consider Easy Ups as their preferred choice for potty training pants.

Monitoring and Adaptation: Pampers continually monitors the market and gathers feedback from parents to ensure the Easy Ups sub-brand remains relevant and effective. They collect data on sales, customer reviews, and engagement metrics to assess the product's performance and make necessary adjustments. Based on market trends and customer insights, Pampers may introduce new features, designs, or marketing strategies to better cater to the evolving needs and preferences of the target demographic.

Outcomes and Impact: By targeting parents of active toddlers who are transitioning from diapers to training pants, Pampers has expanded its product offerings and captured a larger share of the diaper market. This has led to increased sales and market penetration, resulting in a higher market share for Pampers.

Pampers Easy Up has also strengthened brand loyalty among existing Pampers customers. By providing a seamless transition from traditional diapers to training pants, parents are more likely to remain loyal to the Pampers brand throughout their child's diapering journey. This has resulted in repeat purchases and long-term customer loyalty, contributing to the overall brand equity of Pampers.

Furthermore, Pampers Easy Up has successfully met the specific needs of parents with active toddlers. The design and features of the training pants offer convenience and practicality for parents while providing comfort for toddlers. By addressing these needs, Pampers has established itself as a trusted and preferred brand for parents seeking reliable and functional training pants.

The introduction of Pampers Easy Up has also helped differentiate Pampers from its competitors in the diaper market. The sub-brand offers a unique product line that specifically caters to toddlers in the transition phase. This differentiation allows Pampers to stand out and position itself as a leader in meeting the evolving needs of parents and their children.

Moreover, the success of Pampers Easy Up has created opportunities for brand extensions and product diversification within the Pampers portfolio. Pampers can further expand its offerings by introducing complementary products, such as wipes or diaper accessories, specifically tailored for active toddlers. This allows the brand to capitalize on the recognition and success of

Pampers Easy Up and strengthen its presence in the toddler care market.

Through its Pampers Easy Ups sub-brand, Pampers effectively targets the demographic market segment of parents or caregivers navigating the potty training stage. By understanding this segment's specific needs and challenges, Pampers developed a product line that offers convenience, comfort, and engagement, making the potty training journey more manageable for parents and toddlers alike.

Example 02: Glossier Play

Glossier is a beauty brand that was founded in 2014 by Emily Weiss. The brand is known for its simple, millennial-friendly products and its focus on social media marketing. In 2018, Glossier launched a sub-brand called Glossier Play, specifically targeted to Gen Z consumers.

Gen Z is the generation that was born between 1995 and 2012. This generation is known for being more experimental and daring than previous generations. They are also more likely to be interested in beauty products that are bold and colourful.

Glossier Play was launched as a separate line within the brand to cater to this more adventurous and experimental customer segment. The sub-brand offers a range of products that are designed to help Gen Z consumers express their individuality and creativity.

Market Segment: The target market for Glossier Play is beauty enthusiasts who are looking for bold, vibrant, and playful makeup options. This segment consists of young, trend-conscious individuals who enjoy experimenting with different looks and expressing their creativity through makeup.

Product Features and Benefits: Glossier Play distinguishes itself from Glossier's main line by offering a range of makeup products that are characterized by their vibrant colours, intensity, and impact. These products aim to promote self-expression and encourage customers to step outside their comfort zones in terms of their makeup choices. The line includes a diverse selection of colorful makeup options, such as eye shadows, lipsticks, and highlighters. These products feature highly pigmented formulas that allow customers to create bold and dramatic looks, whether it be for special occasions or simply when they want to make a statement. In addition to their vibrant colours, Glossier Play products stand out with their playful and eye-catching packaging. The packaging design reflects the brand's fun and adventurous approach, resonating with the target market and creating a sense of excitement and anticipation when using the products. Despite the emphasis on vibrant colors and intense impact, Glossier Play ensures that its products maintain the high-quality standards associated with the Glossier brand. The formulas are carefully developed to be long-lasting, blendable, and easy to use, enabling customers to effortlessly achieve their desired looks while maintaining the performance and reliability they expect from Glossier.

Brand Fit: Glossier Play aligns well with the parent brand, Glossier, in several ways. While Glossier promotes a minimalist, natural beauty approach, Glossier Play embraces a more playful and experimental aesthetic. Despite this difference, both brands share a commitment to self-expression and inclusivity, connecting them through their overarching brand identity.

Regarding the target audience, both Glossier and Glossier Play cater to millennial and Gen Z consumers. However, Glossier Play specifically appeals to those who are more adventurous and willing to experiment with bold colors, glitter, and unique textures. This sub-brand targets customers who value self-care and self-expression while enjoying the exploration of bolder makeup choices.

Glossier focuses primarily on skincare and natural-looking makeup, while Glossier Play expands the brand's product offering by introducing vibrant eyeshadows, lipsticks, and highlighters. This diversified product range allows customers to explore their creativity and experiment with different looks, complementing the everyday beauty routine encouraged by Glossier.

In terms of visual identity, both Glossier and Glossier Play share a clean and minimalist aesthetic. They employ sleek packaging designs that are Instagram-friendly. This visual coherence helps maintain a connection between the parent and sub-brand, while Glossier Play stands out with its vibrant and eye-catching product packaging.

Both brands align with similar values, such as celebrating individuality and offering high-quality formulations. While Glossier focuses on enhancing natural beauty, Glossier Play encourages self-expression within a more vibrant and experimental context. Both brands maintain their commitment to accessible and user-friendly beauty products.

In the market, Glossier Play occupies a distinct position within the Glossier brand portfolio. It targets customers seeking statement-making and experimental makeup options, offering a differentiated product line from Glossier's main range of everyday essentials. This positioning allows Glossier Play to tap into a different market segment while maintaining a cohesive brand identity within the Glossier portfolio.

Brand Portfolio Architecture: Glossier Play is a distinct sub-brand within the Glossier portfolio, offering bold and vibrant makeup options that differentiate it from Glossier's minimalistic everyday beauty products. It targets a specific market segment of customers who seek more experimental and playful beauty experiences.

Despite its differentiation, Glossier Play maintains a cohesive brand identity within the Glossier portfolio. It shares common brand elements, such as user-friendly formulations, high-quality products, and inclusive messaging. This coherence ensures that Glossier Play is recognizable as part of the Glossier family and leverages the trust and reputation built by the parent brand.

The brand portfolio architecture fit also enables cross-promotion and cross-selling opportunities between Glossier and Glossier Play. Customers familiar with Glossier's minimalistic products may be enticed to explore the more vibrant and playful offerings of Glossier Play. Likewise, Glossier Play customers may discover and become interested in the everyday essentials of Glossier. This cross-pollination enhances brand awareness and loyalty within the Glossier portfolio.

By incorporating Glossier Play, Glossier expands its product offerings and captures a wider market share. It taps into the growing trend of bold and experimental makeup, attracting customers with different preferences than the core Glossier audience. This strategic expansion strengthens the overall brand portfolio and positions Glossier as an innovative and inclusive beauty brand that caters to various customer needs.

Communication and Marketing Strategies: Glossier Play utilizes various marketing and communication strategies to reach its target market effectively. These strategies include:

1. Vibrant Visual Identity: Glossier Play embraces a bold and colourful visual identity that sets it apart from the parent brand. The packaging, product designs, and marketing materials feature vibrant hues and eye-catching visuals, creating a sense of playfulness and intrigue.
2. Social Media Engagement: Glossier Play heavily utilizes social media platforms to connect with its audience. By leveraging platforms like Instagram, Glossier Play shares visually appealing content, showcases creative looks using its products, and encourages user-generated content through hashtags and challenges. This strategy promotes engagement, creates a community around the brand, and generates buzz.
3. Influencer Collaborations: Glossier Play partners with influencers and beauty enthusiasts who align with the brand's image and target audience. These collaborations involve influencers creating content featuring Glossier Play products, sharing their experiences, and endorsing the brand to their followers. This strategy helps reach a wider audience and leverage the influence and credibility of these individuals.
4. Experiential Marketing: Glossier Play embraces experiential marketing by hosting events, pop-up shops, and interactive experiences. These activations allow customers to explore and try out the products, create personalized looks, and interact with brand representatives. By providing immersive experiences, Glossier Play strengthens the emotional connection between the audience and the brand.

5. Storytelling and Brand Narrative: Glossier Play develops a compelling brand narrative that emphasizes the fun, experimental, and empowering aspects of makeup. Through storytelling in their marketing campaigns, they showcase how Glossier Play products can be used to express one's individuality, enhance creativity, and have fun with beauty.

6. Limited Edition Releases and Product Drops: Glossier Play often releases limited edition products or launches new items through highly anticipated drops. This strategy creates a sense of exclusivity, urgency, and excitement among customers, driving sales and encouraging brand loyalty.

7. Collaborative Product Development: Glossier Play involves its customers in the product development process by soliciting feedback, conducting surveys, and actively listening to their preferences. This customer-centric approach ensures that Glossier Play is creating products that resonate with its target audience and meet their needs.

Through these communication and marketing strategies, Glossier Play encourages self-expression, fosters brand loyalty, and drives sales.

Monitoring and Adaptation: Glossier Play closely monitors trends and customer feedback to adapt its products and marketing strategies. The brand actively seeks input from its target market through social media interactions, surveys, and customer reviews. This feedback loop allows Glossier Play to make product improvements, introduce new shades or formulations, and stay relevant in the ever-changing beauty industry.

Outcomes and Impact: Some of the outcomes and impacts of Glossier Play:

1. Increased Brand Reach: With the introduction of Glossier Play, the parent brand, Glossier, expanded its reach and captured a new segment of customers. Glossier Play's focus on bold, experimental makeup products attracted a wider audience interested in expressive and vibrant beauty looks.

2. Engaged and Growing Community: Glossier Play successfully built an engaged community of beauty enthusiasts and makeup lovers. Through its social media presence, Glossier Play encourages customers to share their looks, experiences, and product recommendations, creating a sense of community and fostering brand advocacy.

3. Enhanced Brand Perception: Glossier Play's innovative and playful approach to makeup has enhanced the overall brand perception of Glossier. The introduction of Glossier Play demonstrated the brand's ability to cater to diverse beauty needs and preferences, positioning Glossier as a comprehensive beauty brand.

4. Revenue Growth: The launch of Glossier Play has contributed to the revenue growth of Glossier as a whole. The introduction of new product lines and the expansion into the vibrant and experimental makeup segment has attracted new customers and increased sales.

5. Differentiation and Market Positioning: Glossier Play has allowed Glossier to differentiate itself in the highly competitive beauty industry. By offering a distinct line of bold and creative makeup products, Glossier Play stands out from traditional beauty brands and has established a unique market positioning.

6. Influencer and Celebrity Endorsements: Glossier Play's innovative and visually appealing products have garnered attention and endorsements from influencers and celebrities. These partnerships have increased brand visibility and credibility, further expanding Glossier Play's reach and impact.

7. Product Development and Innovation: Glossier Play's introduction has also stimulated product development and innovation within the broader Glossier brand. The success of Glossier Play has encouraged ongoing creativity and experimentation in the development of new products, ensuring the brand remains at the forefront of beauty trends and consumer demands.

Through its distinct and playful approach to makeup, Glossier Play has solidified Glossier's position as a dynamic and forward-thinking beauty brand in the industry.

Glossier Play is a successful example of a sub-brand that targets a specific demographic market segment within the beauty industry. By understanding the desires and preferences of its adventurous and trend-conscious target audience, Glossier Play offers a unique and vibrant product line that encourages self-expression and creativity.

* * *

4

Psychographic Segmentation

P sychographic segmentation involves dividing a market into distinct groups based on psychological characteristics such as values, interests, opinions, personality traits, and lifestyle choices. By analyzing these aspects, brands can gain valuable insights into the deeper motivations and preferences of their customers, allowing them to tailor their marketing efforts effectively.

Brands need psychographic segmentation for several reasons. Firstly, it allows them to go beyond demographic data and uncover the underlying psychological factors that influence consumer behaviour. By understanding the values, beliefs, and aspirations of different psychographic segments, brands can create marketing strategies that resonate on a deeper level. This understanding enables brands to establish emotional connections with their audience, fostering loyalty and long-term relationships.

Furthermore, psychographic segmentation helps brands identify niche markets and target specific consumer groups with precision. By identifying shared interests, attitudes, or lifestyle choices within a psychographic segment, brands can develop specialized products, services, or messaging that cater to those specific desires. This targeted approach increases the relevance and appeal of the brand to the intended audience, enhancing its competitive advantage in the market.

While psychographic segmentation is valuable, brands may face the challenge of effectively reaching and engaging with multiple psychographic segments within their target market. This is where sub-brands come into play.

Using sub-brands allows brands to craft tailored strategies for each segment. Each sub-brand can have its own unique positioning, messaging, and visual identity that resonates with the psychographic characteristics of its target audience. By doing so, brands can establish a stronger connection with consumers, as they feel that the brand truly understands their values and aspirations.

Psychographic Variables

Psychographic segmentation involves dividing a market based on consumers' psychological characteristics, attitudes, values, interests, opinions, lifestyle choices, and personality traits. Unlike demographic segmentation, which focuses on observable and measurable traits, psychographic segmentation delves deeper into the motivations, aspirations, and behaviours of individuals. Understanding psychographic variables is essential for developing effective sub-branding strategies that resonate with consumers on a deeper emotional level.

Here are key psychographic variables and their relevance to sub-branding:

1. Values: Values refer to the fundamental beliefs and principles that individuals hold. They shape consumers' decision-making processes and influence their preferences and behaviours. Sub-brands can align with specific values to connect with target consumers who share those values. For example, a sub-brand focusing on sustainability and environmental consciousness may appeal to consumers who prioritize eco-friendly practices.

2. Attitudes: Attitudes represent individuals' positive or negative evaluations and feelings toward certain objects, ideas, or experiences. Sub-

brands can cater to specific attitudes to establish an emotional connection with consumers. For instance, a sub-brand promoting body positivity and self-acceptance may resonate with consumers who appreciate inclusive messaging and reject unrealistic beauty standards.

3. Lifestyle: Lifestyle encompasses the activities, interests, opinions, and behaviours that reflect an individual's way of living. Sub-brands can align with specific lifestyles to cater to consumers' preferences and aspirations. For example, a sub-brand targeting adventure enthusiasts might offer products and experiences tailored to their active and outdoor-oriented lifestyle.

4. Personality: Personality traits capture individuals' enduring patterns of thoughts, emotions, and behaviours. Sub-brands can embody certain personality traits to attract consumers who resonate with those traits. For instance, a sub-brand projecting an image of sophistication and elegance may appeal to consumers with a preference for refined experiences.

5. Interests and Hobbies: Interests and hobbies reflect consumers' specific areas of focus and recreational pursuits. Sub-brands can align with consumers' interests to create a sense of affinity and relevance. For example, a sub-brand targeting gamers might develop products or experiences tailored to the gaming community's interests and needs.

Sub-branding strategies that align with consumers' psychographic profiles can foster strong brand-consumer relationships, increase brand loyalty, and drive long-term success.

Example 01: GoPro Hero

GoPro Hero is a sub-brand of GoPro, a leading company in the action camera industry. GoPro Hero was developed to target a specific psychographic market segment composed of adventure enthusiasts, thrill-seekers, and individuals who are passionate about capturing and sharing their experiences.

Psychographic Segmentation: The target market for GoPro Hero consists of individuals who share common psychographic characteristics, such as a love for adventure, a desire to document their experiences, and a passion for sharing those moments with others. These individuals are active and adventurous and seek to push their boundaries, whether it's through extreme sports, travel, or outdoor activities.

Product Features and Benefits: GoPro Hero action cameras offer a range of features and benefits that align with the psychographic profile of adventure-seeking individuals.

One key feature of GoPro Hero cameras is their durability and versatility. Built with rugged environments and extreme conditions in mind, these cameras are made from durable materials and are water-resistant. This allows users to confidently capture footage during activities such as surfing, snowboarding, or rock climbing. Additionally, their compact and lightweight design makes them highly portable and suitable for various mounting options.

Another standout feature of GoPro Hero cameras is their ability to capture high-quality footage. These cameras are renowned for their exceptional image and video quality. They offer high-resolution recording capabilities, advanced image stabilization technology, and wide-angle lenses. This combination allows users to capture stunning, immersive footage that vividly showcases their adrenaline-fueled moments.

GoPro Hero cameras also prioritize user-friendliness. With a user-friendly interface, these cameras make navigating through settings, modes, and options easy for users. The intuitive controls ensure a seamless experience, allowing users to quickly capture the action without being distracted or hindered by complicated configurations.

Brand Fit: GoPro Hero aligns well with the parent brand, GoPro, in several ways:

1. Brand Values and Identity: Both brands prioritize adventure, exploration, and capturing epic moments. The GoPro Hero sub-brand embodies

the spirit of the parent brand and carries forward its commitment to empowering individuals to document and share their experiences.

2. Product Innovation: GoPro is renowned for its continuous innovation in the action camera industry. The GoPro Hero sub-brand maintains this commitment by offering cutting-edge camera technology and features that cater to the needs of adrenaline seekers and outdoor enthusiasts. The sub-brand leverages the parent brand's expertise and resources to introduce new, advanced camera models that capture high-quality footage in extreme conditions.

3. Durability and Reliability: GoPro has established a reputation for man-ufacturing durable, reliable cameras that can withstand rugged envi-ronments and extreme sports activities. The GoPro Hero sub-brand upholds these qualities, ensuring that its cameras are built to withstand challenging conditions and deliver exceptional performance. This consistency in durability and reliability reinforces the brand fit between GoPro Hero and the parent brand.

4. Community and User-generated Content: GoPro has a strong community of users who actively share their captured footage and engage with the brand. The GoPro Hero sub-brand encourages user-generated content and provides platforms for users to showcase their adventures. By fostering a community of like-minded individuals, both the parent and sub-brand create a sense of belonging and shared experiences.

5. Marketing and Communication: GoPro's marketing strategies and communication tactics are well-aligned with the GoPro Hero sub-brand. Both brands focus on showcasing real-life experiences, emphasizing the versatility and capabilities of the cameras, and inspiring consumers to capture their own adventures. The consistent marketing approach reinforces the brand fit and ensures a unified brand message across the parent brand and sub-brand.

6. Distribution and Retail Presence: The GoPro Hero sub-brand benefits from the extensive distribution and retail presence established by the parent brand. GoPro has a strong global presence, with its products available in various retail outlets and online platforms. This broad

distribution network ensures that the GoPro Hero sub-brand reaches its target audience effectively and enhances its brand fit with the parent brand.

Brand Portfolio Architecture: The GoPro Hero sub-brand fits well within the brand portfolio architecture of GoPro, enhancing the overall product offerings and capturing a specific segment of the market. Here's a closer look at the brand portfolio architecture fit of GoPro Hero:

1. Brand Cohesion: The GoPro Hero sub-brand maintains a strong brand cohesion with the parent brand, GoPro. Both brands share a common purpose of enabling individuals to capture and share their adventures. The GoPro Hero cameras align with the parent brand's commitment to delivering high-quality, action-oriented cameras that are synonymous with the GoPro name.

2. Product Diversification: The GoPro Hero sub-brand expands the product portfolio of GoPro, offering a range of camera models tailored to different customer needs and budgets. The GoPro Hero cameras are designed to cater to a broader consumer base, offering a balance between performance and affordability. They provide many essential features in higher-end GoPro cameras but may have certain limitations or trade-offs to achieve a more accessible price point.

3. Target Market Segmentation: GoPro primarily targets adventure enthusiasts, extreme sports athletes, and content creators who require rugged and high-quality cameras to capture their activities. The target segment for GoPro tends to be more professional or semi-professional users who demand advanced features and are willing to invest in top-of-the-line equipment. The GoPro Hero product line expands the target segment to include a wider range of consumers, including hobbyists, casual users, and those who may be new to action cameras. GoPro Hero cameras' affordability and simplified features make them appealing to a broader audience, including travellers, vloggers, and individuals who want to capture their everyday adventures.

4. Price Differentiation: The GoPro Hero sub-brand offers a range of camera models at different price points, providing customers with options that fit their budgets. This price differentiation within the brand portfolio allows GoPro to target a wider range of customers, from entry-level users to professionals, without diluting the brand's overall reputation for quality and performance.

5. Distribution Channels: The GoPro Hero cameras are distributed through the same channels as the parent brand's products, leveraging GoPro's established retail and online distribution network. This seamless integration ensures that customers can easily access and purchase GoPro Hero cameras alongside other GoPro products, reinforcing the brand's presence and visibility in the market.

6. Brand Reputation and Trust: The GoPro Hero sub-brand benefits from the strong reputation and trust established by the parent brand. GoPro has built a solid reputation for manufacturing durable and high-performance cameras, which extends to the GoPro Hero cameras. The association with the trusted parent brand adds credibility to the GoPro Hero sub-brand and instils confidence in customers.

GoPro Hero sub-brand's strategic alignment strengthens the overall brand portfolio of GoPro and enables the company to cater to a wider range of customer needs in the action camera market.

Communication and Marketing Strategies: The GoPro Hero sub-brand employs various communication and marketing strategies to effectively promote its cameras and engage with its target audience. Here are some key strategies used by GoPro Hero:

1. Emphasizing Adventure and Action: The communication and marketing materials for GoPro Hero cameras revolve around adventure and action. The brand showcases thrilling and adrenaline-pumping moments captured with their cameras, highlighting the product's durability and performance in extreme conditions. This approach appeals to the target

audience of outdoor enthusiasts and adventure seekers who want to capture their experiences.

2. User-Generated Content: GoPro Hero leverages user-generated content as a powerful marketing tool. The brand encourages customers to share their GoPro footage, photos, and stories on social media platforms using specific hashtags. This strategy not only showcases the capabilities of the cameras but also creates a community of GoPro users who can inspire and connect with one another.

3. Influencer Partnerships: GoPro Hero collaborates with influencers, athletes, and content creators who align with its brand values and target audience. These partnerships involve featuring influencers using GoPro cameras in their adventures and sharing their experiences with their followers. The influencers' credibility and reach help increase brand visibility and influence purchasing decisions among their dedicated fan base.

4. Engaging Social Media Presence: GoPro Hero maintains an active and engaging presence on social media platforms like Instagram, YouTube, and Facebook. The brand regularly shares compelling visuals and videos captured with its cameras, showcasing the product's capabilities and inspiring potential customers. GoPro Hero also interacts with its audience through comments, responding to queries, and featuring user-generated content.

5. Event Sponsorship and Activation: GoPro Hero sponsors and participates in events related to adventure sports, outdoor activities, and extreme sports. These sponsorships provide opportunities for the brand to showcase its cameras in action, engage with the target audience, and create memorable experiences. The brand often sets up interactive booths or displays where attendees can test out the cameras and interact with brand representatives.

6. Educational Content: GoPro Hero produces educational content that helps users maximize the capabilities of their cameras. This content includes tutorials, tips, and tricks on capturing the best footage, editing techniques and using different camera features. By providing valuable

resources, GoPro Hero enhances the user experience and establishes itself as a trusted authority in the action camera industry.

7. Retail Partnerships: GoPro Hero collaborates with retail partners to ensure its cameras are prominently displayed and accessible to customers. This includes strategic placement in retail stores, dedicated sections or displays for GoPro products, and knowledgeable sales staff who can provide guidance and recommendations to customers.

Through these communication and marketing strategies, GoPro Hero effectively communicates the unique features and benefits of its cameras, establishes a strong brand presence in the adventure and action camera market, and engages with its target audience.

Monitoring and Adaptation: GoPro Hero continuously monitors market trends, customer feedback, and technological advancements to adapt its products and strategies. The brand actively engages with its customers through social media, forums, and customer surveys to gather insights and understand their evolving needs and preferences. This feedback-driven approach enables GoPro Hero to introduce new features, enhance existing products, and stay ahead of the competition.

Outcomes and Impact: The GoPro Hero sub-brand has achieved significant outcomes and made a substantial impact in the action camera market. Here are some key outcomes and impacts of GoPro Hero:

1. Market Leadership: GoPro Hero has established itself as a market leader in the action camera industry. The brand's cameras are widely recognized and preferred by adventure enthusiasts, athletes, and content creators around the world. GoPro Hero's innovative features, rugged design, and high-quality video capabilities have set a benchmark in the industry, making it the go-to brand for capturing action-packed moments.

2. Brand Recognition and Reputation: GoPro Hero has built strong brand recognition and reputation. The brand is synonymous with adventure,

action, and high-quality camera technology. GoPro Hero's distinctive branding, iconic logo, and consistent messaging have contributed to its brand equity, making it instantly recognizable and associated with capturing extraordinary moments.

3. User-Generated Content Community: GoPro Hero has successfully created a vibrant and engaged user-generated content community. The brand's call to action for users to share their footage and experiences has resulted in a massive collection of captivating content across social media platforms. This user-generated content not only serves as a powerful marketing tool for GoPro Hero but also fosters a sense of community among GoPro users, encouraging them to inspire and connect with one another.

4. Social Media Influence: GoPro Hero has a significant impact on social media platforms. The brand's content, including stunning visuals and thrilling videos captured with its cameras, generates high engagement and virality. GoPro Hero's social media presence, combined with its active engagement with followers, has helped create a loyal and passionate fan base. The brand's influence on social media extends beyond its own channels, with users and influencers sharing GoPro content and creating a ripple effect of brand advocacy.

5. Inspiring Adventure and Creativity: GoPro Hero has inspired a new generation of adventurers and content creators to push their limits and capture extraordinary moments. The brand's cameras have empowered individuals to document and share their adventures in innovative and creative ways. GoPro Hero's impact goes beyond the products themselves, as it has become synonymous with encouraging people to explore, experience, and document their passions.

6. Media and Industry Recognition: GoPro Hero has received widespread media coverage and industry recognition for its cameras and marketing efforts. The brand's innovative products, captivating campaigns, and user-generated content have been featured in various publications, television programs, and online platforms. This recognition further solidifies GoPro Hero's position as a leader and innovator in the action

camera market.

7. Business Success: The success of the GoPro Hero sub-brand has trans-lated into positive business outcomes for GoPro as a company. The brand's strong market presence, customer loyalty, and continuous product innovation have contributed to revenue growth and increased market share. GoPro Hero's success has enabled the company to expand its product portfolio, explore new markets, and establish partnerships with other industry leaders.

GoPro Hero has solidified its position as a go-to brand for capturing action-packed moments and has empowered individuals to document and share their extraordinary experiences.

Example 02: Airbnb Plus

Airbnb Plus is a sub-brand of Airbnb, a renowned online marketplace for short-term lodging and vacation rentals. Airbnb Plus was developed to target a specific psychographic market segment composed of travellers who value premium accommodations and seek unique and memorable experiences during their stays.

Psychographic Segmentation: The target market for Airbnb Plus consists of individuals who share common psychographic characteristics, such as a preference for high-quality accommodations, attention to detail, and a desire for personalized experiences. These individuals prioritize comfort, aesthetics, and uniqueness when selecting accommodations for their travels.

Product Features and Benefits: Airbnb Plus offers a curated selection of verified and premium accommodations that meet specific quality standards. Key features and benefits of the Airbnb Plus sub-brand include:

1. Verified Quality: Airbnb Plus properties undergo a rigorous verification

process to ensure they meet high standards of cleanliness, comfort, and design. Each property is visited and inspected by Airbnb representatives, who evaluate various criteria, including interior design, amenities, cleanliness, and overall guest experience.

2. Thoughtful Design: Airbnb Plus properties are carefully designed to create a welcoming and comfortable environment for guests. They feature stylish interiors, high-quality furnishings, and thoughtful touches that enhance the overall guest experience. This attention to design appeals to the target market, as they value aesthetically pleasing and well-appointed accommodations.

3. Personalized Recommendations: Airbnb Plus provides personalized recommendations based on each guest's preferences and travel history. The platform uses data and algorithms to suggest properties that align with the guest's previous bookings, reviews, and stated preferences. This customization helps guests discover accommodations that match their unique travel preferences.

Brand Fit: Airbnb Plus aligns well with the parent brand, Airbnb, in several ways:

1. Brand Values Alignment: Airbnb Plus aligns seamlessly with the parent brand's core values. Both brands prioritize the idea of providing unique and authentic travel experiences to guests. Airbnb's mission of creating a sense of belonging and promoting cultural exchange resonates with Airbnb Plus, which aims to offer a higher-end, curated selection of homes that meet certain quality standards.

2. Enhanced Customer Experience: Airbnb Plus enhances the overall customer experience by providing a premium selection of verified and quality-assured homes. It offers an elevated level of comfort, design, and amenities compared to standard listings on Airbnb. This aligns with Airbnb's commitment to offering diverse and exceptional accommodations to cater to different traveler preferences.

3. Brand Reputation and Trust: Airbnb Plus benefits from the strong brand reputation and trust established by Airbnb. As a sub-brand, it leverages the parent brand's credibility, customer base, and global presence. Guests who are familiar with and trust Airbnb are more likely to choose Airbnb Plus as it offers an added layer of assurance and quality.

4. Quality Assurance and Consistency: Airbnb Plus maintains a consistent level of quality across its listings. The sub-brand goes through a rigorous inspection process to ensure that homes meet a set of design and amenity standards. By offering a curated selection of homes that meet these criteria, Airbnb Plus instills confidence in guests, reassuring them that they will have a high-quality and reliable experience.

5. Differentiation and Segment Penetration: Airbnb Plus caters to a specific segment of travellers who seek more premium and upscale accommodations. This sub-brand allows Airbnb to tap into the luxury and higher-end travel market, capturing a new customer segment that values quality, design, and comfort. It enables Airbnb to diversify its offerings and target a broader range of travellers.

6. Seamless Integration: Airbnb Plus integrates seamlessly into Airbnb's online platform. The sub-brand maintains a consistent user interface and booking process, ensuring a smooth and familiar experience for users. This integration strengthens the association between Airbnb Plus and the parent brand, allowing guests to easily identify and choose premium accommodations within the larger Airbnb ecosystem.

7. Global Reach and Expansion: Airbnb Plus benefits from the parent brand's extensive global reach and established presence in the travel industry. It can leverage Airbnb's marketing efforts, partnerships, and user base to expand its reach and attract a wider audience. This global reach enhances the visibility and accessibility of Airbnb Plus listings, increasing its potential for success.

Through shared brand values, enhanced customer experiences, brand reputation and trust, quality assurance, differentiation in the market, seamless integration, and global reach and expansion opportunities, Airbnb Plus effectively aligns with and complements the overarching brand strategy of Airbnb.

Brand Portfolio Architecture: The Brand Portfolio Architecture fit of Airbnb Plus within the larger brand portfolio of Airbnb can be analyzed as follows:

1. Extension of Core Brand: Airbnb Plus serves as an extension of the core Airbnb brand, offering a premium subset of accommodations to cater to travellers seeking a higher-end experience. It operates within the same marketplace and platform, leveraging the existing infrastructure, user base, and brand recognition of Airbnb.

2. Segmentation and Targeting: Airbnb Plus strategically targets a specific segment of travellers who are willing to pay a premium for enhanced quality, design, and amenities in their accommodations. This sub-brand allows Airbnb to segment its offerings and cater to the needs and preferences of different customer segments, including those seeking luxury and upscale accommodations.

3. Differentiation and Positioning: By introducing Airbnb Plus, the brand creates differentiation within its portfolio. It positions itself as a provider of not only standard accommodations but also a curated selection of higher-quality homes. This allows Airbnb to differentiate itself from competitors and cater to a wider range of travellers with varying budgets and preferences.

4. Quality Control and Assurance: Airbnb Plus incorporates a rigorous verification and quality assurance process for its listings. This ensures that the accommodations meet specific standards of design, amenities, cleanliness, and comfort. By maintaining these quality controls, Airbnb Plus enhances its brand reputation and establishes itself as a trusted source for premium accommodations.

5. Upselling and Revenue Generation: Airbnb Plus presents an opportunity for revenue generation by upselling premium listings and charging a higher fee for these verified and higher-quality accommodations. By offering a tiered pricing structure, Airbnb can capture additional revenue

from guests seeking a more upscale travel experience.

6. Coherence and Consistency: Despite being a sub-brand, Airbnb Plus maintains coherence and consistency with the parent brand. It aligns with the overall brand aesthetic, user experience, and booking process of Airbnb. This coherence ensures a seamless transition for users when exploring and booking accommodations on the platform, reinforcing the association between Airbnb Plus and the broader Airbnb brand.

7. Portfolio Expansion and Growth: Airbnb Plus expands the brand's portfolio by introducing a new offering that caters to a different market segment. This expansion allows Airbnb to tap into the luxury travel market, attract a new customer base, and capture additional market share. It supports the brand's growth strategy by diversifying its offerings and revenue streams.

By strategically incorporating Airbnb Plus into its portfolio, Airbnb enhances its overall brand value proposition and provides a more comprehensive range of travel accommodation options to its customers.

Outcomes and Impact: The outcomes and impact of Airbnb Plus, the sub-brand of Airbnb, have been significant in terms of enhancing the guest experience, expanding the offerings on the platform, and driving business growth. Here are some key outcomes and impacts of Airbnb Plus:

1. Enhanced Guest Experience: Airbnb Plus has successfully provided guests with a higher level of comfort, quality, and assurance. By curating a collection of verified and premium accommodations, Airbnb Plus ensures that guests have a consistent and exceptional experience when booking these listings. The focus on design, amenities, and overall quality has elevated the guest experience and garnered positive feedback from users.

2. Differentiation and Brand Positioning: Airbnb Plus has allowed Airbnb to differentiate itself in the market and target a more upscale segment of travellers. The sub-brand's emphasis on verified and premium accommodations sets it apart from standard listings on the platform,

creating a distinct brand positioning. Airbnb Plus has established itself as a premium offering within the broader Airbnb ecosystem.

3. Increased Trust and Credibility: The rigorous verification process of Airbnb Plus, which includes in-person inspections and adherence to quality standards, has boosted trust and credibility among guests. The thorough vetting gives guests confidence that they can trust the accuracy of the listings and expect a certain level of quality. This increased trust has positively impacted the overall reputation of Airbnb and has contributed to the growth of the platform.

4. Business Growth and Revenue Generation: Airbnb Plus has contributed to the growth and revenue generation of Airbnb as a whole. By attracting a more discerning and upscale clientele, Airbnb Plus listings can command higher rates, resulting in increased revenue for hosts and the platform. The introduction of Airbnb Plus has expanded the market reach of Airbnb and has attracted new hosts who can offer premium accommodations.

5. Expansion of Accommodation Options: With the launch of Airbnb Plus, Airbnb has expanded its range of accommodation options to include verified and premium listings. This has allowed the platform to cater to a wider range of travellers who seek higher-quality accommodations. Expanding the Airbnb Plus collection has provided more choices for guests, further solidifying Airbnb's position as a leading online travel platform.

6. Influencing Industry Standards: The introduction of Airbnb Plus has raised the bar for quality standards in the vacation rental industry. By setting specific design and comfort criteria for listings, Airbnb Plus has influenced industry standards and encouraged hosts on the platform to improve the quality of their accommodations. This has had a positive ripple effect on the overall vacation rental market, benefiting both guests and hosts.

7. Inspiration for Other Platforms: The success of Airbnb Plus has inspired other travel and accommodation platforms to introduce similar premium offerings. The concept of curating verified and high-quality accommodations has been replicated by competitors, highlighting the influence

and impact of Airbnb Plus on the broader industry.

Airbnb Plus is an exemplary sub-brand that effectively targets the psychographic segment of travellers seeking premium accommodations and personalized experiences. By curating a selection of verified and thoughtfully designed properties, Airbnb Plus caters to the desires of guests who prioritize quality, aesthetics, and unique stays. Through strategic marketing, visual storytelling, and guest feedback, Airbnb Plus has successfully positioned itself as a premium option within the Airbnb marketplace, appealing to travellers seeking exceptional and personalized travel experiences.

* * *

5

Behavioural Segmentation

I n the world of marketing, understanding consumer behaviour is key to developing successful strategies and building lasting relationships with customers. Behavioural segmentation is a powerful approach that allows brands to group consumers based on their purchasing behaviour, brand loyalty, usage patterns, and other observable actions. By analyzing these behaviours, brands can tailor their marketing efforts to specific segments, maximizing their impact and effectiveness.

Creating sub-brands for behavioural segmentation takes this strategy a step further. It involves developing distinct brands or product lines within a company's portfolio, each targeting a specific behavioural segment. By doing so, brands can cater to the unique needs, preferences, and motivations of different consumer groups, providing tailored offerings and experiences that resonate with their specific behaviours.

Sub-branding for behavioural segmentation offers numerous benefits. Firstly, it enables brands to deepen their understanding of consumer behaviour. By analyzing data and insights related to purchase frequency, brand loyalty, usage patterns, and other behavioural indicators, brands can gain valuable insights into the motivations and preferences of different segments. This understanding allows for the development of targeted marketing strategies that address the specific needs and desires of each segment.

Secondly, sub-brands allow brands to create personalized experiences for different behavioural segments. By developing distinct brand identities, messaging, and product offerings, brands can cater to the unique preferences and behaviours of each segment. For example, a sub-brand could focus on offering exclusive rewards and benefits to highly loyal customers, while another sub-brand could target price-sensitive consumers with more affordable options. This customization enhances customer satisfaction and loyalty, fostering stronger relationships with each segment.

Furthermore, sub-brands help brands mitigate the risk of diluting their main brand image. By creating separate identities for different behavioural segments, brands can ensure that each sub-brand is aligned with the specific expectations and preferences of its target audience. This clarity and consistency enable consumers to easily identify and connect with the sub-brand that best matches their behaviours and preferences, enhancing brand loyalty and reducing confusion.

Behavioural Variables

Behavioural segmentation focuses on understanding how consumers interact with products or services, their purchasing habits, brand loyalty, and the benefits they seek. Here are key behavioural variables and their relevance to sub-branding:

1. Usage Occasions: Usage occasions refer to the specific situations or contexts in which consumers use a product or service. Sub-brands can be developed to cater to different usage occasions, providing tailored solutions that align with consumers' specific needs. For example, a sub-brand of skin care products may target consumers looking for a daily skincare routine, while another sub-brand from the same company may focus on specialized treatments for occasional use.

2. Benefits Sought: Benefits sought represent the specific outcomes or advantages that consumers seek from a product or service. Behavioural seg-

mentation based on benefits sought helps brands understand different consumer motivations and tailor sub-brands to deliver specific benefits. For instance, a sub-brand of energy drinks may target consumers seeking a boost in physical performance, while another sub-brand may cater to those seeking mental focus and concentration.

3. Loyalty Status: Loyalty status refers to consumers' degree of loyalty to a brand. Behavioural segmentation based on loyalty status allows brands to identify and cater to different segments, such as loyal customers, switchers, or brand-agnostic consumers. Sub-brands can be designed to nurture brand loyalty among existing customers or attract switchers by offering unique value propositions or rewards.

4. User Status: User status differentiates between potential customers, first-time users, and frequent users. Sub-brands can be developed to target each user status segment differently. For example, a sub-brand for first-time users may focus on trial offers, educational content, or introductory pricing, while a sub-brand for frequent users may emphasize loyalty programs, exclusive benefits, or personalized experiences.

5. Occasion-Based Segmentation: Occasion-based segmentation considers consumers' behaviours and preferences during specific events or occasions. Sub-brands can be created to align with these occasions and provide tailored experiences or offerings. For instance, a sub-brand of greeting cards may focus on occasions like birthdays, anniversaries, or holidays, catering to the unique needs and sentiments associated with each occasion.

Behavioural segmentation ensures that sub-brands are strategically positioned to deliver the right solutions, benefits, and experiences that drive consumer engagement, satisfaction, and loyalty.

Example 01: Starbucks Rewards Program

Starbucks, a global coffeehouse chain, has successfully implemented a sub-brand for behavioural segmentation through its Starbucks Rewards program. The program is designed to cater to the specific behaviours and preferences of its loyal customers, creating a personalized and rewarding experience. Let's delve into the details.

Understanding the Target Segment: Starbucks recognized that its customer base comprised individuals who frequently visited their stores and exhibited specific behavioural patterns. These behaviours included regular coffee consumption, repeat purchases, and a preference for a personalized and convenient experience. To tap into this segment and drive loyalty, Starbucks introduced the Starbucks Rewards program.

Product Features and Benefits: The Starbucks Rewards Program offers various product features and benefits that aim to enhance the overall customer experience and incentivize continued patronage. Some of the product features and benefits of the Starbucks Rewards Program:

1. Points Accumulation: One of the program's key features is the ability for customers to accumulate points for their purchases. Members earn stars for every transaction they make at Starbucks stores or through the Starbucks mobile app. The more stars they collect, the closer they get to redeeming rewards and benefits.
2. Personalized Offers and Discounts: Starbucks Rewards members enjoy personalized offers and discounts tailored to their preferences and purchasing history. The program uses data analytics to understand individual customer preferences and send targeted promotions, ensuring that members receive offers that are relevant to their tastes and preferences.
3. Free Drinks and Food: Members can redeem their accumulated stars for free drinks or food items through the Starbucks Rewards Program. This allows loyal customers to enjoy complimentary treats as a reward

for their continued patronage. The program offers a sense of value and appreciation to members by giving them the opportunity to indulge in their favourite Starbucks products without additional cost.

4. Birthday Rewards: Starbucks Rewards members receive special rewards on their birthdays, such as a free drink or food item of their choice. This personalized birthday perk adds an extra touch of celebration and makes members feel valued and appreciated on their special day.

5. Mobile Order and Pay: The program lets members conveniently place orders and pay using the Starbucks mobile app. This feature allows for a seamless and time-saving experience, as members can bypass the usual queues and pick up their orders directly. The mobile order and pay feature enhances convenience and efficiency, catering to the needs of busy customers on the go.

6. Early Access to New Products and Promotions: Starbucks Rewards members often enjoy exclusive early access to new menu items, limited-edition beverages, and promotional offers. This gives members a sense of exclusivity and allows them to be among the first to try and experience new offerings from Starbucks.

7. Digital Rewards Card: The Starbucks Rewards Program provides members with a digital rewards card accessible through the Starbucks mobile app. This eliminates the need for physical loyalty cards and streamlines the rewards process. Members can easily track their stars, view their rewards, and manage their account digitally, enhancing convenience and ease of use.

8. Gamification and Social Elements: Starbucks incorporates gamification elements within the Rewards program to further engage customers. Members can participate in challenges, earn bonus stars, and unlock exclusive benefits. Additionally, Starbucks fosters a sense of community by allowing members to connect and share their experiences through the app and social media platforms.

The program enhances the overall Starbucks experience and incentivizes customers to continue choosing Starbucks as their preferred coffee destination.

Brand Fit: The Starbucks Rewards Program sub-brand exhibits a strong brand fit with its parent brand, Starbucks. Let's analyze the brand fit between the Starbucks Rewards Program and its parent brand:

1. Alignment with Customer-centric Approach: The Starbucks Rewards Program is designed to cater to the needs and preferences of Starbucks' loyal customers. It offers personalized rewards, discounts, and exclusive perks based on individual customer behaviour and preferences. This aligns with Starbucks' commitment to providing a personalized and exceptional customer experience where customers feel valued and appreciated.

2. Consistency in Brand Identity: The Starbucks Rewards Program maintains a consistent brand identity with the parent brand. It utilizes the same visual elements, such as the Starbucks logo and iconic green colour scheme, ensuring immediate recognition and association with Starbucks. This consistency in brand identity creates a seamless and integrated experience for customers, strengthening the connection between the sub-brand and the parent brand.

3. Reinforcement of Brand Loyalty: The Starbucks Rewards Program reinforces brand loyalty by rewarding customers for their continued patronage. By offering free drinks, personalized offers, and other exclusive benefits, the program encourages customers to choose Starbucks over competitors, fostering long-term loyalty. This aligns with Starbucks' goal of building strong and lasting relationships with its customers.

4. Integration with Starbucks' Digital Strategy: The Starbucks Rewards Program leverages digital technology and the Starbucks mobile app to provide members a seamless and convenient experience. The program's mobile ordering and payment features align with Starbucks' focus on digital innovation and enhancing customer convenience through technology. The integration of the program with the Starbucks mobile app also supports Starbucks' broader digital strategy and its goal of engaging customers through digital channels.

5. Enhancing the Starbucks Experience: The Starbucks Rewards Program enhances the overall Starbucks experience for customers. By offering

personalized offers, birthday rewards, and early access to new products, the program adds value and excitement to the customer journey. It encourages customers to explore new offerings and engage more deeply with the Starbucks brand, aligning with Starbucks' mission of inspiring and nurturing the human spirit.

The program's focus on rewarding and engaging customers while driving business results strengthens the connection between the sub-brand and the parent brand, ultimately benefiting both Starbucks and its loyal customers.

Brand Portfolio Architecture: The Starbucks Rewards Program sub-brand fits well within Starbucks' brand portfolio architecture. Let's examine how the sub-brand aligns with the overall brand portfolio strategy:

1. Extension of Starbucks' Core Offering: The Starbucks Rewards Program is a natural extension of Starbucks' core offering, which is providing high-quality coffee and a unique customer experience. By introducing a rewards program, Starbucks enhances its value proposition and creates an additional layer of loyalty and engagement with its customers.

2. Integration with the Starbucks Ecosystem: The Starbucks Rewards Program integrates seamlessly with the broader Starbucks ecosystem, including its physical stores, mobile app, and online platforms. Customers can easily earn and redeem rewards at Starbucks locations, making the program a central part of the Starbucks experience. This integration strengthens the brand portfolio architecture by creating a cohesive ecosystem that reinforces customer loyalty and engagement.

3. Differentiation within the Market: The Starbucks Rewards Program sets Starbucks apart from competitors by offering a unique and tailored rewards program. It adds value for customers, incentivizing them to choose Starbucks over other coffee chains. This differentiation strengthens the brand portfolio architecture by giving customers more reasons to engage with Starbucks and its offerings.

4. Complementary to Other Sub-Brands: The Starbucks Rewards Program

complements other sub-brands within the Starbucks brand portfolio. For example, it works synergistically with the Starbucks mobile app, allowing customers to conveniently earn and track rewards through digital channels. It also complements the Starbucks Reserve sub-brand by offering exclusive rewards and experiences related to premium coffee offerings. This complementary nature enhances the overall brand portfolio architecture by creating a cohesive and interconnected system of sub-brands.

5. Reinforcement of Starbucks' Brand Equity: The Starbucks Rewards Program reinforces Starbucks' brand equity by strengthening customers' emotional connection and loyalty to the brand. By providing personalized rewards and exclusive benefits, the program deepens customers' affinity for Starbucks, which in turn strengthens the overall brand portfolio architecture.

These factors collectively enhance the brand portfolio architecture, creating a stronger and more comprehensive brand portfolio for Starbucks.

Communication and Marketing Strategies: The Starbucks Rewards Program utilizes various communication and marketing strategies to engage customers, promote loyalty, and drive participation in the program. Here are some key strategies employed by the sub-brand:

1. Personalized Email and Mobile Marketing: Starbucks leverages customer data collected through the rewards program to send its members personalized emails and mobile notifications. These communications include tailored offers, promotions, and new product or reward updates. By delivering relevant content directly to customers' inboxes and mobile devices, Starbucks aims to keep members engaged and encourage repeat visits.

2. In-Store Promotions and Signage: Starbucks prominently displays signage and promotional materials in its stores to raise awareness of the rewards program and its benefits. This includes posters, counter

displays, and digital screens showcasing the perks of being a rewards member. By making the program visible within its physical locations, Starbucks encourages customers to enrol and participate in the program.

3. Digital and Social Media Advertising: Starbucks utilizes digital advertising platforms and social media channels to promote the rewards program. They run targeted ad campaigns on platforms like Facebook, Instagram, and Google, reaching potential customers who may be interested in joining the program. These ads highlight the program's benefits, such as free drinks, personalized offers, and member-exclusive events.

4. Integration with the Starbucks Mobile App: The Starbucks Rewards Program is seamlessly integrated into the Starbucks mobile app. The app serves as a hub for customers to track their rewards, view available offers, and place mobile orders. Starbucks actively promotes the app and its rewards features through app store optimization, push notifications, and app-specific promotions, ensuring customers are aware of the benefits of using the app to enhance their rewards experience.

5. Influencer Partnerships and Collaborations: Starbucks collaborates with influencers and brand ambassadors to create buzz around the rewards program. Influencers may share their experiences with the program, showcase rewards earned, or highlight exclusive promotions. By leveraging the reach and influence of these individuals, Starbucks expands its reach and attracts new customers to join the rewards program.

6. Seasonal and Limited-Time Promotions: Starbucks introduces seasonal and limited-time promotions tied to the rewards program to create excitement and urgency among customers. These promotions may include bonus stars for specific purchases, limited-edition rewards, or exclusive member events. By offering time-sensitive incentives, Starbucks motivates customers to actively participate in the program and maximize their rewards.

7. Referral and Member-Get-Member Programs: Starbucks encourages its reward members to refer friends and family to join the program through referral incentives. Existing members may receive bonus stars or exclusive rewards when their referrals sign up and make qualifying

purchases. This referral program helps expand the membership base and drives word-of-mouth marketing for the rewards program.

The communication and marketing strategies of the Starbucks Rewards Program are designed to engage customers, increase enrollment and participation, and foster brand loyalty.

Outcomes and Impact: The Starbucks Rewards Program has had significant outcomes and impacts on both Starbucks and its customers. Here are some key outcomes and impacts of the program:

1. Increased Customer Loyalty: The Rewards Program has been successful in fostering customer loyalty. By offering rewards, personalized offers, and exclusive perks, Starbucks has incentivized customers to choose Starbucks over competitors and to make repeat visits. This has resulted in increased customer retention and a higher level of brand loyalty among program members.

2. Higher Customer Engagement: The program has effectively engaged customers by providing them with a sense of belonging and recognition. Customers are motivated to earn stars and unlock higher tiers within the program, which encourages them to continue visiting Starbucks and making purchases. The interactive nature of the program keeps customers engaged and invested in the Starbucks brand.

3. Repeat Business and Increased Sales: The Rewards Program has contributed to increased sales and repeat business for Starbucks. Members of the program are more likely to visit Starbucks frequently and spend more money on their purchases in order to earn rewards and stars. This has led to a positive impact on Starbucks' revenue and overall sales performance.

4. Data-Driven Insights: The program allows Starbucks to collect valuable customer data and insights. By analyzing customer preferences, purchase patterns, and behaviours, Starbucks can tailor its offerings and marketing strategies to better meet customer needs. This data-driven approach enables Starbucks to make informed business decisions and

create personalized experiences for its customers.

5. Positive Word-of-Mouth and Brand Advocacy: Starbucks's Rewards Program has generated positive word-of-mouth. Satisfied program members are likely to share their positive experiences with friends and family and on social media, which in turn helps attract new customers to join the program and visit Starbucks. The program's benefits and rewards create brand advocates who actively promote Starbucks to others.

6. Increased App Adoption and Mobile Ordering: The integration of the Rewards Program into the Starbucks mobile app has encouraged customers to download and use the app for ordering and payment. This has streamlined the ordering process and enhanced the overall customer experience. The convenience of mobile ordering and the ability to track rewards and offers within the app has contributed to increased app adoption and usage.

7. Continued Program Innovations: The success of the Rewards Program has driven Starbucks to continuously innovate and introduce new features. Starbucks regularly updates the program with new rewards, seasonal promotions, and member-exclusive offerings to keep customers engaged and excited. This commitment to program enhancements demonstrates Starbucks' dedication to meeting customer expectations and evolving its loyalty program.

The program's positive outcomes have contributed to Starbucks' continued success and growth in the highly competitive coffee industry.

Example 02: Sephora Beauty Insider Program

Sephora, a leading beauty retailer, has successfully implemented a sub-brand for behavioural segmentation through its Beauty Insider program. The program caters to beauty enthusiasts' specific behaviours and preferences, creating a personalized and engaging experience.

Understanding the Target Segment: Sephora recognized that its customer base consisted of individuals who exhibited specific behavioural patterns related to their interest in beauty products. These behaviours included regular purchases, engagement with beauty trends and tutorials, and a desire for personalized recommendations. To tap into this segment and drive loyalty, Sephora introduced the Beauty Insider program.

Product Features and Benefits: The Sephora Beauty Insider Program offers a range of product features and benefits designed to enhance the shopping experience and reward customer loyalty. Here are the detailed product features and benefits of the Sephora Beauty Insider Program:

1. Tiered Rewards System: The Beauty Insider Program operates on a tiered rewards system, allowing customers to earn points for every purchase made at Sephora. Customers can unlock different membership tiers, including Beauty Insider, VIB (Very Important Beauty Insider), and Rouge as they accumulate points. Each tier offers its own set of exclusive benefits and rewards, such as early access to product launches, seasonal promotions, and special events.

2. Points Redemption: One of the program's main features is the ability to redeem accumulated points for various rewards. Customers can choose from a selection of beauty products, samples, and even experiences, allowing them to try new products or indulge in their favourites. This feature encourages continued engagement and repeat purchases as customers strive to earn more points to redeem for desirable rewards.

3. Birthday Gifts: Beauty Insider Program members receive special birthday gifts as a token of appreciation from Sephora. These gifts can include mini-sized beauty products, exclusive samples, or discounts, providing an additional incentive for customers to shop during their birthday month and reinforcing the personalization aspect of the program.

4. Exclusive Offers and Promotions: Members of the Beauty Insider Program gain access to exclusive offers and promotions throughout the year. Sephora often runs limited-time discounts, free gifts with purchase,

and special sales events exclusively for program members. These exclusive offers add value to the shopping experience and create a sense of exclusivity for program members.

5. Personalized Recommendations: The Beauty Insider Program leverages customer purchase history and preferences to provide personalized product recommendations. Program members receive tailored product suggestions based on their beauty profile, previous purchases, and reviews. This feature helps customers discover new products that align with their preferences and enhances their overall shopping experience.

6. Insider Community: The program fosters a sense of community among beauty enthusiasts by providing access to an online community of like-minded individuals. Members can participate in discussion boards, share product reviews, and engage with Sephora's beauty experts and other customers. This creates a space for customers to connect, exchange beauty tips, and seek advice, further enhancing their overall experience with Sephora.

7. Exclusive Beauty Events: Beauty Insider Program members have the opportunity to attend exclusive beauty events hosted by Sephora. These events can include makeup tutorials, beauty workshops, and meet-and-greets with industry experts or brand representatives. These events offer unique experiences and insights into the latest beauty trends and products, making them highly sought-after benefits of the program.

The Sephora Beauty Insider features and benefits encourage customer engagement, repeat purchases, and a sense of belonging, ultimately strengthening the relationship between Sephora and its customers.

Brand Fit: The Sephora Beauty Insider Program has a strong brand fit with its parent brand, Sephora. Let's analyze the brand fit between the Beauty Insider Program and Sephora:

1. Alignment with Sephora's Values: Sephora is known for its commitment to providing a diverse range of beauty products, exceptional customer

service, and creating an inclusive beauty community. The Beauty Insider Program aligns perfectly with these values by offering a personalized and inclusive experience for customers. It promotes diversity through its wide range of product offerings, encourages engagement with a vibrant beauty community, and delivers personalized recommendations based on individual preferences.

2. Reinforcement of Customer Loyalty: Sephora places a strong emphasis on building and nurturing customer loyalty. The Beauty Insider Program plays a vital role in strengthening customer loyalty by rewarding customers for their purchases and engagement. The tiered rewards system, exclusive offers, and personalized recommendations incentivize customers to continue shopping at Sephora, reinforcing their loyalty and encouraging repeat purchases.

3. Enhancing the Shopping Experience: Sephora is known for its immersive and enjoyable shopping experience. The Beauty Insider Program enhances this experience by offering additional benefits and exclusive access to rewards, events, and promotions. By providing personalized recommendations, birthday gifts, and insider community engagement, the program adds value and creates a more personalized and memorable shopping journey for Sephora customers.

4. Extension of Brand Identity: The Beauty Insider Program seamlessly extends Sephora's brand identity. It retains the brand's reputation for offering a vast selection of beauty products and expertise while adding an extra layer of personalization and rewards. The program reinforces Sephora's image as a beauty authority, offering customers an elevated and rewarding experience within the beauty industry.

5. Customer-Centric Approach: Sephora places a strong emphasis on customer satisfaction and understanding their needs. The Beauty Insider Program demonstrates this customer-centric approach by tailoring rewards, recommendations, and offers based on individual preferences and behaviours. It shows that Sephora values its customers' loyalty and is dedicated to providing them with a personalized and enjoyable beauty shopping experience.

The Sephora Beauty Insider program complements and strengthens Sephora's overall brand strategy, allowing the company to deepen its relationship with customers and maintain its position as a leading beauty retailer.

Outcomes and Impact: Some of the outcomes and impacts of the program:

1. Customer Loyalty and Engagement: The Beauty Insider Program has been successful in fostering customer loyalty and engagement. By offering exclusive benefits, personalized rewards, and a sense of community, Sephora has created a strong bond with its customers. The program incentivizes customers to continue shopping at Sephora and encourages repeat purchases, resulting in increased customer loyalty and engagement.

2. Increased Customer Lifetime Value: The Beauty Insider Program has positively impacted the customer lifetime value for Sephora. By rewarding customer purchases and encouraging members to earn points and redeem rewards, Sephora has increased customer spending and incentivized higher-value purchases. The program's tiered structure also motivates customers to reach higher membership tiers, leading to increased spending over time.

3. Customer Data and Insights: The program provides Sephora with valuable customer data and insights. Through the Beauty Insider Program, Sephora collects information about customers' preferences, purchase history, and beauty preferences. This data enables Sephora to better understand its customers, personalize their experiences and tailor marketing efforts to their specific needs and preferences.

4. Word-of-Mouth and Brand Advocacy: The Beauty Insider Program has generated positive word-of-mouth and brand advocacy for Sephora. Satisfied program members often share their experiences and rewards with friends and family, leading to increased brand awareness and new customer acquisition through referrals. The program's exclusive perks and personalized benefits create a sense of excitement and loyalty among members, which they are likely to share with others.

5. Enhanced Customer Experience: The Beauty Insider Program has contributed to an enhanced customer experience at Sephora. Members receive personalized recommendations, early access to new products, and special promotions, making their shopping experience more enjoyable and rewarding. The program also offers educational resources, beauty tips, and interactive community features, further enriching the overall customer experience.

6. Competitive Advantage: The Beauty Insider Program has given Sephora a competitive advantage in the beauty retail industry. The program's comprehensive rewards system, personalized benefits, and community engagement differentiate Sephora from its competitors. The program's success and popularity have positioned Sephora as a leading beauty retailer that goes beyond offering products to providing a rewarding and immersive beauty experience.

7. Data-Driven Marketing and Personalization: The customer data collected through the Beauty Insider Program allows Sephora to implement data-driven marketing strategies. Based on individual customer preferences, Sephora can personalize its marketing efforts, including email campaigns, promotions, and product recommendations. This level of personalization helps Sephora target customers more effectively and create a more relevant and engaging experience.

The Beauty Insider program has strengthened Sephora's brand reputation, increased customer satisfaction, and positioned Sephora as a leader in the beauty industry.

* * *

6

Product Line Expansion

A product line extension is a strategy that involves introducing new products to an existing product line. The new products are typically similar to the existing products in terms of quality, price, and target market. However, they may offer new features or benefits, or they may be targeted at a different segment of the market.

There are several reasons why a company might launch a product line extension. One reason is to increase sales. By adding new products to the product line, the company can appeal to a wider range of customers and generate more revenue. Another reason is to compete with other companies. By introducing new products, the company can stay ahead of the competition and maintain its market share.

There are several ways to launch a product line extension. One way is to introduce the new products under the same brand name as the existing products. This is the simplest and most cost-effective way to launch a product line extension. However, it can also be the least effective, as it may not give the new products enough differentiation from the existing products.

Another way to launch a product line extension is to introduce new products under a sub-brand. A sub-brand is a subsidiary brand that is closely associated with the parent brand, but it has its own unique name, identity, and positioning. This can be a more effective way to launch a product line extension, as it can give the new products the differentiation they need to succeed.

Example 01: Procter & Gamble (P&G)

P&G is a multinational consumer goods company known for its diverse brand portfolio. One notable example of product expansion through sub-brands is the "Pampers" brand.

Pampers, initially launched as a single brand offering disposable diapers, recognized the importance of catering to the diverse needs of parents and babies. To better serve different customer segments and address specific requirements, P&G expanded the Pampers brand by introducing various sub-brands.

One sub-brand under the Pampers umbrella is "Pampers Swaddlers," specifically designed for newborns. Swaddlers feature a soft and gentle design with an umbilical cord notch, ensuring comfort and protection for newborn babies. P&G recognized the unique needs of this segment, such as delicate skin and the need for a snug fit, and tailored the Swaddlers sub-brand accordingly.

Another sub-brand, "Pampers Cruisers," was developed to cater to active babies who are constantly on the move. Cruisers offer excellent mobility and flexibility, allowing babies to explore and play freely while still providing the comfort and absorption Pampers is known for. This sub-brand addresses the needs of parents with more active babies who require diapers that can keep up with their movements.

Pampers also launched the "Pampers Pure" sub-brand, targeting parents seeking natural and hypoallergenic options for their babies. Pure diapers are made with carefully selected materials and are free from chlorine bleaching, fragrance, and parabens. This sub-brand appeals to environmentally conscious parents who prioritize using products with minimal impact on their baby's skin and the environment.

By introducing these sub-brands, P&G effectively segmented the market and expanded the Pampers brand to accommodate different customer needs. Each sub-brand within the Pampers family caters to a specific age group or addresses unique preferences, ensuring that parents can find the right diaper solution for their baby.

The sub-brands under Pampers allow P&G to capture a broader market share within the highly competitive baby care segment. By offering tailored solutions, Pampers has positioned itself as a trusted and reliable brand that understands the distinct requirements of parents and babies at various stages of development.

The sub-brands under Pampers exemplify how product expansion through sub-branding can enable companies to better serve specific customer segments, strengthen brand loyalty, and achieve market success.

Example 02: Volkswagen's "Volkswagen ID"

Volkswagen introduced the sub-brand "Volkswagen ID" to represent its electric vehicles (EVs) and drive its transition to sustainable mobility. This sub-brand specifically targets consumers seeking eco-friendly transportation options. By focusing on EVs under the Volkswagen ID name, the company tailored its messaging, design, and features to meet the unique needs of this target market.

The Volkswagen ID sub-brand aligns with the company's broader commitment to sustainability and innovation. The name "ID" represents "Intelligent Design," highlighting Volkswagen's emphasis on advanced technology, futuristic design, and eco-friendliness. This association strengthens Volkswagen's reputation for quality and reliability while signalling its dedication to sustainable mobility.

Creating the Volkswagen ID sub-brand allowed the company to differentiate its EV lineup from traditional combustion engine vehicles. The Volkswagen ID vehicles showcase cutting-edge electric drivetrain technology, longer driving ranges, and advanced connectivity features that cater to EV users. This differentiation positions Volkswagen as a player in the growing electric mobility market and appeals to consumers seeking greener alternatives.

Furthermore, the sub-brand strategy enables Volkswagen to adapt to evolving market trends and regulations in the electric mobility space. By focusing on EVs under the Volkswagen ID name, the company can align its product development, marketing efforts, and customer experience to meet electric vehicle owners' unique requirements and expectations.

Through comprehensive marketing and communication strategies, Volkswagen effectively launched and managed the Volkswagen ID sub-brand. The company utilized various channels, such as digital marketing, events, and partnerships, to raise awareness about its EV lineup, highlight the benefits of electric mobility, and address customer concerns like range anxiety and charging infrastructure.

In summary, creating the Volkswagen ID sub-brand positions Volkswagen as a leader in the electric vehicle market. By segmenting its product portfolio and aligning with environmentally conscious consumers, Volkswagen successfully differentiates its EV offerings, demonstrates its commitment to sustainable mobility, and adapts to the changing automotive industry landscape.

In conclusion, creating a sub-brand for product/service expansion is a strategic decision that can offer numerous benefits to a company. By developing a sub-brand, businesses can effectively target specific market segments, differentiate their offerings, and extend their brand into new product or service categories. This strategy allows companies to leverage their existing brand equity while tailoring their messaging, positioning, and value proposition to meet the unique needs and preferences of the target market.

* * *

7

New Product Categories or Industries

When a company decides to venture into a new product category or industry, it often faces the challenge of establishing a presence and building credibility in an unfamiliar market. In such situations, creating a sub-brand can be a strategic approach to leverage the company's existing brand equity and customer trust while entering new territory.

A sub-brand allows the company to introduce new products or services that cater to a different customer segment or fulfil specific needs within a new product category or industry. By creating a sub-brand, the company can maintain a sense of continuity with its existing brand while differentiating its offerings for the new market.

Creating a sub-brand for entering a new product category or industry involves careful strategic planning and brand management. It requires a thorough understanding of the target market, customer preferences, and competition in the new industry. The sub-brand should be positioned strategically to address the unique requirements and expectations of the new market segment while aligning with the parent brand's overall brand strategy.

The sub-brand's name, visual identity, messaging, and product offerings should be carefully developed to create a strong brand presence and resonate with the target audience. Effective communication and consistent brand messaging are crucial to establishing credibility, building awareness, and gaining market acceptance for the sub-brand.

By creating a sub-brand, companies can mitigate the risks associated with entering a new product category or industry. They can leverage the reputation and customer loyalty of the parent brand to establish credibility and trustworthiness in the new market. Additionally, the sub-brand allows for flexibility in product development, marketing strategies, and brand positioning specific to the new market segment.

Example 01: Apple's "AirPods"

Apple, a renowned technology company, successfully launched the sub-brand "AirPods" to expand into the wireless earphones market. The introduction of AirPods exemplifies Apple's strategic approach to brand extension and its ability to enter new product categories.

Reason for Sub-Brand Creation: Apple recognized the growing demand for wireless audio devices and identified an opportunity to cater to the needs of its existing customer base while attracting new customers. As technology advanced and smartphones eliminated the traditional headphone jack, the trend towards wireless audio solutions became more prominent. This prompted Apple to introduce AirPods, leveraging its brand equity, design expertise, and seamless integration with its existing product ecosystem to offer a premium and innovative wireless earbuds experience.

By creating the sub-brand AirPods, Apple was able to differentiate the product from the competition and position it as a leader in the wireless earbuds market. While other wireless earbuds existed, AirPods stood out as the first truly wireless option, setting a new standard in the industry. The sub-branding strategy allowed Apple to create a distinct category of product and establish itself as the premier provider within that category.

Moreover, AirPods were strategically targeted at a younger, fashion-conscious market, diverging from Apple's traditional customer base.

Brand Fit: Some of the key points of brand fit analysis—

1. Design and Aesthetics: The Apple AirPods sub-brand aligns seamlessly with Apple's design philosophy and aesthetic. The AirPods feature a sleek, minimalist design that reflects Apple's commitment to elegance and simplicity. The clean lines, smooth surfaces, and white colour palette resonate with Apple's overall brand identity, creating a cohesive and recognizable product within the Apple ecosystem.

2. Innovation and Technology: Apple is renowned for its focus on innovation and cutting-edge technology. The AirPods sub-brand exemplifies this by introducing wireless, Bluetooth-enabled earbuds with advanced features like seamless connectivity, intelligent sensors, and voice-activated assistance through Siri. The integration of these technological advancements showcases Apple's commitment to pushing the boundaries of innovation and delivering breakthrough products to its customers.

3. User Experience: Apple has consistently emphasized user experience in its products, aiming for intuitive interfaces and seamless interactions. The AirPods sub-brand extends this emphasis by offering a hassle-free user experience. From effortless pairing with Apple devices to automatic ear detection and seamless switching between devices, the AirPods provide a user-friendly and convenient experience that aligns with Apple's customer-centric approach.

4. Ecosystem Integration: The AirPods sub-brand integrates seamlessly into Apple's ecosystem of devices and services. The AirPods offer a streamlined connection and integration with iPhones, iPads, Macs, and other Apple devices, allowing users to enjoy a seamless experience across their Apple products. This integration enhances the overall value proposition for Apple customers and reinforces brand loyalty within the Apple ecosystem.

5. Brand Reputation: Apple has built a strong reputation for delivering high-quality, premium products with a focus on craftsmanship and attention to detail. The AirPods sub-brand upholds this reputation by offering

a well-crafted, reliable, and durable product. The use of premium materials, precision engineering, and rigorous quality standards reflect Apple's commitment to delivering products that meet or exceed customer expectations.

6. Marketing and Branding: The AirPods sub-brand benefits from Apple's extensive marketing and branding efforts. Apple's strong global presence, iconic advertising campaigns, and brand equity contribute to the success and recognition of the AirPods. The Apple logo on the AirPods packaging and marketing materials reinforces the association between the sub-brand and its parent brand, further enhancing the brand fit.

The seamless integration of the AirPods into the Apple ecosystem and the marketing support from Apple further strengthen the brand fit, creating a cohesive and compelling product offering for customers.

Brand Architecture: The Apple AirPods sub-brand aligns well with Apple's brand portfolio architecture strategy. Here's an analysis of the brand fit within the portfolio:

1. Product Synergy: Apple's brand portfolio consists of various product categories, including iPhones, iPads, Macs, Apple Watches, and more. The AirPods sub-brand complements these product categories by offering a wireless audio solution that enhances the overall user experience. The seamless integration of AirPods with Apple devices creates a synergistic relationship, as users can enjoy the convenience of wireless audio while leveraging the functionalities of other Apple products. This synergy strengthens the overall appeal of Apple's ecosystem and encourages cross-product adoption.

2. Premium Positioning: Apple has positioned itself as a premium brand, offering high-quality, innovative, and premium-priced products. The AirPods sub-brand aligns with this positioning by delivering a premium audio experience. The use of advanced technology, premium materials, and attention to detail in the design and manufacturing of AirPods

reinforce the premium brand image of Apple. The AirPods' pricing also reflects this positioning, allowing Apple to maintain its reputation as a provider of high-value, premium products within its brand portfolio.

3. Brand Consistency: Apple is known for its consistent brand identity and messaging across its product portfolio. The AirPods sub-brand maintains this consistency by incorporating Apple's iconic design elements, such as the white colour palette, sleek aesthetics, and minimalist approach. The Apple logo prominently displayed on AirPods packaging and marketing materials further reinforces the brand's consistency and association with the parent brand.

4. Ecosystem Enhancement: Apple's brand portfolio architecture strategy focuses on enhancing its ecosystem of products and services. The AirPods sub-brand contributes to this strategy by expanding the functionality and integration within the Apple ecosystem. Users can seamlessly connect AirPods to their Apple devices, allowing for a seamless transition between audio experiences. This ecosystem enhancement strengthens customer loyalty and encourages users to stay within the Apple ecosystem, fostering a deeper engagement with Apple's broader product lineup.

5. Differentiation and Competitive Advantage: The AirPods sub-brand provides Apple with a competitive advantage in the audio accessories market. By leveraging Apple's expertise in technology, design, and user experience, AirPods stand out from competitors and offer a unique value proposition. The combination of superior technology, seamless integration, and Apple's brand reputation differentiates AirPods in the market and contributes to Apple's overall competitive advantage.

The Apple AirPods sub-brand synergizes with existing product categories, maintains brand consistency, enhances the ecosystem, and provides a competitive advantage. This strategic fit enables Apple to leverage its brand equity, expand its product offerings, and create a cohesive and compelling brand portfolio for customers.

Communication and Marketing Strategies: Apple adopts various communication and marketing strategies to promote its AirPods sub-brand. Here are some key strategies employed by Apple:

1. Emphasizing Innovation and Technology: Apple highlights AirPods' cutting-edge technology and innovative features in its marketing campaigns. The focus is on features such as wireless connectivity, seamless integration with Apple devices, active noise cancellation, and spatial audio. Through demonstrations and visuals, Apple showcases how AirPods offer a unique and advanced audio experience.

2. Showcasing Design and Aesthetics: Apple is known for its sleek and minimalist product design, and this is emphasized in the marketing of AirPods. The clean and elegant aesthetics of the AirPods are showcased through high-quality visuals and close-ups, highlighting the product's premium build and attention to detail. Apple emphasizes the simplicity and elegance of AirPods' design, aligning with the brand's overall design philosophy.

3. Lifestyle and User Experience: Apple positions AirPods as a lifestyle accessory, focusing on how they seamlessly integrate into users' daily lives. Marketing campaigns often showcase individuals using AirPods in various settings, such as during workouts, commuting, or leisure activities. By emphasizing the convenience, portability, and enhanced audio experience AirPods offer, Apple connects with consumers on an emotional level, appealing to their desire for a seamless and enjoyable user experience.

4. Celebrity Endorsements and Influencer Marketing: Apple leverages the power of celebrity endorsements and influencer marketing to promote AirPods. Well-known personalities and influencers are often seen using AirPods in their daily lives or featured in Apple's marketing campaigns. This strategy helps create aspirational associations with AirPods and highlights their desirability among trendsetters and opinion leaders.

5. Integration with Apple Ecosystem: Apple promotes the seamless integration of AirPods with its broader ecosystem of products and services. Marketing materials often highlight how AirPods effortlessly connect

and sync with iPhones, iPads, Macs, and Apple Watches. This integration reinforces AirPods's convenience and value proposition for existing Apple customers and encourages cross-product adoption.

6. Engaging Digital and Social Media Presence: Apple utilizes its strong digital and social media presence to reach a wide audience. It creates engaging content and advertisements for platforms like YouTube, Instagram, and Twitter. The use of short videos, customer testimonials, and user-generated content helps generate excitement and word-of-mouth promotion for AirPods.

7. Retail Experience: Apple's brick-and-mortar retail stores play a significant role in marketing AirPods. Customers can visit Apple stores to try out AirPods, receive personalized assistance from Apple's knowledgeable staff, and learn about the product's features. The in-store experience aligns with Apple's emphasis on providing exceptional customer service and creates opportunities for direct engagement with potential customers.

These communication and marketing strategies collectively position AirPods as a premium, innovative, and desirable audio accessory within Apple's product portfolio. By highlighting the product's features, design, integration, and user experience, Apple effectively promotes AirPods to its target audience, driving awareness, engagement, and sales.

Outcomes and Impact: Here are some key outcomes and impacts of the Apple AirPods sub-brand launch:

1. Market Disruption: The launch of AirPods disrupted the wireless earphone market by introducing a new form factor and seamless integration with Apple devices. It set a new standard for wireless audio technology and established Apple as a leader in the category. AirPods' success has influenced the market and prompted other companies to develop their own wireless earphone offerings.

2. Brand Extension: The launch of AirPods expanded Apple's brand pres-

ence beyond its core product lines. It demonstrated Apple's ability to innovate in new product categories and provided an opportunity to diversify its revenue streams. AirPods contributed to strengthening Apple's brand image as a company that consistently delivers high-quality, innovative products.

3. Sales Growth: AirPods quickly became a commercial success for Apple. Since its launch, the sub-brand has experienced strong sales growth, contributing to Apple's overall revenue and profitability. AirPods have become a significant revenue driver and one of Apple's fastest-growing product lines.

4. User Adoption and Loyalty: AirPods have gained a loyal customer base, with users praising their convenience, audio quality, and integration with Apple devices. The product's ease of use and seamless connectivity have contributed to a positive user experience and high levels of customer satisfaction. This has led to increased customer loyalty and repeat purchases within the Apple ecosystem.

5. Cultural Icon and Fashion Statement: AirPods have transcended their role as mere audio accessories and have become cultural icons. When worn, their distinctive design and visual prominence have made them a fashion statement and status symbol for many users. AirPods' popularity in popular culture, music videos, and social media further solidifies their cultural status.

6. Market Influence: The success of AirPods has influenced the broader wireless audio market. Competitors have sought to emulate AirPods' design and features, leading to the market proliferation of similar wireless earphone products. AirPods' impact has pushed the industry to prioritize seamless connectivity, improved audio quality, and innovative features.

7. Brand Reinforcement: The launch of AirPods has reinforced Apple's brand as an innovator and trendsetter. It has demonstrated Apple's ability to create products that seamlessly integrate hardware, software, and services to deliver exceptional user experiences. AirPods' success has contributed to enhancing Apple's brand reputation and differentiation

from competitors.

The launch of Apple AirPods has driven sales growth, expanded Apple's brand presence, and solidified its position as a leader in wireless audio technology. AirPods' success has generated financial success and contributed to shaping cultural trends and consumer preferences in the audio accessory market.

Example 02: Amazon Prime

Amazon, the multinational e-commerce company, successfully launched the sub-brand "Amazon Prime" to expand its services beyond online retail. The introduction of Amazon Prime showcases the company's strategic approach to brand extension and its ability to enter new product categories while enhancing customer loyalty.

Reason for Sub-Brand Creation: Amazon created the sub-brand Amazon Prime to expand its offerings beyond its core e-commerce business and enter new product categories and services. This decision was driven by Amazon's recognition of evolving consumer needs and expectations. The company aimed to provide a comprehensive membership program that would not only enhance the overall customer experience but also offer additional benefits beyond traditional online shopping.

With the introduction of Amazon Prime as a subscription service, the company sought to offer convenience, value, and exclusivity to its members. By doing so, Amazon positioned itself as more than just an online retailer. The primary motivation behind creating the Amazon Prime sub-brand was to diversify the company's revenue streams and extend its presence into new areas of consumer spending.

One of the key aspects of Amazon Prime was its offering of free and expedited shipping, which provided a compelling value proposition to attract and retain loyal customers. In addition to this, the sub-brand provided access to a vast library of streaming entertainment, exclusive deals, and other perks. This move allowed Amazon to extend its reach into the entertainment industry and compete with established streaming platforms like Netflix and Hulu.

Furthermore, Amazon Prime acted as a gateway to other Amazon services and offerings, such as Prime Video, Prime Music, Prime Reading, and more. This cross-promotion and cross-selling strategy within Amazon's ecosystem fostered customer loyalty and engagement.

The creation of the Amazon Prime sub-brand enabled Amazon to leverage its existing customer base, brand reputation, and distribution infrastructure to enter new product categories and services. It provided an opportunity to diversify revenue streams, enhance customer loyalty, and differentiate itself from competitors in the e-commerce and streaming industries.

Value Proposition: The Amazon Prime sub-brand offers a unique value proposition that goes beyond traditional online shopping and encompasses various services and perks that enhance the overall customer experience.

The key elements of the value proposition of Amazon Prime are as follows:

1. Free and Fast Shipping: One of the primary benefits of Amazon Prime is the inclusion of free two-day shipping on eligible items. This value proposition appeals to customers who prioritize convenience and want their orders delivered quickly without incurring additional shipping costs.

2. Unlimited Streaming of Movies, TV Shows, and Music: Amazon Prime subscribers have access to a vast library of streaming content, including movies, TV shows, and music. This benefit adds entertainment value to the membership, offering subscribers a wide range of options for their viewing and listening pleasure.

3. Exclusive Deals and Discounts: Amazon Prime members gain early access to exclusive deals, discounts, and promotions. This value proposition appeals to customers who seek cost savings and enjoy accessing special offers before non-members. The exclusive deals can span across various product categories, encouraging members to make more purchases and maximize their savings.

4. Prime Video Originals and Content: Amazon Prime offers a collection of original content, including TV shows, movies, and documentaries produced exclusively for the platform. This unique content attracts subscribers who are interested in exploring new and exclusive entertainment options.

5. Prime Reading and Audible: Amazon Prime includes access to Prime Reading, which offers a selection of e-books, magazines, and other reading materials. Additionally, subscribers can access a rotating selection of audiobooks through Audible Channels. These features cater to readers and audiobook enthusiasts, enhancing the value proposition for those who enjoy consuming written or audio content.

6. Prime Wardrobe and Fashion Benefits: Amazon Prime provides fashion-related benefits, such as Prime Wardrobe, which allows members to try on clothing and accessories before purchasing. The program also includes exclusive fashion deals and early access to select fashion collections. These features appeal to fashion-conscious customers and provide added value in the realm of online fashion shopping.

7. Whole Foods Market Benefits: Amazon Prime members who shop at Whole Foods Market enjoy additional benefits, including exclusive discounts and access to special deals. This value proposition appeals to customers who prioritize organic and natural food products and want to save on their grocery purchases.

The value proposition of the Amazon Prime sub-brand centres around convenience, cost savings, entertainment options, and a comprehensive suite of benefits that cater to a wide range of customer needs.

Brand Fit: The Amazon Prime sub-brand seamlessly integrates with Amazon's core values, customer-centric approach, and mission to provide exceptional customer experiences. The brand fit between Amazon Prime and Amazon can be analyzed in the following aspects:

1. Customer-Centric Approach: Both Amazon and Amazon Prime are

built on a foundation of prioritizing the customer. Amazon's focus on delivering convenience, selection, and competitive pricing aligns with the value proposition of Amazon Prime, which offers a wide range of benefits and services to enhance the customer experience. The sub-brand reinforces Amazon's commitment to meeting customer needs and exceeding their expectations.

2. Service Excellence: Amazon is known for its commitment to service excellence, and Amazon Prime upholds this reputation by offering various perks and benefits to its members. The sub-brand expands on Amazon's promise of exceptional service by providing free and fast shipping, exclusive deals, access to streaming content, and other valuable services. The brand fit ensures that Amazon Prime aligns with the high standards of quality and service that customers associate with Amazon.

3. Trust and Reliability: Amazon has established itself as a trusted and reliable brand, and Amazon Prime inherits this trustworthiness. Customers have confidence in Amazon's ability to deliver on its promises, and this extends to the Amazon Prime sub-brand. The brand fit reinforces customers' trust and reliability with Amazon, encouraging them to subscribe to Amazon Prime and enjoy its benefits.

4. Brand Recognition and Awareness: Amazon is a highly recognized and widely known brand globally. The strong brand awareness of Amazon helps in the successful launch and adoption of the Amazon Prime sub-brand. Customers are already familiar with Amazon's reputation and offerings, making it easier to introduce and promote the benefits of Amazon Prime. The brand fit leverages the existing brand equity of Amazon and strengthens the overall brand presence.

5. Cross-Selling and Upselling Opportunities: The brand fit between Amazon and Amazon Prime allows for effective cross-selling and upselling opportunities. Amazon can leverage its existing customer base and promote the benefits of Amazon Prime to encourage customers to subscribe. Conversely, Amazon Prime members are more likely to engage in additional purchases on Amazon's platform, further driving revenue for the parent brand.

The sub-brand enhances and complements the parent brand's offerings, reinforcing Amazon's commitment to delivering exceptional customer experiences and driving customer loyalty.

Brand Architecture: The Amazon Prime sub-brand is an integral part of Amazon's brand portfolio architecture, strategically designed to enhance and expand the offerings of the parent brand. The brand portfolio architecture strategy ensures a strong fit between Amazon Prime and the overall brand portfolio in the following ways:

1. Complementary Offerings: Amazon Prime fits well within Amazon's brand portfolio by providing additional value and benefits to customers. While Amazon offers a wide range of products and services, Amazon Prime serves as a subscription-based membership program that complements and enhances the overall customer experience. It offers a suite of exclusive benefits, such as free and fast shipping, access to streaming content, discounts, and more. This complementary nature ensures that Amazon Prime expands upon the core offerings of the parent brand.

2. Customer Segmentation: The brand portfolio architecture strategy recognizes the diverse needs and preferences of different customer segments. Amazon Prime caters to a specific segment of customers who value convenience, savings, and access to exclusive perks. By offering this subscription-based service, Amazon effectively targets and serves this customer segment, while other parts of the brand portfolio cater to different segments with their specific needs. This strategy allows Amazon to capture a broader market and maintain a strong position in the e-commerce industry.

3. Cross-Promotion and Upselling: The brand portfolio architecture enables cross-promotion and upselling opportunities between Amazon and Amazon Prime. The parent brand can leverage its extensive customer base to promote the benefits of Amazon Prime, encouraging customers to subscribe and enjoy the additional perks. Conversely, Amazon Prime members are more likely to engage in frequent purchases on Amazon's

platform, contributing to increased sales and customer loyalty. The integration of Amazon Prime within the brand portfolio creates synergies and maximizes the value generated by each customer.

4. Brand Cohesion: Amazon Prime aligns seamlessly with Amazon's brand identity, values, and customer promise. Both brands share a focus on customer satisfaction, convenience, and delivering exceptional experiences. The brand portfolio architecture ensures that Amazon Prime maintains brand cohesion and reinforces the overall brand image of Amazon as a customer-centric and innovative company. The sub-brand's offerings and benefits are consistent with the values and promises of the parent brand, creating a unified and cohesive brand experience.

The inclusion of Amazon Prime enhances the overall brand portfolio and reinforces Amazon's position as a customer-centric and innovative company in the e-commerce industry.

Communication and Marketing Strategies: The communication and marketing strategies of Amazon Prime, as a sub-brand, play a crucial role in promoting its value proposition and attracting new subscribers. Some key strategies employed by Amazon to effectively communicate and market Amazon Prime include:

1. Clear Value Proposition: Amazon Prime's communication focuses on clearly conveying its value proposition to customers. The key benefits, such as free and fast shipping, access to exclusive deals and discounts, streaming services, and more, are highlighted to showcase the value that subscribers receive. The messaging emphasizes how Amazon Prime enhances the overall shopping and entertainment experience.

2. Multi-Channel Approach: Amazon utilizes a multi-channel approach to reach a wide audience and communicate the benefits of Amazon Prime. This includes advertising on various platforms, including television, digital media, social media, and email marketing. By utilizing multiple channels, Amazon can effectively target different customer segments

and increase brand visibility.

3. Personalization: Amazon leverages data and customer insights to per-sonalize its communication and marketing efforts. Tailored recom-mendations and offers are sent to customers based on their shopping preferences and browsing history. This personalized approach enhances the customer experience and encourages engagement with Amazon Prime.

4. Free Trial and Promotional Offers: Amazon employs the strategy of offer-ing a free trial of Amazon Prime to new customers. This allows potential subscribers to experience the benefits firsthand before committing to a paid subscription. Additionally, promotional offers, such as discounted subscription fees or limited-time deals, are periodically introduced to incentivize new sign-ups and create a sense of urgency.

5. Cross-Promotion: Amazon leverages its vast product and service ecosys-tem to cross-promote Amazon Prime. Prominent placement of Amazon Prime messaging can be seen on the Amazon website, during the checkout process, and through product recommendations. This integration ensures that customers are constantly exposed to the benefits of Amazon Prime while engaging with other Amazon services.

6. Influencer Collaborations: Amazon partners with influencers and celebri-ties to promote Amazon Prime and showcase its benefits. Influencers often share their personal experiences and recommendations, creating buzz and generating interest among their followers. These collaborations help reach a broader audience and enhance the credibility and desirability of Amazon Prime.

7. Customer Testimonials and Reviews: Amazon incorporates customer testimonials and reviews in its communication to highlight the positive experiences of existing Amazon Prime subscribers. These testimonials serve as social proof and help build trust and credibility among potential subscribers.

8. Retention and Engagement Strategies: Amazon employs various strate-gies to keep existing Amazon Prime subscribers engaged and satisfied. This includes personalized recommendations, exclusive content, early

access to deals, and special events. By continuously providing value to subscribers, Amazon aims to foster long-term loyalty and reduce churn.

Through these communication and marketing strategies, Amazon effectively promotes Amazon Prime, highlights its unique benefits, and drives customer acquisition and retention. The strategies focus on creating awareness, conveying the value proposition, and delivering personalized experiences to attract and retain subscribers.

Outcomes and Impact: The launch of Amazon Prime as a sub-brand has had significant outcomes and impact on both Amazon and its customers. Here are some of the key outcomes and impacts of the Amazon Prime sub-brand launch:

1. Enhanced Customer Loyalty: Amazon Prime has been instrumental in building and strengthening customer loyalty. The program offers a range of benefits, such as free two-day shipping, access to Prime Video streaming, exclusive deals, and more. These benefits have incentivized customers to become Prime members, leading to increased customer retention and repeat purchases.
2. Increased Customer Engagement: Amazon Prime has created a deeper level of engagement with customers. The program offers additional services and features that encourage customers to interact with Amazon more frequently. Features like Prime Video, Prime Music, and Prime Reading provide entertainment and convenience, keeping customers engaged within the Amazon ecosystem.
3. Revenue Growth: The launch of Amazon Prime has significantly impacted Amazon's revenue growth. Prime membership fees, coupled with increased customer spending due to the program's benefits, have contributed to a substantial increase in Amazon's overall revenue. The recurring subscription revenue from Prime memberships provides a stable and predictable income stream for the company.
4. Market Differentiation: Amazon Prime has set Amazon apart from its

competitors. The program's comprehensive benefits and seamless user experience have created a unique selling proposition that distinguishes Amazon from other online retailers. This market differentiation has helped Amazon maintain its position as a leader in the e-commerce industry.

5. Expansion into New Services: The success of Amazon Prime has allowed Amazon to expand its services beyond e-commerce. The program's popularity and customer trust have paved the way for the introduction of additional services, such as Prime Video, Prime Music, and Prime Reading. These expansions have diversified Amazon's offerings and allowed the company to tap into new revenue streams.

6. Brand Perception and Trust: Amazon Prime has positively influenced the brand perception and trust in Amazon. The program's benefits, such as fast and reliable shipping, exclusive deals, and access to entertainment content, have created a positive association with the Amazon brand. Customers perceive Amazon as a trustworthy and customer-centric company, further enhancing its reputation.

7. Competitive Advantage: The launch of Amazon Prime has given Amazon a significant competitive advantage. The program's extensive benefits and seamless user experience have set a high bar for competitors to match. It has become a benchmark for customer loyalty and satisfaction in the e-commerce industry, making it challenging for competitors to replicate its success.

8. Customer Acquisition and Retention: Amazon Prime has been instrumental in acquiring new customers and retaining existing ones. The program's attractive benefits and convenience have enticed customers to join Prime, and once they become members, they are more likely to continue shopping on Amazon and utilizing the program's offerings.

The success of Amazon Prime has solidified Amazon's position as a leader in the e-commerce and subscription-based services industry.

The case of Amazon Prime demonstrates the successful creation of a sub-brand for a new product category and industry expansion. By providing a compelling value proposition, leveraging its existing customer base, and continuously expanding its services, Amazon enhanced customer loyalty, drove revenue growth, and expanded its market presence in various industries.

Brand Extension Without Sub-Brand: Potential Challenges and Implications

When a brand extends into a new category without using a sub-brand, it can lead to confusion among customers. Brands often become strongly associated with a specific product or category in consumers' minds, and when the same brand name is used for a completely different product, it can create cognitive dissonance and a sense of conflict.

Example 01: Colgate's Frozen Dinner

In the 1980s, Colgate, a well-established oral care brand, ventured into the frozen dinner market with a product line called "Colgate Kitchen Entrees." The brand extension aimed to capitalize on Colgate's strong brand recognition and trust in an attempt to enter the food industry. However, this extension turned out to be a notable failure, primarily due to the lack of a sub-brand and the subsequent confusion it created among consumers.

The primary reason for the failure of Colgate's brand extension was the significant misalignment between the brand's association with oral care and its entry into the food category. Consumers found it challenging to reconcile the notion of a toothpaste brand branching out into frozen dinners, as it contradicted their existing perceptions and expectations of the Colgate brand. The absence of a sub-brand or clear distinction between the oral care and food categories amplified this confusion.

The Colgate brand extension failure underscores the importance of thorough market research and understanding consumer behaviour before embarking on a new product category. It is essential to evaluate whether the brand's core values and associations align with the intended category and whether there is a strong customer need or desire for the brand to expand into that area.

In hindsight, Colgate's attempt to enter the frozen dinner market without a sub-brand or clear differentiation proved to be a significant strategic misstep. The brand's credibility and expertise in oral care did not translate seamlessly into the realm of food products. Consumers were unable to make the cognitive leap from toothpaste to frozen dinners, and the lack of clarity left them confused and sceptical.

Example 02:Harley-Davidson Perfume

Harley-Davidson is an iconic motorcycle brand that attempted to extend its brand into the perfume market without using a sub-brand. The company wanted to leverage its strong brand equity and appeal to a wider audience by introducing a line of perfumes for both men and women.

However, the brand extension faced several challenges. The primary issue was the lack of alignment between the brand's image as a rugged, masculine motorcycle brand and the association with perfumes, which are typically seen as a more feminine and delicate product category. The attempt to bridge the gap between these contrasting brand images proved unsuccessful and led to confusion and rejection among consumers.

Harley-Davidson enthusiasts, who were predominantly male and passionate about the brand's motorcycles, found it difficult to connect with the perfume line, as it deviated from their expectations and the brand's core identity. Moreover, the introduction of perfumes under the same brand name diluted the brand's association with its core products and created cognitive dissonance for consumers.

The lack of a sub-brand or clear differentiation between the motorcycle line and the perfume line caused significant brand dilution and eroded the trust and authenticity associated with the Harley-Davidson name. The perfume line failed to attract its intended target market and faced resistance from both existing brand enthusiasts and potential new customers.

As a result, Harley-Davidson decided to discontinue the perfume line after a relatively short period. The failure of the brand extension emphasized the importance of maintaining a strong brand identity and carefully considering the fit between the brand's core values and the new product category. Without a sub-brand to differentiate the perfume line and manage consumer expectations, the brand extension lacked credibility and failed to resonate with consumers.

In conclusion, creating sub-brands to extend the brand into new product categories or industries can be a powerful market growth and diversification strategy. It allows companies to leverage their existing brand equity, customer base, and resources while entering new markets and appealing to different customer segments. Companies can successfully launch sub-brands that resonate with consumers and drive business success by carefully analyzing brand fit, considering brand architecture, and implementing effective marketing strategies.

* * *

8

New Geographic Markets

C reating sub-brands for geographic market expansion refers to the strategic decision of developing separate brand identities or product lines tailored to specific geographic regions or markets. It involves adapting the brand to local preferences, cultures, and market dynamics to establish a stronger presence in new geographic territories.

The importance of creating sub-brands for entering new geographic markets lies in the opportunities for business growth and market diversification it offers. Some key reasons include:

1. Market Expansion: Entering new geographic markets allows businesses to tap into untapped customer bases and expand their reach beyond existing markets. By creating sub-brands tailored to local preferences, businesses can establish a stronger foothold and gain market share in diverse regions.

2. Cultural Relevance: Every geographic market has unique cultural nuances, traditions, and consumer behaviours. Creating sub-brands enables businesses to adapt their offerings to align with local cultures and preferences, enhancing their relevance and resonance with the target audience.

3. Market Differentiation: In highly competitive markets, creating sub-

brands helps businesses differentiate themselves from competitors by catering to specific local needs and tastes. This differentiation can lead to increased customer loyalty, market positioning, and competitive advantage.

4. Adaptation to Local Regulations: Geographic markets often have specific regulations, standards, and compliance requirements. By creating sub-brands, businesses can navigate these regulations more effectively and establish a stronger presence while complying with local laws and regulations.

5. Market Learning: Entering new geographic markets offers businesses valuable opportunities to learn about diverse consumer behaviours, market trends, and preferences. The process of creating sub-brands involves conducting market research, understanding local customer needs, and adapting strategies accordingly, allowing businesses to gain insights and expand their knowledge base.

6. Localization of Marketing and Communication: By creating sub-brands, businesses can develop localized marketing and communication strategies tailored to specific geographic markets. This includes adapting language, imagery, messaging, and promotional activities to resonate with the target audience in each region. Effective localization enhances brand perception, customer engagement, and market penetration.

7. Building Trust and Relationships: Local customers often prefer brands that have a strong presence and understanding of their specific market. Creating sub-brands demonstrates a commitment to the local market, builds trust, and fosters deeper relationships with customers. It shows that the business is invested in meeting its unique needs and preferences, which can result in increased customer loyalty and advocacy.

8. Flexibility and Agility: Different geographic markets may have varying product demands, pricing sensitivities, and distribution channels. Creating sub-brands allows businesses to be more flexible and agile in adapting their product offerings, pricing strategies, and distribution networks to suit local market conditions. This responsiveness enhances competitiveness and helps capture market opportunities more effectively.

9. Risk Mitigation: Geographic market expansion can involve risks such as cultural misalignment, regulatory challenges, or unexpected market dynamics. By creating sub-brands, businesses can mitigate risks by focusing their resources, investments, and brand positioning in specific regions. This targeted approach minimizes the impact of potential challenges and allows for better risk management.

10. Portfolio Diversification: Geographic market expansion through sub-brands enables businesses to diversify their product portfolio and revenue streams. By entering new markets with tailored offerings, businesses reduce their reliance on a single market or product category. This diversification strengthens the overall business resilience, mitigates risks, and creates opportunities for long-term growth.

In summary, creating sub-brands for geographic market expansion allows businesses to adapt to local preferences, establish relevance, and grow their presence in new markets.

Example 01: KFC China

When KFC entered the Chinese market, they recognized that food played a central role in Chinese society, deeply tied to national and regional cultures. To win over Chinese consumers and establish a strong presence, KFC understood that it needed to go beyond being perceived as a fast-food chain and instead become a part of the local community. To overcome these barriers and establish a strong presence in the market, KFC created a geographic sub-brand called "KFC China" They embarked on a strategy to stretch the brand by offering a diverse range of flavours and creating an inviting ambience that would resonate with Chinese customers.

One key step KFC took was to enlarge its outlets in China, making them approximately twice the size of those in the United States. This allowed for bigger kitchens and more dining floor space, enabling customers to linger and creating a welcoming atmosphere for extended families and groups. By accommodating the Chinese preference for communal dining experiences, KFC aimed to become a destination where families and friends could gather and enjoy their meals together.

To cater to the diverse palate of Chinese consumers, KFC China developed an expansive menu comprising approximately 50 items, compared to about 29 in the United States. The menu featured a wide array of offerings, including spicy chicken, rice dishes, soy milk drinks, egg tarts, fried dough sticks, wraps with local sauces, and fish and shrimp burgers on fresh buns. Understanding the importance of spice levels in Chinese cuisine, KFC ensured that the spiciness of their dishes aligned with regional preferences. They listened to customer feedback and adjusted their recipes accordingly, making them milder in Shanghai and more flavorful and spicy in Sichuan and Hunan.

KFC China also embraced innovation and introduced approximately 50 new products each year, some of which were available for a limited time. This continuous product development allowed KFC to keep its menu fresh, exciting, and responsive to evolving customer tastes and preferences.

Through these strategic initiatives, KFC successfully bridged cultural gaps and established a strong connection with Chinese consumers. The larger outlets, diverse menu options, regional customization, and focus on creating a welcoming dining experience aligned with the Chinese culture and preferences. As a result, KFC China has become one of the leading fast-food chains in the country, deeply ingrained in the fabric of Chinese society.

Example 02: Coca-Cola Cherry

Coca-Cola Cherry in North America and Coca-Cola with Lime in various international markets are examples of creating geographic sub-brands to cater to local preferences and enhance market relevance.

Coca-Cola Cherry (North America)

In North America, Coca-Cola introduced the sub-brand Coca-Cola Cherry to expand its product offerings and appeal to consumers who desired a cherry-flavoured soda. The recognition of the popularity of cherry-flavoured beverages in the North American market drove the decision to create Coca-Cola Cherry.

By launching this sub-brand, Coca-Cola aimed to capture a specific segment of consumers who preferred the taste of cherry in their soft drinks.

Brand Fit: Coca-Cola Cherry aligns with the overall Coca-Cola brand by leveraging its reputation for quality and taste. It maintains the core brand's visual identity, packaging, and messaging while offering a distinct flavour variation.

Brand Architecture: Coca-Cola Cherry operates as a sub-brand under the Coca-Cola umbrella, leveraging the parent brand's established reputation and consumer trust.

Challenges: One of the challenges faced by Coca-Cola in introducing Coca-Cola Cherry was ensuring that it differentiated itself enough from the original Coca-Cola flavour while still being recognizable as part of the Coca-Cola family. Balancing the new flavour profile with the familiarity of the original brand was crucial to its success.

Outcomes: Coca-Cola Cherry has achieved significant success in North America, attracting consumers who specifically seek out the cherry-flavoured variant. It has become a popular choice for consumers who prefer a sweeter and fruitier cola experience.

Coca-Cola with Lime (International Markets)

Coca-Cola with Lime is another example of geographic sub-branding by Coca-Cola. This sub-brand was launched in various international markets to cater to the preferences of consumers who desired a hint of lime in their Coca-Cola beverage. Lime is a popular flavour in many countries, and Coca-Cola recognized the opportunity to tap into this market by introducing Coca-Cola with Lime.

Brand Fit: Coca-Cola with Lime maintains the core attributes of the Coca-Cola brand while infusing it with the refreshing taste of lime. The sub-brand aligns with the overarching Coca-Cola brand's values and quality standards.

Brand Architecture: Coca-Cola with Lime operates as a sub-brand under the Coca-Cola portfolio, leveraging the parent brand's strong global presence and brand recognition.

Challenges: One of the challenges faced by Coca-Cola was ensuring that the addition of lime flavour did not overpower or significantly alter the original Coca-Cola taste. Striking the right balance to maintain the familiar Coca-Cola flavour profile while incorporating the lime twist required careful formulation and testing.

Outcomes: Coca-Cola with Lime has been well-received in international markets where lime-flavoured beverages are popular. It has provided consumers with an alternative Coca-Cola experience that combines the classic taste with a refreshing citrus note.

In conclusion, creating sub-brands to enter new geographic markets is a strategic approach that allows companies to adapt to local preferences, overcome cultural barriers, and enhance market relevance. By understanding consumers' unique needs and preferences in different regions, companies can develop sub-brands that resonate with the target audience, establish a local presence, and drive business growth.

The importance of creating sub-brands for geographic market expansion lies in the ability to tailor products, services, and marketing strategies to suit the specific market dynamics of each region. By doing so, companies can build stronger connections with local consumers, establish brand loyalty, and gain a competitive edge in new markets.

* * *

9

Lifestyle Branding

L ifestyle branding is a strategic approach that focuses on creating a brand identity and positioning that resonates with specific consumer segments defined by their lifestyles and subcultures. It goes beyond selling products or services and aims to establish an emotional connection with consumers who share similar values, interests, and aspirations.

Lifestyle branding allows brands to speak directly to these consumer segments' unique needs and desires. By understanding their preferences, behaviours, and identities, brands can craft tailored experiences and offerings that align with their target audience's way of life.

The benefits of creating sub-brands for lifestyle branding are numerous. Firstly, it allows brands to establish a stronger presence within specific lifestyle segments, enhancing brand relevance and resonance. By creating sub-brands that align with the unique values and aspirations of these segments, brands can become an integral part of their consumers' lifestyles.

Secondly, sub-brands enable brands to expand their reach and tap into new consumer markets. By targeting specific lifestyles and subcultures, brands can penetrate niche markets and connect with previously untapped consumer segments. This opens up opportunities for growth and diversification.

Furthermore, sub-brands provide the flexibility to experiment with different brand identities and offerings without diluting the overall brand equity. Brands can tailor their messaging, visual identity, and product/service offerings to better suit the specific lifestyle segments they are targeting. This customization strengthens the connection between the brand and its target audience, fostering loyalty and advocacy.

Challenges and Opportunities in Lifestyle Branding

While lifestyle branding offers exciting opportunities to connect with specific consumer segments and create sub-brands that resonate with their lifestyles, it also presents its own set of challenges. Understanding and addressing these challenges is essential for brands to leverage the full potential of lifestyle branding. Let's explore some common challenges and opportunities in lifestyle branding:

Authenticity: One of the key challenges in lifestyle branding is maintaining authenticity. Consumers are increasingly seeking genuine and meaningful experiences with brands. It is essential for brands to ensure that their sub-brands authentically represent the values, interests, and aspirations of the target lifestyle or subculture. Any perceived inauthenticity can lead to mistrust and disengagement from the audience. Brands should strive to create sub-brands embodying the desired lifestyle, ensuring consistency across all touchpoints.

Niche Targeting: Lifestyle branding often involves targeting niche consumer segments or subcultures with specific needs and preferences. This can be a challenge as these segments may be relatively small in size, making it difficult to achieve mass reach and scale. Brands need to carefully balance the appeal of niche targeting with the need for sustainable business growth.

Cultural Sensitivity: Lifestyle branding often involves navigating cultural nuances and sensitivities when targeting specific lifestyles or subcultures. Brands need to ensure they understand and respect the cultural context of their target audience to avoid misinterpretation or offence. Failing to address cultural sensitivities can lead to backlash and damage the brand's reputation.

Evolving Consumer Trends: Lifestyles and subcultures are dynamic, influenced by evolving consumer trends and societal shifts. Brands operating in lifestyle branding must stay agile and adaptable to keep up with these changes. Failing to evolve and stay relevant can result in the sub-brand losing its appeal and becoming disconnected from the target audience.

By prioritizing authenticity, carefully targeting niche segments, embracing cultural sensitivity, and staying adaptable to evolving trends, brands can overcome the challenges and leverage lifestyle branding as a powerful strategy for connecting with consumers, building strong brand communities, and driving long-term business success.

Identifying Target Lifestyles and Consumer Subcultures

When creating sub-brands for lifestyle branding, it is crucial to identify the target lifestyles and consumer subcultures that align with the brand's values and offerings. This process involves a thorough understanding of various factors that define and differentiate these segments. Here are some key factors to consider when identifying target lifestyles and consumer subcultures:

1. Values and Beliefs: Target lifestyles and subcultures often share specific values and beliefs that guide their choices and behaviours. Brands need to identify these core values and align their sub-brands with them to establish a genuine connection. For example, outdoor apparel brands targeting adventure enthusiasts may focus on values such as exploration, sustainability, and connecting with nature.

2. Interests and Hobbies: Different lifestyle segments are driven by unique interests and hobbies. By understanding these passions, brands can create sub-brands that cater to specific needs and desires. For instance, a sub-brand targeting fitness enthusiasts might offer specialized workout apparel, equipment, and nutritional products.

3. Demographics: Demographic factors, such as age, gender, income level, and occupation, play a role in shaping lifestyles and subcultures. Brands must analyze demographic data to identify the segments most

relevant to their offerings. For example, a luxury fashion brand may create a sub-brand targeting affluent millennials with a more casual and contemporary style.

4. Psychographics: Psychographic factors include personality traits, attitudes, and lifestyle choices. Brands need to delve into the psychographic profiles of their target audience to understand their motivations, preferences, and aspirations. This knowledge helps in crafting sub-brands that resonate deeply with their desired consumer base.

5. Social and Cultural Influences: Lifestyle choices and subcultures are often influenced by social and cultural factors. Brands must consider the social contexts in which their target audience lives and determine how their sub-brands can tap into these cultural influences. For example, a skincare brand may create a sub-brand specifically for Asian consumers, taking into account their unique skincare rituals and preferences.

To identify target lifestyles and consumer subcultures, brands can conduct market research, surveys, and focus groups. They can also leverage data analytics and social listening tools to gain insights into consumer behaviour and preferences. By combining quantitative and qualitative data, brands can comprehensively understand their target audience and make informed decisions regarding sub-brand creation.

Note: The Overlap of Lifestyle Branding with Psychographic and Behavioral Segmentation

Lifestyle branding closely aligns with psychographic segmentation as it seeks to understand and target consumers based on their attitudes, interests, beliefs, and values. The company needs to understand its customer's desires, aspirations, and motivations, allowing them to create a brand experience that resonates personally and emotionally.

Furthermore, lifestyle branding also overlaps with behavioural segmentation. By analyzing consumers' behaviours, including their purchasing habits, activities, and interactions with the brand, lifestyle brands can tailor their messaging and offerings to align with those behaviours.

The beauty of lifestyle branding lies in its ability to capture the essence of both psychographic and behavioural segmentation. By considering the mindset and behaviours of their target audience, lifestyle brands can develop a comprehensive understanding of their customers' lifestyle choices. This allows them to create relevant and meaningful brand experiences that truly resonate with their audience, fostering a sense of connection, loyalty, and community.

Example 01: GoPro and GoPro Lifestyle

GoPro, a leading action camera brand, recognized the market opportunity to expand its customer base beyond extreme sports enthusiasts. The company observed that there was a growing trend among consumers who enjoyed adventure, travel, and outdoor activities and wanted to capture and share their experiences. By studying consumer behaviour and market trends, GoPro identified a significant demand for a lifestyle-focused sub-brand that could cater to a broader range of individuals seeking to document and share their exciting moments.

Value Proposition of GoPro Lifestyle: GoPro Lifestyle positioned itself as a brand that empowers individuals to capture and share their adventures, regardless of their skill level or the intensity of their activities. The sub-brand's value proposition revolved around providing high-quality, durable cameras that could withstand various environments and deliver stunning footage. GoPro Lifestyle emphasized the simplicity of capturing moments and highlighted the ease of sharing content with others. The brand aimed to inspire and connect with consumers who were passionate about adventure and exploration.

GoPro Lifestyle vs GoPro:

- **GoPro Lifestyle:** GoPro Lifestyle is a sub-brand of GoPro that focuses on products that are designed for everyday use. These products are typically smaller and more affordable than the standard GoPro cameras, and they are often used for activities such as vlogging, travel, and fitness.

- **GoPro:** GoPro is the main brand of GoPro, and it focuses on products that are designed for extreme sports and activities. These products are typically larger and more expensive than Lifestyle products, and they often have features such as rugged construction, waterproof housings, and high frame rates.

Brand Fit: GoPro Lifestyle, as a sub-brand for Lifestyle Branding, has a strong brand fit with the parent brand, GoPro. Here is a brand fit analysis between GoPro Lifestyle and its parent brand:

1. Alignment with Brand Purpose: GoPro is known for its mission to capture and share life's most incredible moments through action cameras. GoPro Lifestyle aligns perfectly with this purpose by expanding the brand's reach into the lifestyle segment. It allows GoPro to cater to a wider audience and capture everyday adventures and experiences.
2. Consistency in Brand Values: GoPro is associated with values such as adventure, exploration, authenticity, and creativity. GoPro Lifestyle complements these values by showcasing how GoPro cameras can be integrated into various aspects of everyday life, from travel and leisure activities to family moments and creative endeavours. The sub-brand reinforces and extends the core values of the parent brand.
3. Target Audience Overlap: GoPro has traditionally targeted active and adventurous individuals who engage in outdoor sports and activities. GoPro Lifestyle expands the target audience to include a broader range of consumers who are passionate about documenting and sharing their everyday experiences. The sub-brand appeals to individuals seeking to capture their lifestyle moments with high-quality action cameras.
4. Brand Experience Continuity: GoPro is known for its rugged and durable cameras that can withstand challenging environments. GoPro Lifestyle maintains the same quality and durability standards, ensuring that

customers can rely on their cameras in various lifestyle scenarios. The sub-brand extends the brand experience from extreme sports to everyday adventures seamlessly.

5. Visual and Design Consistency: GoPro has a distinctive visual identity characterized by its compact, versatile cameras and immersive action shots. GoPro Lifestyle maintains this visual consistency, ensuring that the sub-brand's products and marketing materials are in line with the overall aesthetics of the parent brand. This consistency strengthens brand recognition and association.

6. Leveraging Brand Reputation: GoPro has established a strong reputation as a leader in action cameras and content creation. GoPro Lifestyle leverages this reputation to enter the lifestyle market, benefiting from the trust and credibility built by the parent brand. The sub-brand's association with GoPro enhances its perceived quality and reliability among consumers.

7. Extension of Brand Reach: GoPro Lifestyle allows the parent brand to expand its market presence and reach new customer segments. By diversifying into lifestyle branding, GoPro can tap into additional revenue streams and capitalize on the growing demand for documenting and sharing everyday experiences. The sub-brand strengthens GoPro's position as a comprehensive solution for capturing all aspects of life.

GoPro Lifestyle extends the reach of GoPro and capitalizes on the growing interest in documenting and sharing everyday lifestyle moments.

Brand Architecture: GoPro Lifestyle, as a sub-brand for Lifestyle Branding, has a strong brand portfolio strategy fit. Here is an analysis of the brand portfolio strategy fit between GoPro Lifestyle and its parent brand, GoPro:

1. Diversification within the Brand Portfolio: GoPro Lifestyle represents a strategic diversification within the GoPro brand portfolio. While the parent brand primarily focuses on action cameras for extreme sports and adventure, GoPro Lifestyle expands the brand's offerings into the

lifestyle segment. This diversification allows GoPro to tap into new markets and reach a broader range of customers who are interested in documenting their everyday experiences.

2. Complementary Product Range: GoPro Lifestyle complements the existing product range of GoPro by offering cameras and accessories that are tailored to lifestyle activities. It expands the portfolio beyond action sports to include travel, family, leisure, and creative pursuits. This allows GoPro to cater to its customer's evolving needs and preferences and capture additional market share.

3. Leveraging Brand Equity: GoPro has established a strong brand reputation and equity in the action camera industry. By leveraging this equity, GoPro Lifestyle benefits from the parent brand's association with quality, durability, and innovation. Customers already familiar with and trusting the GoPro brand are more likely to consider GoPro Lifestyle a reliable, high-quality option for their lifestyle-focused camera needs.

Communication and Marketing Strategies: The communication and marketing strategies used by GoPro Lifestyle focus on showcasing the brand's lifestyle-oriented positioning and engaging with the target audience. Here are some key strategies employed by GoPro Lifestyle:

1. Lifestyle-Centric Messaging: GoPro Lifestyle communicates a lifestyle-oriented message that emphasizes adventure, exploration, and capturing unique moments. The brand showcases the idea that owning a GoPro camera enhances and enriches one's lifestyle, enabling users to document and share their exciting experiences.

2. Compelling Visual Content: GoPro Lifestyle relies heavily on visual content to tell engaging stories and inspire its audience. The brand creates high-quality videos and images that showcase the versatility and capabilities of GoPro cameras in various lifestyle activities such as extreme sports, outdoor adventures, travel, and creative pursuits.

3. User-Generated Content: GoPro Lifestyle encourages users to share their content captured with GoPro cameras through its "Photo of the Day"

or "Video of the Week" campaigns. The brand creates an authentic and relatable connection with its audience by showcasing user-generated content on its website, social media channels, and marketing materials.

4. Social Media Engagement: GoPro Lifestyle maintains an active presence on popular social media platforms such as Instagram, YouTube, and TikTok. The brand shares compelling visuals, engages with followers through comments and direct messages and encourages users to share their GoPro experiences using branded hashtags.

5. Influencer Marketing: GoPro Lifestyle collaborates with influential content creators and athletes who align with the brand's adventurous and active lifestyle image. These influencers create sponsored content that highlights their experiences with GoPro cameras, showcasing the brand's products in action and reaching a wider audience.

6. Partnerships and Sponsorships: GoPro Lifestyle forms partnerships and sponsorships with lifestyle brands, events, and organizations that share similar target audiences. This includes collaborating with outdoor gear companies, sports competitions, travel agencies, and adventure-focused brands to create joint marketing campaigns and cross-promotional activities.

7. Content Creation and Distribution: GoPro Lifestyle produces a wide range of content, including tutorials, tips, and behind-the-scenes videos, that educate and inspire its audience. This content is distributed through various channels, including the GoPro website, social media platforms, and partner websites, to provide valuable information and build brand credibility.

8. Retail Presence and Experiential Marketing: GoPro Lifestyle utilizes experiential marketing techniques in retail stores, pop-up shops, and events. This includes allowing customers to test and experience the products firsthand, offering interactive displays, and organizing events and workshops to directly engage with the target audience.

9. Community Building: GoPro Lifestyle fosters a sense of community among its customers through online forums, social media groups, and customer support channels. The brand encourages users to share their

stories, ask questions, and connect with fellow GoPro enthusiasts, creating a dedicated and passionate community around the brand.

By implementing these communication and marketing strategies, GoPro Lifestyle effectively communicates its lifestyle-oriented messaging, engages with its target audience, and strengthens its brand presence within the adventure and lifestyle market.

Outcomes and Impact: The launch of GoPro Lifestyle as a sub-brand has had significant outcomes and impacts on the brand and its target audience. Firstly, it has expanded GoPro's target audience beyond extreme sports enthusiasts, attracting a broader range of consumers interested in capturing and sharing everyday experiences. This expansion has increased brand relevance and demonstrated GoPro's ability to adapt to evolving consumer trends.

Moreover, the introduction of GoPro Lifestyle has positively influenced brand perception, showcasing GoPro as a versatile and innovative camera brand catering to diverse consumer lifestyles. The sub-brand has also diversified GoPro's product offerings, introducing new camera models, accessories, and software features tailored to lifestyle-oriented needs. This diversification has likely resulted in increased sales and revenue for the brand.

Additionally, GoPro Lifestyle has deepened brand loyalty by aligning with the lifestyle aspirations of its target audience, fostering stronger emotional connections. The launch has facilitated partnerships and collaborations with lifestyle brands, content creators, and influencers, expanding GoPro's reach and exposure to new audiences.

Lastly, the sub-brand's emphasis on sharing everyday adventures and experiences has encouraged social media engagement and user-generated content creation, serving as a valuable source of marketing for GoPro. In summary, the launch of GoPro Lifestyle has extended the brand's reach, diversified its product portfolio, strengthened customer loyalty, and increased engagement with a broader audience of lifestyle-oriented consumers.

Example 02: Bose and Bose Frames

Bose, a renowned audio technology company, identified a market opportunity to expand beyond traditional audio products and tap into the growing demand for wearable technology. Through consumer behaviour analysis, Bose recognized that people wanted seamless integration of audio devices into their daily lives, particularly in the realm of fashion and personal style. This insight led to the development of a sub-brand that catered to consumers seeking a combination of audio functionality and fashionable accessories.

Value Proposition of Bose Frames: Bose Frames positioned itself as a sub-brand that offered stylish sunglasses integrated with high-quality audio technology. The value proposition centred around providing users with an immersive audio experience while enjoying the benefits of wearing fashionable eyewear. Bose Frames aimed to replace the need for separate headphones or earphones by embedding discreet speakers into the frames, enabling users to listen to music, take calls, and access voice assistants hands-free.

Brand Fit: Here is a brand fit analysis highlighting the alignment between Bose Frames and the parent brand:

1. Audio Expertise: Bose is renowned for its expertise in audio technology and sound quality. Bose Frames seamlessly integrates this core brand value into its sub-brand by incorporating high-quality speakers directly into the frames of stylish sunglasses. This integration ensures that consumers can enjoy immersive audio experiences while also protecting their eyes from the sun.
2. Innovation and Technology: Bose is known for its commitment to innovation and pushing the boundaries of technology. Bose Frames reflects this brand value by introducing cutting-edge features like built-in Bluetooth connectivity, touch-sensitive controls, and augmented reality capabilities. These technological advancements enhance the user experience and differentiate Bose Frames.

3. Design and Aesthetics: Bose is recognized for its sleek and sophisticated product design. Bose Frames embodies this design philosophy by offering stylish sunglasses that are functional and fashionable. The frames are designed to appeal to consumers who value both technology and aesthetics, creating a brand fit that aligns with the parent brand's focus on design excellence.

4. Brand Reputation and Trust: Bose has established a strong reputation for producing high-quality audio products that deliver exceptional performance. This reputation for quality and reliability extends to the Bose Frames sub-brand, instilling confidence in consumers that they are purchasing a premium product backed by the trusted Bose name.

5. Target Audience: Bose Frames caters to a lifestyle-oriented target audience who values both music and fashion. This aligns with the parent brand's target audience, including individuals who appreciate immersive audio experiences and seek products seamlessly integrated into their lifestyles.

6. Marketing and Branding: Bose Frames leverages the parent brand's established branding and marketing efforts. The sub-brand incorporates the Bose logo, visual identity, and messaging in its marketing materials, creating a consistent and recognizable brand presence that resonates with existing Bose customers.

The sub-brand effectively leverages the parent brand's reputation, technology, and marketing efforts to establish itself as a lifestyle-oriented product that seamlessly integrates audio technology into fashionable sunglasses.

Brand Architecture: Bose Frames, as a sub-brand for Lifestyle Branding, exhibits a strong fit within the brand portfolio strategy of Bose. Here's an analysis of the brand portfolio strategy fit:

1. Diversification: Bose Frames represents a strategic diversification for the Bose brand, expanding beyond traditional audio products like head-phones and speakers. By introducing a product that combines audio

technology with fashion-forward sunglasses, Bose is able to tap into new market segments and reach a broader audience interested in both style and audio experiences.

2. Lifestyle Extension: The introduction of Bose Frames aligns with the brand's strategy to extend its presence into the lifestyle category. Bose recognizes that consumers seek products that seamlessly integrate into their everyday lives, and sunglasses with built-in audio capabilities offer a unique and desirable lifestyle-oriented solution. This extension allows Bose to connect with consumers in new ways and become a part of their daily routines.

3. Synergy and Cross-Promotion: Bose Frames leverages the existing brand equity and customer base of Bose to drive the adoption and acceptance of the new sub-brand. By cross-promoting the product through Bose's established distribution channels, retail partnerships, and marketing efforts, the brand can effectively introduce Bose Frames to a wide audience of loyal customers. This synergy strengthens the overall brand portfolio and enhances the visibility and success of the sub-brand.

4. Brand Reputation and Trust: Bose has built a strong reputation as a leading audio technology company known for its quality and innovation. This brand reputation and trust directly transfer to Bose Frames, assuring customers that they can expect the same level of excellence and performance in their sunglasses with integrated audio. This alignment enhances the credibility and acceptance of the sub-brand within the brand portfolio.

The sub-brand aligns with the overall brand strategy of Bose, expanding its market reach and delivering innovative products that integrate seamlessly into consumers' lifestyles.

Outcomes and Impact: The launch of Bose Frames had a significant impact on the brand. It increased brand visibility and awareness among consumers through targeted marketing campaigns and collaborations, positioning Bose as a lifestyle brand that merges technology and fashion.

Furthermore, Bose successfully expanded into a new product category by introducing smart audio sunglasses, attracting a broader consumer base and diversifying its offerings. The launch of Bose Frames also reinforced the brand's reputation as an innovative and quality-driven company, showcasing its commitment to cutting-edge technology and superior audio experiences. The positive consumer perception generated by Bose Frames, with its combination of style and convenience, further contributed to the brand's success.

Additionally, Bose was able to differentiate itself from competitors by offering a unique product that combines audio technology with fashionable sunglasses, carving out a niche market for itself. Lastly, the personalized features and seamless integration of smart assistants in Bose Frames enhanced customer engagement and loyalty, making customers advocates for the brand. These outcomes have helped Bose to strengthen its position in the market and attract new customers while retaining existing ones.

In conclusion, creating a sub-brand for lifestyle branding is a strategic approach that enables companies to connect with specific consumer segments and cater to their unique preferences, interests, and values. By understanding target lifestyles and consumer subcultures, companies can identify market opportunities and develop sub-brands that resonate with their target audience on a deeper level.

Through lifestyle branding, companies can enhance relevance and establish a strong emotional connection with consumers. Sub-brands allow for a more focused and tailored approach to meet the needs and aspirations of specific consumer segments, offering products or experiences that align with their desired lifestyle.

* * *

10

Price Segmentation

P rice segmentation is a market segmentation strategy that involves dividing customers into distinct segments based on their price sensitivity, purchasing power, and willingness to pay for products or services. It recognizes that customers have different perceptions of value and are willing to pay different prices for similar offerings.

The importance of price segmentation lies in its ability to cater to the diverse needs and preferences of customers. Not all customers have the same budget constraints or willingness to spend, and by offering different price points, businesses can effectively target and attract customers across various income levels and price ranges.

Price Segmentation and Brand Reputation

Many consumers associate price with the perceived value of a product. In some cases, a low-priced product may be perceived as having lower quality compared to higher-priced alternatives. This association between price and quality can have an impact on the overall brand perception.

When a brand with a reputation for offering high-quality products wants to enter the lower-priced market segment, it can face challenges. Lowering the price of their existing product may send a contradictory message to consumers, potentially damaging the brand's reputation for quality. This is where the concept of creating a separate sub-brand becomes relevant.

By creating a new sub-brand specifically targeting the low-priced market segment, the brand can address the pricing expectations of that particular market without compromising its existing brand image and perceived value. This allows the brand to maintain its premium reputation while extending its reach to a different customer segment.

The sub-brand can be designed to have its own distinct positioning, messaging, and product offerings that align with the expectations and preferences of the low-priced market. This enables the brand to create a separate identity and value proposition tailored to that segment's needs.

Additionally, creating a sub-brand allows the brand to effectively manage customer perceptions and mitigate the potential negative impact on its existing brand equity. Consumers will understand that the sub-brand represents a separate offering with its own set of characteristics and value propositions separate from the brand's existing high-priced products.

By adopting this strategy, the brand can capture new market opportunities, expand its customer base, and effectively cater to customers with different price sensitivities. It allows the brand to balance its premium positioning while addressing the demand for more affordable options.

Example 01: Intel Celeron

In the late 1990s, the demand for low-cost PCs was on the rise, and Intel recognized the need to cater to this emerging market segment. However, they faced a challenge in leveraging their existing Pentium brand, which was associated with premium and high-performance processors. Launching a low-cost product under the Pentium brand could potentially dilute its premium image and confuse customers.

To address this opportunity, Intel introduced the sub-brand "Celeron", specifically targeted at the value segment. The decision to create a sub-brand was driven by the need to differentiate the low-cost offering from the premium

Pentium brand and avoid jeopardizing the reputation of Pentium.

Analyzing brand fit:

1. Target Segment: Intel positioned itself as a leading provider of high-performance processors for a wide range of computing devices, including desktops, laptops, and servers. Celeron, on the other hand, targeted price-conscious consumers who sought affordable computing solutions without compromising basic performance needs. This targeting allowed Celeron to address a specific segment within Intel's larger market while maintaining the overall reputation of the parent brand.

2. Brand Values: Intel is renowned for its innovation, advanced technology, and reliable performance in the computer processor industry. As a sub-brand, Celeron positioned itself to offer a cost-effective solution without compromising essential computing capabilities. While not as powerful as Intel's flagship processors, Celeron was designed to deliver adequate processing power for everyday computing tasks. It upheld Intel's commitment to quality and reliability, even at a lower price point. By providing a reliable and budget-friendly option, Celeron catered to users with less demanding computing needs while staying true to Intel's reputation for excellence.

3. Brand Identity: Celeron is a line of budget-friendly microprocessors. Intel is known for its high-performance microprocessors. Celeron and Intel have different brand identities, but they align with the parent company's values of performance, innovation, and accessibility.

4. Brand Promise: Celeron promises to "deliver great performance at an affordable price." Intel's brand promise is to "deliver the best performance in the market." The two brands have different brand promises, but they are both aligned with the parent company's values of performance and accessibility.

5. Brand Synergy: Intel's expertise in processor technology and manufacturing supported the development and production of Celeron processors. The synergy between the parent brand and the sub-brand allowed for

the efficient utilization of resources and enabled Celeron to benefit from Intel's reputation and distribution channels.

6. Brand Personality: Celeron's brand personality is affordable, reliable, and efficient. Intel's brand personality is high-performance, innovative, and cutting-edge. The two brands have different brand personalities, but they are both consistent with the parent company's values.

Brand architecture: Intel adopted an indirectly linked endorsement brand architecture for the Celeron sub-brand. This means that the Intel brand was associated with Celeron but not explicitly integrated into the brand name. This approach allowed Intel to leverage its strong brand reputation and provide reassurance to customers about the quality and reliability of the Celeron processors.

1. Brand Extension: Intel Celeron leverages the reputation and brand equity of the parent brand, Intel, known for its innovation, reliability, and technological expertise. By using the Intel brand name, Celeron inherits the trust and recognition associated with Intel, providing consumers with confidence in the product's quality despite its lower price point.

2. Market Coverage: The inclusion of Intel Celeron in the brand portfolio allows Intel to cater to a wider range of customers and address different market segments. By offering a variety of processors at different price points, Intel can reach more consumers and fulfil their specific needs, enhancing market coverage and competitiveness.

3. Upgradability Path: Intel Celeron also serves as an entry point for consumers to experience Intel's ecosystem. While Celeron processors may be suitable for basic computing needs initially, customers can upgrade to higher-performance Intel processors in the future as their requirements evolve. This provides a seamless transition within Intel's product lineup and encourages customer loyalty.

Celeron enables Intel to effectively cater to the budget-conscious market segment while maintaining the overall brand reputation and positioning.

Outcomes and Impact: The launch of the Intel Celeron sub-brand has had significant outcomes and impacts on the market. Firstly, it has increased Intel's market reach by targeting price-conscious consumers who previously may not have considered Intel processors due to budget constraints. The affordability of Celeron processors has attracted this segment of customers, expanding Intel's customer base.

Additionally, the sub-brand has gained significant traction in the entry-level computing segment, offering cost-effective solutions for basic computing needs. This positioning has made Intel Celeron a popular choice for budget-friendly laptops, desktops, and Chromebooks. The sub-brand has also contributed to building brand loyalty and trust among price-conscious consumers by delivering reliable performance at an affordable price point. This has further strengthened Intel's reputation and customer relationships. The launch of the Intel Celeron sub-brand has provided Intel with a competitive advantage in the entry-level computing market, enabling them to effectively compete against other processor manufacturers in this segment.

Moreover, the success of the sub-brand has opened up new market expansion opportunities for Intel, particularly in emerging markets and regions where affordability is a critical factor in purchasing decisions.

Lastly, the launch has contributed to a positive industry perception of Intel as a company that offers a diverse range of processors to meet different customer needs, showcasing their commitment to addressing various market segments.

Through careful brand management and strategic differentiation, Intel effectively used the Celeron sub-brand to cater to different price segments and extend its market reach. The decision to create a separate sub-brand for low-cost processors proved to be a strategic move, enabling Intel to meet the demands of diverse customer segments while preserving the reputation and value of its premium brand.

Example 02: Old Navy by Gap Inc.

In the late 1990s, Gap Inc., a leading retail company, recognized the need to cater to a broader customer base beyond its existing Gap brand. They observed an opportunity to target price-sensitive consumers who were looking for affordable yet fashionable clothing options.

Value proposition: Old Navy's value proposition centred around offering trendy and affordable clothing for the entire family. The brand focused on providing fashionable designs at lower price points compared to the main Gap brand.

Old Navy positioned itself as a go-to destination for budget-conscious shoppers who wanted to stay stylish without breaking the bank.

Analyzing brand fit: Gap Inc. had already established itself as a reputable brand known for its casual and classic clothing. To cater to price-sensitive consumers without diluting the Gap brand's image, Gap Inc. decided to create a sub-brand called Old Navy. The goal was to position Old Navy as a more affordable and value-oriented option within the Gap Inc. portfolio.

1. Brand Positioning: Old Navy is positioned as a "democratic" clothing brand that offers high quality, stylish clothes at an affordable price. The brand's positioning is reflected in its tagline, "The everyday essential."
2. Brand Identity: Gap Inc. is known for its casual, classic styles. Old Navy is known for its affordable prices and trendy styles. The two brands have different brand identities, but they are both aligned with the parent company's values of quality, fashion, and value.
3. Brand Promise: Old Navy's brand promise is to "make everyone feel good." The brand promises to offer clothes that are comfortable, stylish, and affordable. Old Navy's brand promise is reflected in its products, which are designed to flatter all body types and to be worn for everyday activities.
4. Brand Personality: Old Navy's brand personality is fun, approachable,

and inclusive. The brand's personality is reflected in its marketing campaigns, which often feature humour and lightheartedness. Old Navy's brand personality is also reflected in its stores, which are designed to be inviting and comfortable.

5. Brand Synergy: Gap Inc's expertise in retail operations and brand management provided support for Old Navy's growth and expansion. The synergy between the parent brand and the subsidiary brand allowed for efficient sourcing and economies of scale, enabling Old Navy to deliver affordable fashion to its target market.

Brand architecture: Gap Inc. adopted a distinct sub-brand architecture for Old Navy. While Old Navy was associated with Gap Inc., it had its own separate brand identity, including a unique logo, store design, and marketing campaigns. This allowed Gap Inc. to maintain brand differentiation and target different customer segments effectively.

1. Differentiation: Old Navy is positioned as a value-focused, family-oriented brand within the Gap Inc. portfolio. It differentiates itself from other Gap Inc. brands, such as Gap and Banana Republic, by offering affordable and trend-driven clothing options for the whole family. This differentiation allows Old Navy to cater to a specific market segment and avoid direct competition with other brands in the portfolio.

2. Target Market Focus: Old Navy primarily targets budget-conscious consumers who are looking for stylish and affordable clothing options. The brand caters to a wide range of demographics, including men, women, and children, and offers a variety of sizes and styles to meet the diverse needs of its customer base. By focusing on this target market, Old Navy can effectively position itself as a go-to destination for affordable fashion.

3. Brand Positioning: Old Navy is positioned as a fun, inclusive, and accessible brand. It aims to create a positive shopping experience by offering a wide range of on-trend clothing options at affordable prices.

The brand emphasizes its commitment to inclusivity by offering extended sizes and inclusive advertising campaigns that reflect the diversity of its customer base.

4. Brand Integration: While Old Navy operates as a separate brand within the Gap Inc. portfolio, it benefits from the resources, infrastructure, and expertise of its parent company. Gap Inc. provides operational support, including sourcing, supply chain management, and distribution, which enables Old Navy to efficiently deliver its products to customers.

5. Retail Expansion: Old Navy has pursued an aggressive retail expansion strategy, opening standalone stores and expanding its e-commerce presence. This strategy allows the brand to increase its market presence and reach a wider customer base. Old Navy's retail expansion also complements the presence of other Gap Inc. brands, as it allows for cross-shopping opportunities and synergy within the portfolio.

Outcomes and Impact: Creating Old Navy as a sub-brand for price segmentation proved highly successful for Gap Inc. The brand quickly gained popularity among budget-conscious shoppers, attracting a wide customer base seeking affordable fashion options. Old Navy's value-oriented approach, trendy designs, and strategic marketing helped Gap Inc. capture a significant market share within the price-sensitive segment.

Old Navy's success contributed to Gap Inc.'s overall growth and diversification. By addressing the needs of price-conscious consumers through a separate sub-brand, Gap Inc. expanded its customer base and strengthened its position in the retail industry.

Premium Price Segmentation

Example: Toyota Lexus

Toyota recognized the opportunity to expand into the luxury car market segment, targeting customers who desired high-end features, superior performance, and luxury craftsmanship. By creating a sub-brand Lexus, Toyota aimed to cater to these specific customer needs and tap into the growing demand for luxury vehicles.

Value proposition: Lexus was positioned as a premium brand, offering luxurious and technologically advanced vehicles with exceptional performance, comfort, and craftsmanship. The brand's emphasis on quality, refinement, and attention to detail differentiated it from the mainstream Toyota models and appealed to customers seeking a more elevated driving experience.

Analyzing brand fit: Toyota's main brand was known for its reliable, durable, and affordable vehicles, primarily targeting the mass market. Launching luxury cars under the Toyota brand could potentially dilute its value-focused image and confuse customers. Therefore, the creation of a separate sub-brand, Lexus, allowed Toyota to position itself in the luxury segment while maintaining the reputation and value proposition of the Toyota brand for its existing customer base.

1. Target Segment: Lexus targeted a more affluent and discerning customer base seeking luxury and high-performance vehicles. This targeting allowed Lexus to differentiate itself from Toyota and tap into the premium automotive market.
2. Brand Identity: Toyota is known for its reliability, safety, and affordability. Lexus is a luxury automotive brand that is known for its high-quality, stylish vehicles. The two brands have different brand identities, but they are both aligned with the parent company's values of quality, innovation, and customer satisfaction.
3. Brand Positioning: Toyota is positioned as a "mainstream" automotive brand that offers reliable, affordable vehicles. Lexus is positioned as

a "luxury" automotive brand that offers high-quality, stylish vehicles. The two brands have different brand positionings, but they are both complementary. Toyota's positioning appeals to a wide range of consumers, while Lexus's positioning appeals to a more affluent segment of the market.

4. Brand Promise: Toyota's brand promise is to "deliver outstanding quality and reliability." Lexus's brand promise is to "provide the finest in luxury and performance." The two brands have different brand promises, but they are both aligned with the parent company's values of quality and customer satisfaction.

5. Brand Personality: Toyota's brand personality is reliable, safe, and family-friendly. Lexus's brand personality is sophisticated, luxurious, and exclusive. The two brands have different brand personalities, but they are both consistent with the parent company's values.

6. Brand Synergy: Toyota's expertise in automotive engineering and manufacturing provided a strong foundation for Lexus to deliver high-quality luxury vehicles. The synergy between the two brands ensured that Lexus could benefit from Toyota's established reputation for reliability and quality while incorporating its own unique design language and features.

Brand architecture: Toyota adopted a separate endorsement brand architecture for the Lexus sub-brand. The Lexus logo prominently featured the Lexus name, while the association with Toyota was communicated subtly. This approach allowed Toyota to leverage its reputation for reliability and engineering excellence while creating a distinct brand identity for the luxury segment.

Outcomes: The introduction of the Lexus sub-brand has been highly successful for Toyota. It allowed them to enter and establish a strong presence in the luxury car market segment, competing with established luxury brands. Lexus became renowned for its exceptional build quality, advanced technologies, and refined driving experience, attracting a loyal customer base seeking premium vehicles.

By creating the Lexus sub-brand, Toyota successfully targeted a different customer segment, expanded its market reach, and increased its overall market share. The brand's reputation for reliability and value, combined with the luxury and sophistication associated with the Lexus brand, allowed Toyota to diversify its product offerings and cater to a broader range of customer preferences.

In conclusion, creating sub-brands with different price points is a strategic approach allowing companies to effectively target and attract diverse customer segments. Businesses can cater to varying customer preferences, purchasing power, and value perceptions by offering products or services at different price levels. Price segmentation helps companies maximize market potential by capturing customers who may have different affordability levels or willingness to pay. It also enables brands to position themselves in different market segments, expand their customer base, and drive overall business growth. However, it is crucial for companies to carefully consider brand fit, value proposition, brand architecture, and communication strategies when introducing sub-brands for different price segments to maintain brand equity and effectively meet customer needs.

* * *

11

Social or Environmental Issues

E stablishing sub-brands dedicated to social or environmental causes refers to creating separate brand entities within an existing brand portfolio focused on promoting and supporting specific social or environmental initiatives. These sub-brands are designed to enhance the brand image and engage with socially conscious consumers by demonstrating a strong commitment to positively impacting society or the environment.

In today's socially aware and environmentally conscious landscape, consumers are increasingly seeking brands that align with their values and actively contribute to meaningful causes. By establishing sub-brands dedicated to social or environmental causes, companies can demonstrate their commitment to corporate social responsibility, sustainability, and making a difference in the world. This not only helps enhance the brand's image but also establishes a strong connection with consumers who prioritize supporting socially responsible brands.

By actively engaging in initiatives that address social or environmental challenges, brands can position themselves as agents of positive change. This, in turn, fosters consumer trust, loyalty, and advocacy. Additionally, connecting with socially conscious consumers can expand the brand's reach and attract a new customer base that values and supports brands with a purpose beyond profit.

Developing A Sub-brand for a Social Cause or Purpose

Developing sub-brands for cause-related initiatives involves implementing strategies that align the brand with a specific social or environmental cause. Here are some key strategies for creating sub-brands dedicated to such initiatives:

1. Identify a Relevant Cause: Conduct research and analysis to identify a cause that aligns with the brand's core values, target audience, and industry. Consider social or environmental issues that resonate with the brand's mission and purpose.

2. Integration of Cause into Brand Values: Integrate the cause into the brand's core values and messaging to ensure a genuine and authentic connection. This involves aligning the brand's existing values and mission with the cause, reflecting a commitment to making a positive impact.

3. Consistent Brand Identity: Develop a consistent brand identity for the sub-brand that aligns with the parent brand while emphasizing the cause. This includes visual elements such as logo, colours, and design that reflect the cause and maintain brand consistency.

4. Clear Messaging and Communication: Craft clear and compelling messaging that communicates the sub-brand's dedication to the cause and its impact. Clearly articulate the connection between the parent brand and the cause-related initiative to ensure transparency and build trust with consumers.

5. Collaborations and Partnerships: Forge collaborations and partnerships with relevant organizations, experts, influencers, or non-profits working in the field of the cause. These partnerships can enhance the sub-brand's credibility, expand its reach, and leverage expertise and resources.

6. Employee and Stakeholder Engagement: Involve employees and stakeholders in the cause-related initiative to foster a sense of ownership and engagement. Encourage employee volunteering, provide training, and actively seek feedback and ideas to create a unified approach.

7. Impact Measurement and Reporting: Implement a system to measure the impact of the cause-related initiative and regularly report the progress and outcomes to stakeholders. Transparent reporting helps build credibility and demonstrates the brand's commitment to the cause.

Integrating a cause into a brand's core values and messaging is crucial for establishing an authentic and meaningful connection with consumers. Today's consumers actively seek out brands that align with their values and actively contribute to social or environmental causes. By integrating the cause into the brand's core values, the sub-brand demonstrates its genuine commitment, builds trust with consumers, and fosters stronger brand loyalty.

When the cause is effectively integrated, it becomes an intrinsic part of the brand's identity, values, and messaging. This integration not only generates a positive social impact but also sets the brand apart in a competitive market. Consumers are more inclined to support and engage with brands that align with causes they care about, leading to heightened brand loyalty and positive brand perception.

Example 01: Patagonia Provisions

One example of a brand that created a sub-brand by identifying a social and environmental cause aligned with its values is Patagonia with its sub-brand, Patagonia Provisions.

Patagonia is an outdoor clothing and gear company known for its commitment to environmental sustainability and activism. The brand's values revolve around protecting the environment and promoting responsible business practices. Recognizing the growing concern about food sustainability and the impact of industrial agriculture on the planet, Patagonia identified an opportunity to extend its brand into the food industry.

Patagonia Provisions was created as a sub-brand dedicated to providing ethically sourced, organic, and sustainable food products. The brand aligns with Patagonia's core values by offering products that support regenerative agriculture, protect biodiversity, and promote fair labour practices. Patagonia Provisions focuses on offering responsibly sourced ingredients and minimal processing to reduce the environmental footprint of the food industry.

The brand-consumer alignment is evident as Patagonia's target audience, which includes outdoor enthusiasts and environmentally conscious consumers, is also concerned about sustainable food choices. By extending its brand into the food industry, Patagonia effectively taps into the values and preferences of its target audience.

Patagonia's commitment to the cause goes beyond just offering sustainable food products. The company actively advocates for policy changes, educates consumers about the importance of regenerative agriculture, and supports grassroots movements to create a more sustainable food system. Through its sub-brand, Patagonia Provisions, the company demonstrates its dedication to its core values and engages with consumers on a deeper level.

Brand Fit Analysis: The brand fit between Patagonia Provisions and its parent brand—

1. Sustainability: Patagonia has established itself as a leader in sustainability within the outdoor industry. This commitment to environmental responsibility and conservation aligns with the core values of Patagonia Provisions, which emphasizes sustainable farming, regenerative agriculture, and minimizing environmental impact in the food industry. The brand fit is strong in terms of their shared commitment to sustainability.

2. Ethical Sourcing: Patagonia has a long-standing commitment to fair labour practices and ensuring the welfare of workers in its supply chain. This ethos extends to Patagonia Provisions, which places a strong emphasis on sourcing organic and responsibly produced ingredients. The brand fit is evident in their shared values of ethical sourcing and social responsibility.

3. Quality and Durability: Patagonia is renowned for its high-quality and durable outdoor apparel, which reflects its commitment to creating long-lasting products. Similarly, Patagonia Provisions focuses on providing

high-quality food products that are nutritious, flavorful, and made to last. This brand fit is evident in their shared dedication to quality and durability.

4. Outdoor Lifestyle: Both Patagonia and Patagonia Provisions cater to individuals who embrace an outdoor lifestyle and have a passion for nature. The brands promote a connection with the environment and encourage sustainable practices among their customers. This shared focus on the outdoor lifestyle strengthens the brand fit between Patagonia Provisions and its parent brand.

5. Brand Personality: The brand personality of Patagonia Provisions aligns closely with the parent brand's personality. It embodies qualities such as authenticity, ruggedness, and environmental consciousness. Patagonia Provisions portrays itself as a brand that is adventurous, passionate about the outdoors, and committed to sustainable practices. This personality resonates with the target audience, who share similar values and beliefs.

6. Brand Promise: Patagonia Provisions promises to deliver high-quality, ethically sourced, and sustainable food products. The brand commits to providing nutritious and flavorful options while prioritizing the health of people and the planet. Patagonia Provisions' brand promise reflects the parent brand's commitment to environmental and social responsibility.

7. Brand Differentiation: While Patagonia Provisions operates as a separate sub-brand, it leverages the parent brand's reputation and expertise in sustainability and outdoor lifestyle. This association allows Patagonia Provisions to differentiate itself from other food brands by highlighting its commitment to environmental stewardship and ethical sourcing. Brand differentiation is achieved through a shared focus on quality, sustainability, and promoting a connection with nature.

Brand Architecture: Patagonia Provisions operates under a sub-brand or sub-division model within the overall brand architecture of Patagonia. This means that it is a distinct brand entity but still maintains a strong connection to the parent brand. The sub-brand leverages the reputation, values, and customer loyalty of the parent brand to establish credibility and trust in the food industry.

Outcomes and Impact:

1. Environmental Stewardship: Patagonia Provisions has made significant strides in promoting environmental stewardship through its sustainable sourcing and regenerative farming practices. By prioritizing organic and regenerative ingredients, the brand has minimized its ecological footprint and contributed to the preservation of natural resources. This commitment to environmental sustainability has resonated with consumers who are increasingly conscious of the impact of their food choices, leading to increased support and loyalty for Patagonia Provisions.

2. Community Empowerment: Patagonia Provisions has had a positive impact on local communities by partnering with small-scale farmers, fishermen, and indigenous communities. These partnerships not only provide economic opportunities but also support traditional and sustainable livelihoods. By working directly with these communities, Patagonia Provisions has helped preserve cultural heritage and fostered a sense of empowerment and self-sufficiency. This community-focused approach has garnered recognition and support from consumers who value ethical and fair trade practices.

3. Education and Awareness: Patagonia Provisions has played a pivotal role in raising awareness about sustainable food systems and the importance of conscious consumption. Through its educational campaigns, documentaries, and partnerships with environmental organizations, the brand has informed and inspired consumers to make more mindful choices regarding their food and its impact on the planet. This increased awareness has sparked conversations and actions around sustainable food production and consumption, contributing to a broader movement towards more sustainable and ethical practices.

Patagonia's creation of the sub-brand Patagonia Provisions showcases how a brand can identify a social or environmental cause aligned with its values and extend its brand to address the issue. The sub-brand strengthens the brand-consumer connection by providing products and initiatives that resonate with the target audience's values and contribute to a more sustainable future.

Example 02: Dove Self-Esteem Project

Unilever, a multinational consumer goods company, is widely known for its diverse range of products across various categories. While Unilever as a whole didn't have a specific social cause or purpose, it recognized an opportunity to make a positive impact in the area of self-esteem and body confidence, particularly among young girls and women. The company identified a gap in the market where many young people face issues related to body image and self-esteem.

To address this issue, Unilever created the Dove Self-Esteem Project as a sub-brand focused on promoting positive body image and self-esteem. The project aims to provide educational resources, workshops, and support to help individuals build confidence and develop a healthy relationship with their bodies.

By creating the Dove Self-Esteem Project as a sub-brand, Unilever was able to channel its resources and expertise toward this specific social cause while maintaining the distinct identity and positioning of its main brand, Dove. The sub-brand's focus on self-esteem and body confidence allowed it to connect with passionate consumers and sought products and initiatives that aligned with its values.

The establishment of the Dove Self-Esteem Project as a sub-brand enabled Unilever to leverage its existing brand recognition and consumer trust to make a meaningful impact in an area of social concern. By associating the sub-brand with a specific social purpose, Unilever expanded its brand portfolio to cater to consumers who valued and supported self-esteem and body image initiatives.

Through the Dove Self-Esteem Project, Unilever not only provided valuable resources and support to individuals but also initiated conversations and raised awareness about the importance of self-esteem and body positivity. The sub-brand's initiatives and partnerships with organizations, experts, and influencers further amplified its impact and reach.

Brand Fit: Let's explore the brand fit between the Dove Self-Esteem Project and its parent brand:

1. Alignment with Brand Purpose: The Dove Self-Esteem Project aligns perfectly with Dove's purpose of promoting self-esteem. It focuses on empowering individuals, especially young people, to develop a healthy relationship with their bodies and boost their self-confidence. This alignment reinforces Dove's commitment to celebrating diverse beauty and challenging societal beauty standards.
2. Shared Values: The Dove Self-Esteem Project reflects the values of inclusivity, authenticity, and self-acceptance that are at the heart of the Dove brand. Both initiatives aim to create a more inclusive and accepting world, encouraging people to embrace their unique qualities and recognize their self-worth beyond physical appearance.
3. Amplifying the Brand Message: By launching the Dove Self-Esteem Project, Dove extends its brand message beyond personal care products. It demonstrates a genuine commitment to making a positive impact on people's lives, building a deeper emotional connection with consumers. The project enhances Dove's brand reputation as a socially responsible and empathetic brand that cares about the well-being of its customers.
4. Leveraging Brand Expertise: Dove's expertise in personal care and beauty allows the brand to provide valuable resources and educational materials through the Dove Self-Esteem Project. By leveraging its knowledge and experience, Dove can offer practical support and guidance to individuals, educators, and parents in nurturing positive self-esteem and body confidence.
5. Reinforcing Brand Loyalty: The Dove Self-Esteem Project reinforces brand loyalty by fostering a sense of community and shared values among consumers. By actively engaging with their target audience and

empowering individuals, Dove builds trust and loyalty, as consumers appreciate the brand's efforts to create a positive social impact beyond its product offerings.

Brand Architecture: The Dove Self-Esteem Project operates as an extension of the Dove brand, utilizing its existing brand equity and recognition. It leverages Dove's resources, credibility, and consumer trust to deliver impactful programs and campaigns.

Outcomes and Impact:

1. Empowering Individuals: The Dove Self-Esteem Project has empowered millions of individuals, particularly young people, by providing them with resources and tools to develop a positive body image and enhance their self-esteem. Through workshops, educational materials, and online platforms, the project has helped individuals build resilience and confidence in their own unique beauty.

2. Positive Social Change: The Dove Self-Esteem Project has contributed to positive social change by challenging societal beauty standards and promoting inclusivity. By raising awareness about the harmful effects of unrealistic beauty ideals and fostering a culture of acceptance, the project has played a significant role in shaping a more diverse and inclusive society.

3. Community Engagement: The project has fostered community engagement by collaborating with educators, parents, and organizations to deliver self-esteem workshops and programs. By engaging these stakeholders, the Dove Self-Esteem Project has created a collective effort to support individuals in developing a healthy relationships with their bodies and promoting positive self-esteem.

4. Brand Perception and Loyalty: The Dove Self-Esteem Project has enhanced the brand perception of Dove by showcasing its commitment to social impact and its genuine concern for individuals' well-being. Through its involvement in promoting self-esteem and body confidence,

Dove has gained loyalty and support from consumers who appreciate the brand's efforts to make a meaningful difference in society.

5. Industry Leadership: The Dove Self-Esteem Project has positioned Dove as a leader in the beauty industry, going beyond product offerings and advocating for positive change. By addressing critical issues related to self-esteem, body image, and media influence, Dove has set a precedent for other brands to prioritize social responsibility and contribute to the well-being of their consumers.

The Dove Self-Esteem Project has profoundly impacted individuals, communities, and the brand itself. The project has empowered individuals, fostered social change, and strengthened brand loyalty by promoting positive body image and self-esteem. Through its efforts, Dove has solidified its position as a purpose-driven brand that values the well-being and self-confidence of its consumers.

In conclusion, establishing sub-brands dedicated to social or environmental causes can be a powerful strategy to enhance brand image. By aligning with causes that resonate with their target audience, brands can demonstrate their commitment to social responsibility and sustainability and connect with socially conscious consumers.

Through effective messaging and storytelling, these sub-brands can communicate their purpose and impact, building trust and loyalty among consumers. The integration of cause-related initiatives into the brand's core values and messaging helps create an authentic and meaningful connection with consumers.

Furthermore, leveraging various marketing channels enables brands to reach and engage a wider audience, spreading awareness about the cause and driving positive change. Ultimately, by establishing sub-brands for social or environmental causes, brands have the opportunity to not only enhance their brand image but also make a tangible difference in the world.

* * *

12

Technology Advancements or Innovation

L aunching sub-brands for technological advancements refers to the strategic creation of separate brand identities within specific product categories to showcase and highlight the brand's commitment to innovation, cutting-edge technology, and advancements in the field. These sub-brands are designed to capture the attention of tech-savvy consumers and position the brand as a leader in technological advancements, offering innovative solutions and products that address the evolving needs of the market. The primary objective is to communicate the brand's commitment to technological excellence, differentiate from competitors, and attract customers who prioritize advanced features and capabilities in their purchasing decisions.

Reasons for Sub-brands

Launching sub-brands for technological advancements or innovation can be driven by several reasons. Here are some key reasons:

1. Highlighting Expertise: By launching a sub-brand dedicated to technological advancements, a company can emphasize its expertise and capabilities in a particular technology or product category. It allows the

brand to position itself as a leader and demonstrate its commitment to pushing the boundaries of innovation in that specific field.

2. Catering to Tech-Savvy Consumers: With the increasing demand for advanced technology and features, many consumers actively seek products that offer the latest advancements. By launching a sub-brand, companies can cater to the needs and preferences of tech-savvy customers who prioritize cutting-edge technology and innovation in their purchasing decisions.

3. Differentiation from Competitors: In a highly competitive market, launching a sub-brand focused on technological advancements provides a clear point of differentiation from competitors. It allows the brand to stand out by showcasing its unique capabilities, innovations, and technological breakthroughs, thereby attracting customers who are seeking innovative solutions.

4. Targeting Niche Markets: Launching a sub-brand can also be a strategic approach to target niche markets or specific customer segments that are particularly interested in advanced technology. By tailoring the sub-brand's offerings and messaging to the needs and preferences of these niche markets, companies can effectively capture their attention and establish a strong market presence.

5. Building Brand Reputation and Perception: A sub-brand dedicated to technological advancements can significantly enhance the overall brand reputation and perception. It demonstrates the brand's commitment to staying at the forefront of technological progress and reinforces its image as an innovative and forward-thinking company.

6. Leveraging Technological Breakthroughs: When a company achieves significant technological breakthroughs or develops game-changing innovations, launching a sub-brand can serve as a platform to showcase and commercialize those advancements. It allows the brand to capitalize on its technological achievements and generate market excitement around the new offerings.

7. Creating Excitement and Buzz: Launching a sub-brand dedicated to showcasing technological advancements can generate excitement and

buzz among consumers. It creates a sense of anticipation and curiosity, driving interest and engagement with the brand. By positioning the sub-brand as the hub for the latest technological innovations, companies can captivate their target audience and create a buzz around their offerings.

8. Demonstrating Continuous Progress: A sub-brand focused on technological advancements allows companies to demonstrate their commitment to continuous progress and staying ahead of the curve. It showcases the brand's dedication to ongoing research and development, pushing the boundaries of what is possible, and delivering cutting-edge solutions. This constant drive for innovation helps the brand maintain relevance and stay competitive in the fast-paced technology landscape.

9. Enhancing Perceived Value: Launching a sub-brand that highlights technological advancements can enhance the perceived value of the brand's products or services. Consumers often associate advanced technology with improved performance, functionality, and overall value. By leveraging the sub-brand to communicate the enhanced capabilities and benefits enabled by the technological advancements, companies can position their offerings as premium and high-value options in the market.

10. Fostering Industry Partnerships and Collaborations: Launching a sub-brand dedicated to technological advancements can attract industry partners and collaborations. Other companies, researchers, or technology experts in the field may be more inclined to work with a brand that has a clear focus on innovation. These partnerships can lead to joint research and development efforts, knowledge sharing, and access to the latest technological advancements, further strengthening the brand's position as an industry leader.

11. Future-Proofing the Brand: In rapidly evolving industries, launching a sub-brand for technological advancements helps future-proof the brand. The brand can adapt to changing market demands and consumer expectations by embracing emerging technologies and showcasing a commitment to innovation. It positions the brand as forward-thinking and adaptable, ensuring its long-term relevance and sustainability in

the ever-changing technology landscape.

By dedicating a sub-brand to technological advancements, companies can effectively communicate their commitment to innovation, drive customer engagement, and generate business growth.

Challenges

Here are the challenges and considerations associated with launching sub-brands to showcase technological advancements:

1. Investment in Research and Development: To maintain a competitive edge and deliver meaningful technological advancements, companies must invest significantly in research and development (R&D). This includes allocating resources for exploring new technologies, conducting experiments, prototyping, testing, and refining innovations. The commitment to ongoing R&D can be a financial and resource-intensive challenge, requiring a long-term strategic vision and investment.

2. Delivering Promised Benefits: When launching a sub-brand for technological advancements, it is crucial to ensure that the showcased innovations deliver on their promised benefits. Technological advancements must live up to consumer expectations in terms of performance, functionality, reliability, and user experience. Failing to deliver on these promises can lead to disappointment, erosion of trust, and damage to the brand's reputation.

3. Managing the Brand Portfolio: When introducing a sub-brand for technological advancements, companies must carefully manage the relationship between the main brand and the sub-brand within the brand portfolio. The sub-brand should align with the overall brand architecture and maintain coherence with the brand's values, positioning, and target audience. Balancing the distinct identity and messaging of the sub-brand while preserving the brand's overarching image can be a complex task.

4. Monitoring Market Trends and Competition: The technological land-scape is constantly evolving, with new advancements and innovations emerging at a rapid pace. Companies launching sub-brands for techno-logical advancements must stay vigilant and monitor market trends and competition. This includes tracking new technologies, understanding consumer preferences and demands, and assessing the competitive landscape to stay ahead and differentiate themselves in the market.

5. Navigating Technological Obsolescence: Technology can become out-dated quickly, and advancements that were once cutting-edge can become obsolete in a short period. Companies must anticipate and navigate technological obsolescence by continuously investing in R&D, staying informed about emerging technologies, and adapting their sub-brands' offerings to meet evolving market needs. This requires agility, adaptability, and a proactive approach to technology adoption and innovation.

6. Ensuring Consistent Brand Experience: While showcasing technological advancements, it is essential to ensure that the brand experience remains consistent across all touchpoints. The sub-brand's messaging, design, and customer interactions should align with the brand's overall identity and promise. Consistency in brand experience helps build trust, maintain brand loyalty, and ensure a seamless transition for customers between the main brand and the sub-brand.

By addressing these challenges and considerations, companies can success-fully navigate the complexities of showcasing technological advancements through sub-brands.

Example 01: NVIDIA GeForce

NVIDIA, a leading technology company, identified a growing demand for high-performance graphics processing units (GPUs) in the gaming and professional visualization markets. They recognized the need for cutting-edge GPUs capable of delivering exceptional graphics rendering, immersive gaming experiences, and accelerated computing for professional applications. To meet these specialized needs, NVIDIA's design team developed an advanced technology for a new GPU.

However, this new product was significantly more advanced than NVIDIA's existing offerings. Recognizing the potential of this technology and the need to differentiate it from its current brand, NVIDIA decided to launch a separate sub-brand called GEFORCE. By creating this sub-brand, NVIDIA aimed to position the new GPU as a distinct and specialized product within the market.

Through the launch of the GEFORCE sub-brand, NVIDIA introduced their highly advanced GPU to the market, targeting gamers and professionals who demanded top-tier graphics performance and computing capabilities. The sub-brand allowed NVIDIA to showcase the new GPU's technological advancements and cutting-edge features while also establishing a separate identity and positioning within the competitive GPU market.

Value Proposition: The value proposition of NVIDIA GeForce as a sub-brand lies in its ability to provide gamers and technology enthusiasts with cutting-edge graphics processing units (GPUs) that deliver exceptional gaming performance, immersive experiences, and advanced visual effects. The key elements of the value proposition include:

1. Unparalleled Gaming Performance: NVIDIA GeForce GPUs are designed to deliver high-performance gaming experiences. With powerful processing capabilities, advanced graphics technologies, and optimized drivers, GeForce GPUs enable smooth gameplay, high frame rates, and enhanced visuals, allowing gamers to fully immerse themselves in their favorite games.

2. Realistic and Immersive Graphics: GeForce GPUs bring lifelike visuals to gaming. With features like real-time ray tracing and AI-powered image upscaling, NVIDIA GeForce GPUs create stunningly realistic graphics, vibrant colors, and detailed environments, enhancing the overall gaming experience and making virtual worlds come to life.

3. Broad Compatibility and Game Support: NVIDIA GeForce GPUs are widely supported by game developers and are compatible with a vast library of games. Whether it's the latest AAA titles or popular indie games, GeForce GPUs ensure seamless compatibility and optimization, allowing gamers to enjoy their favorite games at their best.

4. Technological Advancements: NVIDIA GeForce is at the forefront of GPU technology advancements. From introducing new architectures and advanced features to pushing the boundaries of performance and visual fidelity, GeForce GPUs consistently deliver the latest innovations in gaming graphics. This ensures that gamers have access to the most advanced technologies and features available in the market.

5. Gaming Ecosystem and Support: NVIDIA GeForce provides a comprehensive gaming ecosystem that includes software tools, driver updates, and community support. GeForce Experience software offers features like automatic game optimizations, game streaming, and easy gameplay recording, enhancing the overall gaming experience and providing gamers with added convenience and functionality.

6. Brand Reputation and Trust: NVIDIA is a trusted brand in the gaming industry known for its commitment to innovation, quality, and reliability. GeForce GPUs carry the reputation and trust associated with the NVIDIA brand, giving gamers confidence in their performance, durability, and long-term support.

The value proposition of the NVIDIA GeForce sub-brand is centred around delivering exceptional gaming performance, realistic graphics, advanced technologies, and a comprehensive support ecosystem. By providing the tools and hardware necessary to enhance gaming experiences, NVIDIA GeForce aims to be the preferred choice for gamers seeking top-tier graphics performance and visual fidelity.

Brand Fit: The sub-brand aligned with NVIDIA's main brand by emphasizing its commitment to innovation, superior graphics performance, and immersive gaming experiences. It showcased NVIDIA's expertise in graphics technology and its dedication to pushing the boundaries of GPU capabilities.

1. Technological Expertise: NVIDIA Corporation is globally recognized as a leader in GPU technology and has built a strong reputation for its advancements in graphics processing. The NVIDIA GeForce sub-brand aligns perfectly with the parent brand's core competency, focusing exclusively on the gaming and high-performance computing markets. This brand fit allows NVIDIA to leverage its expertise and showcase the latest innovations in GPU technology through the GeForce sub-brand.

2. Target Market Focus: Both NVIDIA and the GeForce sub-brand target the gaming and high-performance computing markets. The parent brand caters to a diverse range of industries, including gaming, professional visualization, data centers, and automotive. The GeForce sub-brand, specifically designed for gamers, aligns with the parent brand's target market and allows NVIDIA to directly engage with gaming enthusiasts and showcase the capabilities of their GPUs in gaming applications.

3. Brand Reputation and Recognition: NVIDIA has established a strong brand reputation for its GPUs, known for their performance, quality, and reliability. The GeForce sub-brand inherits this positive brand perception and recognition, benefitting from the parent brand's established reputation. The association with the NVIDIA brand further enhances the credibility and trustworthiness of the GeForce sub-brand among gamers and technology enthusiasts.

4. Marketing Synergy: The GeForce sub-brand complements NVIDIA's overall marketing strategy by providing a focused platform to promote its latest GPU technologies. NVIDIA can leverage the strong brand awareness and market presence of the parent brand to effectively communicate the advancements and features of GeForce GPUs to its target audience. This synergy enables NVIDIA to strengthen its position as a leader in GPU technology and drive demand for its products.

5. Product Integration: The GeForce sub-brand is integrated into NVIDIA's overall product lineup, serving as a dedicated brand for gaming-focused GPUs. NVIDIA offers a range of GeForce GPUs tailored to different gaming

needs, from entry-level to high-end performance. This integration ensures a cohesive product portfolio strategy, allowing NVIDIA to address diverse customer requirements and maintain a strong presence in the gaming market.

The sub-brand effectively showcases NVIDIA's expertise in gaming and high-performance computing, leveraging the parent brand's reputation, target market focus, and marketing synergies to drive brand recognition, market presence, and customer loyalty.

Brand Architecture: The key elements of NVIDIA GeForce's brand portfolio architecture and strategy are as follows:

1. Differentiation and Target Market: NVIDIA GeForce is positioned as a premium gaming brand, targeting gamers and technology enthusiasts who value high-performance graphics and immersive gaming experiences. By focusing on this specific segment, NVIDIA GeForce differentiates itself from other brands in the graphics industry and establishes itself as a leader in gaming graphics.

2. Product Line Variation: NVIDIA GeForce offers a range of GPU models that cater to different gaming needs and budgets. This includes flagship models for hardcore gamers seeking top-tier performance, mid-range models for mainstream gamers, and budget-friendly options for entry-level gamers. This product line variation allows NVIDIA GeForce to address a broad range of customer preferences and price points.

3. Technology Advancements and Innovation: NVIDIA GeForce is known for pushing the boundaries of GPU technology and introducing innovative features and advancements. This includes advancements in areas such as real-time ray tracing, AI-powered graphics enhancements, and high refresh rate displays. By consistently delivering cutting-edge technology, NVIDIA GeForce maintains its reputation as a leader in the gaming graphics industry.

4. Brand Consistency and Visual Identity: NVIDIA GeForce maintains a

strong visual identity that is consistent across its product lineup and marketing materials. The brand logo, colour schemes, and visual elements are designed to evoke a sense of excitement and capture the gaming spirit. This consistency helps build brand recognition and reinforces the association of NVIDIA GeForce with high-performance gaming.

By aligning its product offerings and marketing efforts with gamers' specific needs and preferences, NVIDIA GeForce has established a strong presence in the gaming graphics market and continues to drive innovation in the industry.

Outcomes and Impact: The launch of the NVIDIA GeForce sub-brand had significant outcomes and impacts on the market. Firstly, it solidified NVIDIA's dominance in the gaming market by establishing GeForce GPUs as the preferred choice among gamers. The sub-brand's superior performance, advanced features, and optimized game compatibility played a key role in NVIDIA's market leadership. Additionally, the GeForce sub-brand fostered a loyal and enthusiastic community of gamers and graphics enthusiasts who identified strongly with the brand. NVIDIA's continuous innovation and engagement initiatives helped cultivate this dedicated following. The sub-brand's success was further validated by industry recognition and numerous awards received for technological advancements, gaming performance, and contributions to visual arts. These accolades positioned NVIDIA as a respected and sought-after brand in the GPU market. Furthermore, the success of the GeForce sub-brand allowed NVIDIA to expand its market presence beyond gaming. By leveraging its GPU technology for applications such as artificial intelligence, machine learning, and data science, NVIDIA diversified its revenue streams and further solidified its market position.

The launch of the NVIDIA GeForce sub-brand successfully showcased advancements in graphics processing units (GPUs) and positioned NVIDIA as a leader in the gaming and professional visualization markets. The sub-brand's marketing strategies, brand alignment, and continuous technological innovations resulted in positive outcomes, including market dominance, brand loyalty, and industry recognition.

Example 02: Dyson Supersonic

Dyson, a renowned technology company, recognized the need for innovation in the hair care industry. They identified consumer pain points such as long drying times, heat damage, and bulky hairdryers that lacked performance and design appeal. Dyson saw an opportunity to leverage their expertise in engineering and design to revolutionize the hair care market.

Value Proposition: The value proposition of the Dyson Supersonic sub-brand lies in its ability to revolutionize the hair care experience by offering a hair dryer that combines cutting-edge technology, superior performance, and sleek design. The key elements of the Dyson Supersonic's value proposition include:

1. Advanced Technology: The Dyson Supersonic is equipped with innovative technologies that set it apart from traditional hair dryers. It features intelligent heat control to prevent extreme heat damage, powerful digital motors for fast and controlled airflow, and Air Multiplier technology for precise and efficient drying. These technological advancements enhance the hair drying process and deliver salon-quality results.

2. Superior Performance: The Dyson Supersonic delivers exceptional performance with its high-speed airflow and precise heat settings. It offers fast drying times while minimizing heat damage, allowing users to achieve quick and efficient styling. The hair dryer's balanced design and lightweight construction also contribute to its ease of use and comfort during styling.

3. Sleek and Elegant Design: The Dyson Supersonic is known for its sleek and aesthetically pleasing design. It features a modern and ergonomic shape, premium materials, and a range of attractive colour options. The design not only enhances the user experience but also adds a touch of

luxury and sophistication to the hair care routine.

4. User-Focused Features: The Dyson Supersonic incorporates user-focused features that enhance convenience and customization. It includes magnetic attachments for versatile styling options, a cool shot button for setting hairstyles, and easy-to-use controls for adjusting heat and airflow. These features allow users to tailor their hair drying and styling experience to their specific needs and preferences.

5. Brand Reputation: Dyson is recognized globally for its engineering excellence, innovation, and commitment to quality. The Supersonic sub-brand benefits from Dyson's reputation and brand equity, providing consumers with the assurance of a reliable and high-quality product.

The sub-brand offers a premium and innovative solution for those seeking a superior hair drying and styling experience, positioning itself as a leader in the hair care industry.

Brand Fit: The brand fit analysis between Dyson Supersonic and its parent brand can be assessed based on the following factors:

1. Technology and Innovation: Dyson is widely recognized for its focus on advanced technology and innovation in its products. The Dyson Supersonic hair dryer showcases the same commitment to technological advancements by introducing innovative features and design elements that revolutionize the hair drying experience. The use of advanced airflow technology, intelligent heat control, and powerful yet quiet operation aligns with Dyson's overall brand image of cutting-edge technology and innovation.

2. Design and Aesthetics: Dyson products, including the Supersonic hair dryer, are known for their sleek and distinctive design. The Supersonic hair dryer features a modern and ergonomic design, with a focus on user-friendly controls and a visually appealing aesthetic. This design philosophy resonates with Dyson's overarching brand identity, which emphasizes a combination of functionality and stylish aesthetics.

3. Performance and Quality: Dyson is synonymous with high-performance and high-quality products. The Supersonic hair dryer upholds this brand reputation by delivering exceptional performance in terms of fast drying, precise heat control, and minimizing hair damage. The use of advanced engineering and quality materials ensures that the Supersonic hair dryer meets the expectations of consumers who value performance and durability.

4. Brand Reputation and Trust: Dyson has established a strong brand reputation built on trust, reliability, and customer satisfaction. This positive brand perception extends to the Dyson Supersonic sub-brand, instilling confidence in consumers that the hair dryer will deliver on its promises of performance and quality. The existing brand equity of Dyson enhances the perceived value and trustworthiness of the Supersonic hair dryer in the market.

5. Brand Experience and Customer-centric Approach: Dyson places a strong emphasis on the overall brand experience and customer satisfaction. This customer-centric approach is reflected in the Supersonic hair dryer through features like intelligent heat control, personalized settings, and ease of use. The focus on enhancing the user experience aligns with Dyson's commitment to providing innovative and customer-oriented products.

The sub-brand complements Dyson's portfolio of innovative home appliances and reinforces its position as a leader in the technology and design space.

Brand Architecture: The Dyson Supersonic strategically aligns with the parent brand's portfolio in several ways. Firstly, it stands out as a unique and innovative product within the Dyson brand portfolio, offering advanced technology and superior performance in the hair care category. This product differentiation expands Dyson's offerings while maintaining its reputation for technological innovation. Secondly, the Supersonic maintains a strong connection to the parent brand through consistent design language, visual identity, and brand messaging. This brand cohesion reinforces Dyson's values and image. Thirdly, the Supersonic allows Dyson to enter and establish a presence in the beauty and personal care market, complementing the brand's focus on technology and innovation and broadening its market reach. Lastly, by leveraging Dyson's strong brand equity and reputation for premium products, Supersonic gains a competitive advantage and a higher perceived value in the marketplace. Overall, the Dyson Supersonic enhances the Dyson brand portfolio and drives growth in the hair care industry.

Outcomes and Impact: The launch of Dyson Supersonic had several positive outcomes. Firstly, it disrupted the hair care market by introducing a technologically advanced and visually appealing hairdryer, setting a new standard for the industry. This innovation challenged traditional market players and created a wave of excitement and interest. Secondly, the launch of Dyson Supersonic elevated Dyson's brand reputation, positioning the company as a leader in innovation across multiple industries. The sub-brand's premium positioning and unique features reinforced the perception of Dyson as a high-quality and forward-thinking brand. Thirdly, Dyson Supersonic attracted a broader consumer base beyond traditional hair care customers. Its appeal extended to beauty enthusiasts, professional hairstylists, and individuals seeking premium and cutting-edge hair care solutions. Lastly, Dyson Supersonic received recognition and awards for its design, innovation, and performance, further solidifying its credibility and market position. These positive outcomes have contributed to the success of Dyson Supersonic as a sub-brand and strengthened Dyson's overall brand presence in the market.

The launch of Dyson Supersonic as a sub-brand successfully showcased technological advancements in the hair care industry, aligned with Dyson's brand values, and positioned the company as a leader in innovative personal care products.

In conclusion, launching sub-brands to showcase technological advancements or innovation within specific product categories is an effective strategy for brands to differentiate themselves, capture market opportunities, and enhance their overall brand image. By creating sub-brands dedicated to specific product categories, companies can highlight their technological prowess, attract tech-savvy consumers, and generate excitement and buzz around their advancements.

This approach allows brands to emphasize their commitment to innovation, drive consumer interest, and carve out a unique positioning in the market. It enables them to showcase their technological capabilities, differentiate their products from competitors, and establish a reputation for cutting-edge solutions.

However, launching sub-brands for technological advancements also poses challenges, including investment in research and development, ensuring the promised benefits are delivered, managing brand relationships within the brand portfolio, and staying ahead of market trends and competition. Successful implementation requires careful brand fit, alignment with the main brand, effective marketing strategies, and continuous monitoring and adaptation.

* * *

13

Co-branding

C o-branding is a strategic partnership between two or more brands that combines their strengths, resources, and expertise to create a unique sub-brand. By collaborating with complementary brands, companies can leverage each other's reputation, customer loyalty, and market positions to enhance their brand strengths and unlock new opportunities.

This collaborative approach allows brands to tap into new markets, reach a wider audience, and differentiate themselves from competitors. By partnering with brands that share similar values, target audiences, or industry expertise, companies can fill gaps in their product offerings, access new customer segments, and explore new distribution channels.

The value of collaboration lies in the shared benefits and value creation that arise from combining brand strengths. By pooling resources, knowledge, and capabilities, brands can create innovative products, deliver exceptional customer experiences, and make a greater impact in the market. Co-branding enables brands to tap into the unique strengths of their partners, resulting in increased brand awareness, credibility, and market penetration.

Ultimately, co-branding provides a strategic avenue for brands to leverage their strengths, expand their reach, and gain a competitive advantage. By joining forces with complementary brands, companies can create unique offerings that resonate with consumers and drive mutual success. The collaboration between brands enables them to maximize their potential, enhance brand relevance, and create long-term value in the market.

Key Benefits of Co-Branding

Co-branding offers several key benefits for companies that engage in strategic partnerships. Here are some key benefits of the value proposition of co-branding:

1. Enhanced Product or Service Offering: Co-branding allows partners to combine their expertise, resources, and capabilities to create a product or service that offers enhanced features, quality, or performance. By leveraging the unique strengths of each partner, the co-branded offering can provide a superior value proposition compared to what either brand could achieve individually.

2. Increased Perceived Value: Co-branded products or services often carry a higher perceived value in the eyes of consumers. The association with well-known and trusted brands can enhance the perceived quality, credibility, and desirability of the offering. Customers are more likely to perceive the co-branded product as a premium or special edition, resulting in a willingness to pay a higher price.

3. Access to New Customer Segments: Co-branding can help partners reach new customer segments or markets that they may not have been able to access independently. By aligning with a complementary brand, each partner can tap into the existing customer base of the other brand and gain exposure to a wider audience. This expanded customer reach can lead to increased sales and market share.

4. Strengthened Brand Image and Awareness: Collaborating with a reputable brand can positively impact brand image and awareness. Co-branding allows partners to borrow the other brand's positive associations and brand equity, leading to a strengthened overall brand image. It can also generate buzz and excitement among consumers, increasing brand visibility and attracting new customers.

5. Competitive Advantage: Co-branding can provide a competitive advantage by offering unique or differentiated products or services in the market. Both partners' combined strengths, expertise, and resources can create a distinct value proposition that sets the co-branded offering apart from competitors. This differentiation can lead to increased customer loyalty and preference.

6. Shared Marketing Efforts: Co-branding allows partners to pool their marketing efforts and resources, resulting in more impactful and cost-effective campaigns. Partners can reach a larger audience and generate greater brand exposure by sharing marketing channels, advertising expenses, and promotional activities. This shared marketing approach can result in improved ROI and customer engagement.

Identifying Co-branding Partners

Identifying complementary brands for co-branding requires a strategic and thorough evaluation process to ensure alignment in values, target audience, and product/service offerings. Here's an explanation of the process and the importance of shared objectives and mutual benefits:

1. Research and Analysis: Conducting thorough research and analysis is the first step in identifying complementary brands. This involves understanding the target audience, their preferences, and their needs. It also involves analyzing the market landscape to identify brands with a similar target audience or offering complementary products or services.

2. Define Objectives: The next step is for each brand to define its objectives for co-branding clearly. This includes identifying the specific goals they aim to achieve through the collaboration, such as expanding market reach, enhancing brand image, or accessing new customer segments. A clear understanding of objectives helps identify brands that can contribute towards achieving those goals.

183

3. Identify Brand Values: It is crucial to identify brands that share similar values or have a brand ethos that complements each other. Brands with similar values are more likely to have a natural alignment and can create a cohesive and authentic co-branded experience. This alignment helps in maintaining consistency and credibility in the eyes of consumers.

4. Understand Target Audience: Brands should analyze their target audience and identify any overlaps or synergies with potential partner brands. Collaborating with brands that have a similar or complementary target audience allows for better targeting and engagement. It ensures that the co-branded offering resonates with the shared target audience and increases the chances of success.

5. Consumer Insights: Gain insights into the target audience's preferences, buying behaviours, and aspirations. Understand what they value and what resonates with them. This will help in identifying brands that align with these preferences and can effectively engage the target audience.

6. Assess Product/Service Offerings: Brands need to assess how their product or service offerings can complement each other. Look for areas where the strengths of one brand can enhance the offerings of the other brand, creating a more valuable and compelling proposition for customers. The collaboration should bring unique and complementary benefits that neither brand could offer alone.

7. Shared Objectives and Mutual Benefits: Collaboration works best when both brands have shared objectives and can derive mutual benefits from the partnership. This ensures a balanced and mutually beneficial relationship where both brands have something to gain. The collaboration should offer advantages to each brand, such as increased market exposure, access to new distribution channels, or shared resources and expertise.

8. Market Positioning: Assess the market positioning of potential partners to ensure they complement each other. Look for brands that offer a unique selling proposition or occupy a distinct position in the market. This way, the co-branded offering can tap into new segments or provide a differentiated value proposition to existing customers.

9. Competitive Advantage: When identifying complementary brands, it is

essential to evaluate their competitive advantage. Brands should look for partners that bring unique strengths or expertise to the collaboration. This could be in terms of technology, innovation, design, or any other aspect that sets them apart from competitors. The combination of these advantages can create a more compelling and differentiated offering in the market.

10. Resources and Capabilities: Evaluate the resources, capabilities, and expertise of the potential partner brands. Assess their ability to contribute to the co-branded offering in terms of manufacturing capabilities, distribution networks, marketing expertise, or technological advancements. The collaboration should leverage the strengths of both brands to create a stronger and more competitive offering.

11. Legal and Contractual Considerations: Before entering into a co-branding partnership, it is essential to address legal and contractual considerations. Establish clear agreements regarding brand usage, intellectual property rights, financial arrangements, and any other legal aspects to protect the interests of both parties.

By following a systematic approach to identify complementary brands, the co-branding collaboration can be built on shared objectives and mutual benefits. This ensures a strong foundation for a successful partnership that leverages the strengths of each brand, resonates with the target audience, and creates value for both brands involved.

Example 01: Starbucks and Spotify

Starbucks, a renowned coffee chain, and Spotify, a leading music streaming platform, joined forces in a successful sub-brand partnership to enhance the in-store customer experience and leverage the strengths of both brands. This collaboration aimed to revolutionize the in-store music experience by providing unique and curated playlists for Starbucks customers, while also granting Spotify's global fan base access to Starbucks' extensive music library spanning over two decades.

The partnership between Starbucks and Spotify marked a significant milestone as Starbucks opened up its loyalty program, My Starbucks Rewards (MSR), to a third-party partner for the first time. This strategic move allowed Starbucks' loyal customers, who were also members of the MSR program, to earn "Stars as Currency" by subscribing or upgrading to Spotify Premium. This not only provided added value to Starbucks' loyal customers but also contributed to Spotify's growth by expanding its premium subscriber base and generating increased revenue.

Moreover, the collaboration had a broader impact beyond Starbucks' physical stores. By offering Starbucks playlists to all Spotify users, Starbucks significantly increased its brand exposure and introduced its music selection to a wider audience. This allowed Spotify users worldwide to discover and enjoy the music that was synonymous with the Starbucks experience, even if they had not visited a physical Starbucks location before. The partnership effectively extended the reach and influence of both brands, benefiting Starbucks by expanding its digital presence and Spotify by providing an enriched music offering to its users.

Starbucks and Spotify's sub-brand partnership created a win-win situation, where both brands capitalized on their respective strengths to deliver an enhanced customer experience and achieve mutual growth.

Identifying Complementary Brands: Starbucks and Spotify are two brands that are complementary in nature. Starbucks is known for its cosy and inviting ambience, while Spotify is a popular music streaming platform. Both brands saw an opportunity to collaborate and enhance their respective offerings.

Starbucks wanted to enhance its in-store experience with music, so it partnered with Spotify to create a "music ecosystem." This ecosystem allowed Starbucks to play Spotify playlists in its stores, and it also allowed Spotify users to create their own playlists that could be played in Starbucks stores.

On the other hand, Spotify wanted to extend its reach to a new audience by associating with a physical retail environment. The partnership with Starbucks gave Spotify the opportunity to expose its brand to millions of new customers.

Brand Fit: Starbucks has built a brand image centred around quality, convenience, and community. The brand is known for its focus on creating a unique and personalized coffee experience for customers. With a strong emphasis on providing excellent customer service and fostering a sense of belonging, Starbucks has cultivated a loyal customer base.

Spotify has revolutionized how people discover and enjoy music. It has established itself as a go-to destination for personalized music recommendations, curated playlists, and seamless streaming across devices. With a vast library of music from various genres and artists, Spotify has positioned itself as an innovative and user-friendly platform that caters to individual music preferences.

The co-branding partnership between Starbucks and Spotify leverages the strengths of both brands, creating a unique and enhanced brand experience for their customers. By integrating Spotify's music streaming capabilities into the Starbucks mobile app, customers can enjoy personalized music recommendations and access exclusive Starbucks-curated playlists while savouring their favourite coffee at Starbucks stores. This integration aligns with both brands' core values, offering customers a seamless and immersive experience that combines the pleasures of coffee and music.

Both Starbucks and Spotify aim to establish an emotional connection with their customers. Starbucks emphasizes the concept of a "third place," a welcoming space for people to gather and connect outside of home and work. On the other hand, Spotify enhances users' emotional connection to music by providing personalized playlists and curated recommendations. This shared commitment to emotional connections, and personalization creates a strong brand fit between the two companies.

In addition to providing a unique brand experience, Starbucks and Spotify offer cross-promotion and rewards for their customers. Starbucks Rewards members can earn and redeem Stars for Spotify Premium subscriptions, while Spotify Premium subscribers receive Starbucks Rewards Gold status. This mutually beneficial arrangement encourages brand loyalty and enhances the value proposition for customers of both brands. By partnering together, Starbucks and Spotify extend their brand offerings, tap into new customer segments, and reinforce their brand identities as leaders in their respective industries. The collaboration exemplifies the power of co-branding to create synergistic experiences that resonate with customers and strengthen brand loyalty.

Brand Architecture and Alignment with Brand Values: The dominant brand in the Starbucks and Spotify collaboration is Starbucks. As a renowned coffee chain with a strong brand presence, Starbucks serves as the primary brand within its stores. This strategic partnership allowed Starbucks to leverage its strong brand presence and customer loyalty while enhancing the in-store experience through the addition of music streaming capabilities. By aligning their brand architecture and values, Starbucks and Spotify created a cohesive and authentic customer experience that combined the enjoyment of coffee and music. Both brands shared a common commitment to providing memorable experiences and connecting people through the power of music and coffee, making the collaboration a natural fit.

Outcomes and Impact: The co-branding partnership between Starbucks and Spotify has enhanced the customer experience by integrating Spotify's music streaming platform into Starbucks stores, creating a curated and personalized music experience for customers. The collaboration has also extended the reach of Spotify, attracting new users from Starbucks' customer base and driving customer acquisition. Both brands have been perceived as innovative and forward-thinking, differentiating themselves from competitors. The partnership has provided marketing and promotion opportunities, allowing Starbucks and Spotify to cross-promote each other and increase brand visibility. Furthermore, the collaboration has strengthened brand loyalty by offering unique benefits and experiences to customers.

The Starbucks and Spotify co-branding collaboration has exemplified the power of strategic partnerships in creating mutually beneficial outcomes and delivering a compelling brand experience to customers.

Example 02:Nike+ iPod

Nike and Apple, two iconic brands in their respective industries, identified a unique opportunity to combine their strengths and cater to the growing demand for fitness and active lifestyles.

Nike, known worldwide for its innovative sportswear and athletic footwear, shared a common focus with Apple, renowned for its cutting-edge technology and consumer electronics. Both brands recognized the intersection of sports, fitness, and technology as a fertile ground for collaboration.

With a shared target audience of health-conscious individuals passionate about sports and fitness, Nike and Apple saw the potential to create a seamless integration between their products. Leveraging Apple's iPod technology and Nike's expertise in sports performance, they collaborated to revolutionise how people approached their workouts.

The result was the Nike+iPod sub-brand, a groundbreaking system that allowed users to track their workouts, monitor their progress, and listen to music simultaneously. By integrating fitness tracking and music playback, Nike and Apple created a compelling offering that resonated with consumers seeking an immersive and motivating workout experience. Whether running, training, or participating in various sports activities, users could seamlessly synchronize their fitness data and enjoy their favourite music through their Nike+ shoes and the iPod.

This co-branding initiative not only showcased the compatibility of Nike's sportswear expertise with Apple's technological prowess but also demonstrated their shared commitment to innovation and enhancing the consumer experience.

The Nike+iPod sub-brand quickly gained popularity and became a symbol of the intersection between fashion, fitness, and technology. It not only bolstered the brand positions of Nike and Apple but also solidified their connection with health-conscious consumers who valued performance, style, and innovation.

Brand Fit: The co-branding collaboration between Nike and Apple's iPod was a strategic move that leveraged the strengths and brand attributes of both companies to create a seamless and immersive fitness experience for consumers.

1. Shared Target Audience: Nike and Apple identified a shared target audience of health-conscious individuals who were passionate about sports, fitness, and technology. Both brands recognized the growing demand for fitness-focused products and experiences and aimed to cater to the needs of this specific audience segment. Nike brought its expertise in athletic performance and apparel to the partnership. Apple, known for its cutting-edge technology and consumer electronics, provided the iPod's innovative music playback capabilities.

2. Enhanced Fitness Experience: The Nike+iPod co-branding initiative aimed to enhance the fitness experience for consumers. By integrating Nike's sports performance technology with the iPod's music playback features, users could track their workouts, monitor their progress, and listen to their favourite music simultaneously. This integration added a new level of motivation, engagement, and entertainment to fitness activities.

3. Brand Identity: Nike and Apple seamlessly integrated their brand elements and design aesthetics into the Nike+iPod sub-brand. The iconic Nike swoosh and the recognizable Apple iPod branding were combined to create a cohesive and recognizable identity that reflected the collaboration's purpose and values.

4. Brand Values: Both Nike and Apple share a commitment to innovation, performance, and customer experience. The Nike+iPod sub-brand aligned with these values by providing cutting-edge technology that enhanced athletic performance and motivated users to achieve their fitness goals.

5. Mutual Benefits: The co-branding initiative provided mutual benefits for Nike and Apple. Nike gained access to Apple's loyal customer base and the popularity of the iPod, while Apple extended its reach into the fitness and athletic market. The collaboration allowed both brands to tap into new revenue streams and strengthen their market positions.

Brand Architecture: Nike serves as the parent brand in the Nike+iPod co-branding initiative. iPod is the sub-brand in this co-branding collaboration.

Nike's expertise in sports performance and apparel aligns with the fitness-focused objective of the collaboration, while Apple's innovative technology complements Nike's offerings.

In terms of brand hierarchy, Nike maintains a dominant presence in the co-branded products and marketing efforts. The Nike logo and branding elements are prominently featured alongside the iPod branding, emphasizing Nike's position as the parent brand.

The brand architecture of Nike+iPod extends Nike's brand values of athleticism, innovation, and performance into the realm of technology and music. The collaboration enables Nike to expand its brand presence beyond apparel and footwear while also enhancing Apple's association with sports and fitness.

Outcomes and Impact: The Nike+iPod co-branding initiative has had significant outcomes and impacts on both Nike and Apple. Firstly, it has enhanced the customer experience by integrating Nike's sports performance technology with the iPod's music playback capabilities. This unique combination allows users to track their workouts, monitor their progress, and listen to music simultaneously, enhancing motivation and engagement during physical activities. Secondly, the co-branding collaboration has increased brand visibility and reach for both Nike and Apple. By tapping into each other's customer base, they have expanded their audience and gained exposure to new markets. Thirdly, the initiative has strengthened the brand association between Nike and fitness, as well as Apple and technology. Nike's expertise in sportswear, combined with Apple's innovative technology, has solidified their positions as leaders in their respective industries. Fourthly, the collaboration has led to improved product offerings by developing technologically advanced products that cater to the evolving needs of fitness enthusiasts. The integration of fitness tracking features with music playback has added value and provided a comprehensive experience for customers. Furthermore, the co-branding initiative has generated positive consumer perceptions towards both Nike and Apple. Customers appreciate the seamless integration of fitness and music, recognizing the brands' commitment to innovation and convenience. Lastly, the Nike+iPod collaboration has provided a competitive advantage for both brands by differentiating their products in the market. This unique combination appeals to fitness-conscious consumers who seek a holistic and engaging workout solution.

In a nutshell, the collaboration has successfully combined the strengths of both brands, resulting in a powerful and appealing offering for fitness enthusiasts.

Collaborating with complementary brands to create sub-brands is a strategic approach that allows companies to leverage the strengths of both partners and unlock new opportunities. By combining their resources, expertise, and customer bases, brands can create unique sub-brands that offer enhanced value propositions to their target audience.

The benefits of this approach are manifold. It allows brands to tap into new markets, reach a broader customer base, and capitalize on the expertise and reputation of their collaboration partners. Co-branding collaborations can also create a halo effect, where one brand's positive attributes and associations transfer to the sub-brand, boosting its credibility and appeal.

* * *

14

Ingredient Branding

I ngredient branding refers to the practice of developing sub-brands that highlight specific ingredients or components used in products. It involves giving prominence and recognition to the key ingredients within the overall brand strategy.

Highlighting specific ingredients or components is crucial because they play a significant role in shaping the quality, performance, and value of a product. Ingredients can differentiate a product from competitors, provide unique benefits, and influence consumer perceptions. By highlighting these ingredients through sub-brands, brands can effectively communicate their value and importance to consumers.

Sub-brands in ingredient branding serve as a dedicated platform to showcase the key ingredients or components used in a product. They create a distinct identity for the ingredient, allowing it to stand out and be recognized by consumers. Sub-brands help in communicating the value, quality, and benefits associated with the ingredient, thereby enhancing the overall brand image and consumer perception.

Moreover, sub-brands in ingredient branding provide transparency to consumers, enabling them to make informed choices based on their specific needs and preferences. They create a deeper connection between the brand and the consumers by offering a clear understanding of the ingredients and their impact on the product.

Additionally, sub-brands in ingredient branding contribute to the overall brand differentiation and competitive advantage. By highlighting unique and high-quality ingredients, brands can set themselves apart in the market and establish themselves as leaders in specific ingredient categories.

Furthermore, sub-brands in ingredient branding can drive innovation and product development. They provide a platform for brands to introduce new variants or product lines that emphasize different ingredients, catering to evolving consumer preferences and market trends.

The significance of sub-brands in ingredient branding lies in their ability to effectively communicate the value, quality, and benefits of specific ingredients to consumers.

Strategies for Developing Ingredient Sub-Brands

1. Identifying key ingredients or components with unique selling propositions: The first step in developing ingredient sub-brands is to identify key ingredients or components that have unique selling propositions. These are the ingredients that set the product apart from competitors and offer distinct benefits or qualities. Brands need to analyze their product portfolio and identify the ingredients that contribute significantly to the product's value proposition.

2. Conducting market research to understand consumer preferences and perceptions: Market research plays a crucial role in understanding consumer preferences and perceptions regarding specific ingredients. Brands need to gather insights into consumer attitudes, behaviours, and expectations related to ingredients. This research helps in identifying the ingredients that resonate with the target audience and have the potential to create a competitive advantage.

3. Establishing partnerships with ingredient suppliers or manufacturers: To develop ingredient sub-brands, brands often need to establish partnerships with ingredient suppliers or manufacturers. These partnerships

are essential to ensure the availability of high-quality ingredients and to leverage the expertise of the suppliers in promoting the ingredient's benefits. Collaborating with trusted suppliers also adds credibility to the sub-brand and enhances consumer trust.

4. Creating distinct brand identities and visual elements for ingredient sub-brands: To differentiate the ingredient sub-brand and create a strong brand identity, it is important to develop distinct brand elements such as logos, packaging designs, and visual elements. These elements should align with the overall brand architecture while highlighting the specific ingredient. The design and messaging should convey the unique qualities, benefits, and story of the ingredient, creating a compelling brand image.

5. Developing targeted marketing and communication strategies to highlight the ingredient's value: Marketing and communication strategies play a crucial role in showcasing the value of the ingredient sub-brand. Brands must develop targeted messaging and communication channels that effectively communicate the ingredient's benefits, quality, and unique selling propositions to the target audience. This may involve leveraging various marketing channels, such as advertising, social media, influencer collaborations, and educational content, to create awareness and generate interest.

Additionally, brands can consider engaging in partnerships or collaborations with chefs, nutritionists, or other industry experts who can endorse the ingredient and provide credibility. The communication strategy should focus on educating consumers about the ingredient's origins, production methods, sustainability practices, and impact on product quality and performance.

By implementing these strategies, brands can effectively develop ingredient sub-brands that capture consumer attention, differentiate the product, and communicate the value of the specific ingredient. The goal is to create a compelling brand story around the ingredient, building trust, and loyalty, and ultimately driving consumer preference and sales.

Example 01: L'Oréal Paris - "Pro-Retinol" Sub-Brand

L'Oréal Paris, a leading beauty and cosmetics brand, embarked on a journey to address the specific skincare needs of its customers by introducing the "Pro-Retinol" sub-brand. The journey began with extensive market research, including surveys and focus groups, to gain valuable insights into their target audience's skincare concerns and desired outcomes. The findings revealed a strong demand for affordable and accessible anti-ageing solutions that could visibly improve skin texture and appearance.

Armed with these customer insights, L'Oréal Paris set out to identify a key ingredient that could effectively address these skincare needs. Through rigorous scientific research and experimentation, they discovered Pro-Retinol, a potent derivative of Vitamin A known for its remarkable anti-ageing properties. Pro-Retinol has the power to stimulate collagen production, enhance skin elasticity, and reduce the appearance of wrinkles, making it an ideal ingredient to target signs of ageing.

With Pro-Retinol identified as the key ingredient, L'Oréal Paris crafted a range of skincare formulations, including serums, creams, and masks, to cater to different preferences and skincare routines. This strategic approach allowed customers to seamlessly incorporate Pro-Retinol into their daily skincare regimen, ensuring convenience and efficacy.

To ensure the efficacy and safety of Pro-Retinol, L'Oréal Paris invested in scientific research, clinical trials, and dermatological testing. These endeavours were crucial in validating the claims and substantiating the positive effects of Pro-Retinol on the skin. By prioritizing scientific rigour and transparency, L'Oréal Paris built trust among customers, solidifying the Pro-Retinol sub-brand's reputation as a reliable and effective skincare solution.

Understanding the importance of highlighting the benefits of Pro-Retinol, L'Oréal Paris embarked on the creation of an ingredient sub-brand. This would allow them to emphasize the importance and effectiveness of Pro-Retinol as a key ingredient in their skincare products.

By creating an ingredient sub-brand, L'Oréal Paris could establish Pro-Retinol as a recognizable and trusted name in the skincare industry. This approach also would allow them to communicate the specific benefits of Pro-Retinol to their target audience, such as its anti-ageing properties, ability to reduce wrinkles and improve skin texture.

Through prominent branding featuring the Pro-Retinol name and logo on packaging, marketing materials, and product descriptions, L'Oréal Paris ensured that consumers would associate the sub-brand with the exceptional benefits of Pro-Retinol.

The ingredient sub-brand strategy also provided a clear value proposition to customers by simplifying their decision-making process. Customers could easily identify and choose products containing Pro-Retinol, knowing that they were investing in a proven and trusted ingredient. This approach not only catered to customers' specific skincare needs but also instilled a sense of confidence and assurance in their purchase decisions.

Value Proposition: The Pro-Retinol sub-brand by L'Oréal Paris offers a compelling value proposition to consumers seeking effective and accessible anti-aging skincare solutions. By leveraging the power of Pro-Retinol, a potent ingredient known for its anti-aging properties, L'Oréal Paris provides products that reduce wrinkles, improve skin texture, and stimulate collagen production. The sub-brand combines scientific research, product innovation, and affordable pricing to deliver visible results and cater to a wide range of skincare needs. With a commitment to excellence and inclusivity, the Pro-Retinol sub-brand offers consumers a trusted and reputable choice for their anti-aging skincare journey.

Brand Fit: L'Oréal Paris has established itself as a trusted and reputable beauty brand, known for its commitment to innovation, excellence, and inclusivity. The Pro-Retinol sub-brand embodies these values and reinforces L'Oréal Paris' position as a leader in the skincare industry. The brand value of innovation is reflected in the inclusion of Pro-Retinol as a key ingredient in the sub-brand. L'Oréal Paris invests in scientific research and product development to ensure the efficacy and safety of Pro-Retinol, staying true to their commitment to delivering cutting-edge solutions to consumers.

The Pro-Retinol sub-brand showcases L'Oréal Paris' pursuit of excellence through its high-quality and performance-driven products. With a diverse range of formulations, including serums, creams, and masks, the sub-brand effectively targets the signs of ageing and improves skin texture. By upholding stringent product quality standards, L'Oréal Paris continues to uphold its reputation for excellence through the Pro-Retinol sub-brand.

Moreover, L'Oréal Paris strategically positions the Pro-Retinol sub-brand to offer affordable and accessible anti-ageing solutions. By catering to different skincare preferences and routines, L'Oréal Paris provides consumers with a variety of options to incorporate Pro-Retinol into their daily regimen, ensuring inclusivity and accessibility for a wide range of individuals.

The Pro-Retinol sub-brand seamlessly integrates with L'Oréal Paris' overall brand identity, embracing its elegant and sophisticated aesthetic. The packaging and presentation of Pro-Retinol products reflect the brand's visual identity, creating a consistent and cohesive brand experience for consumers. The prominent display of the Pro-Retinol name and logo on packaging and marketing materials serves as a visual cue, distinguishing the sub-brand and reinforcing its association with effective anti-ageing solutions.

Furthermore, the Pro-Retinol sub-brand aligns with L'Oréal Paris' commitment to inclusivity. By offering a range of Pro-Retinol products in various formulations, L'Oréal Paris ensures that individuals with diverse skincare needs and preferences can benefit from the sub-brand's offerings. This approach highlights L'Oréal Paris' dedication to inclusivity and allows a wide range of consumers to access the transformative benefits of Pro-Retinol.

Brand Architecture: The Pro-Retinol sub-brand by L'Oréal Paris operates within the brand's portfolio architecture, which includes a diverse range of skincare and beauty products. Pro-Retinol is positioned as a specialized line of anti-ageing skincare, leveraging L'Oréal Paris' reputation, resources, and distribution channels.

By introducing the Pro-Retinol sub-brand, L'Oréal Paris expands its offerings in the anti-ageing skincare category, delivering targeted solutions for combating signs of ageing and improving skin texture. This strategic approach allows the brand to tap into the growing demand for effective and accessible anti-ageing products.

Benefiting from the brand equity of L'Oréal Paris, the Pro-Retinol sub-brand gains credibility and trust among consumers. L'Oréal Paris' reputation for innovation, excellence, and inclusivity enhances the perceived value and quality of the Pro-Retinol products, reinforcing the brand's position as a leader in the beauty and skincare industry.

Through its brand portfolio architecture, L'Oréal Paris ensures that the Pro-Retinol sub-brand seamlessly integrates with other product lines, creating a cohesive brand experience. This integration strengthens the overall brand equity and allows L'Oréal Paris to effectively leverage its resources and expertise to drive the success of the Pro-Retinol sub-brand.

Outcomes and impact: The Pro-Retinol sub-brand by L'Oréal Paris has achieved significant outcomes and made a notable impact in the beauty and skincare industry. It has experienced strong market success, resonating with consumers seeking effective and affordable anti-ageing solutions. The sub-brand's success is reflected in its sales performance and market share, establishing it as a leading player in the anti-ageing skincare category. Customers have expressed high satisfaction, experiencing visible improvements in their skin texture and reduced signs of ageing. This has reinforced L'Oréal Paris' reputation as a trusted skincare brand.

The sub-brand has enhanced L'Oréal Paris' brand reputation as a skincare innovation pioneer, demonstrating its commitment to scientifically-backed solutions. It has contributed to L'Oréal Paris' overall market share by attracting consumers who prioritize addressing signs of ageing.

The Pro-Retinol sub-brand provides a competitive advantage, differentiating L'Oréal Paris from competitors and capturing customers seeking anti-ageing solutions. It has received industry recognition and accolades, solidifying its credibility and appeal. The sub-brand's accessible and affordable anti-ageing solutions have expanded L'Oréal Paris' customer base and reached new market segments.

By effectively identifying the key ingredient, conducting market research, aligning the sub-brand with the main brand, and implementing targeted marketing strategies, L'Oréal Paris successfully leveraged ingredient branding to enhance its brand positioning, attract the target customer segment, and drive business growth in the anti-ageing skincare market.

Example 02: Intel Inside

The Intel Inside sub-brand exemplifies the concept of ingredient branding, where a specific component or ingredient is emphasized to enhance the value and recognition of the final product.

A few years back, Intel, a leading semiconductor company, faced the dual challenge of differentiating its microprocessors and building consumer trust in the rapidly advancing computer industry. Meanwhile, as computers became increasingly integral to daily life, consumers sought assurance and confidence in the performance and reliability of their devices. They desired a deeper understanding of the components powering their computers to make informed purchasing decisions.

To address these challenges, Intel recognized the need to establish the Intel Inside sub-brand as a direct response to consumer concerns. By prominently featuring the Intel logo and branding on computer advertisements, packaging, and marketing materials, consumers could easily identify devices that contained Intel microprocessors. This visibility allowed Intel to set its microprocessors apart in a highly competitive market.

The Intel Inside sub-brand not only aimed to differentiate the microprocessors but also sought to build trust and transparency with consumers. By associating the Intel logo with computer components, Intel addressed consumer desires for assurance and confidence in the performance and reliability of their devices. This strategic move demonstrated Intel's commitment to delivering high-quality, innovative microprocessors that power their computers.

Intel's branding initiatives went beyond visual prominence. The company actively collaborated with computer manufacturers and retailers to educate consumers about the advantages of Intel microprocessors. Through co-marketing initiatives and product demonstrations, Intel showcased how their microprocessors enhanced computer speed, power efficiency, and overall performance. By highlighting the benefits of Intel Inside, consumers gained a deeper understanding of the value proposition and how it contributed to an improved computing experience.

The need for ingredient branding also arose from the increasing complexity of the computer industry, where differentiating brands based solely on external features or design became challenging. Intel Inside provided a tangible and recognizable component that consumers could associate with performance and reliability. By highlighting the Intel microprocessor as a critical ingredient, computer manufacturers and retailers were able to establish trust and confidence with consumers, thereby influencing their purchasing decisions.

Value Proposition: The Intel Inside sub-brand provides consumers with a value proposition that encompasses several key elements. Firstly, Intel microprocessors are known for their superior performance and power efficiency, ensuring that computers with Intel Inside deliver faster processing speeds, smoother multitasking, and optimized power consumption. This translates into an enhanced computing experience for users.

Secondly, Intel has built a strong reputation for reliability and product quality over the years. When consumers see the Intel Inside logo, they can trust that their computer is powered by a reliable and industry-leading microprocessor. This assurance of reliability and trust is an important factor for consumers when making purchasing decisions.

Another aspect of the value proposition is the compatibility and future-proofing offered by Intel microprocessors. These processors are designed to be compatible with a wide range of software and applications, ensuring seamless performance and compatibility with evolving technologies. Consumers can have peace of mind knowing that their computer with Intel Inside will be capable of handling future advancements and software updates.

Furthermore, Intel is recognized as a leader in semiconductor technology, constantly pushing the boundaries of innovation. By aligning with the Intel Inside sub-brand, consumers can associate themselves with the latest advancements in computer technology. They can benefit from ongoing improvements and updates, staying at the forefront of technological innovation.

Lastly, the Intel Inside sub-brand offers a unique selling proposition for computer manufacturers and retailers. It allows them to differentiate their products in a competitive market by leveraging the strong brand recognition and positive association consumers have with Intel microprocessors. The Intel Inside logo signifies quality and performance, giving manufacturers and retailers a valuable tool to attract customers and stand out from competitors.

Brand Portfolio Architecture: The Intel Inside sub-brand serves as a specialized sub-brand that focuses on promoting and emphasizing the presence of Intel microprocessors in computers. The sub-brand operates within the broader Intel brand portfolio, which includes a range of semiconductor products and computing solutions.

The Intel Inside sub-brand complements Intel's broader brand portfolio by focusing on promoting and emphasizing the presence of Intel microprocessors in computers. It strategically aligns with Intel's focus on microprocessor technology and caters to specific market segments within the computer technology industry. By creating a dedicated sub-brand, Intel can effectively communicate its technological leadership and differentiate its microprocessor offerings. The sub-brand benefits from Intel's strong brand equity and maintains coherence and consistency with the overall Intel brand.

Outcomes and Impact: The Intel Inside sub-brand has had significant outcomes and impact in the technology industry. It has led to strong brand recognition and consumer preference, with the Intel Inside logo becoming influential in associating Intel microprocessors with quality computing devices. This has translated into increased sales and market share for computer manufacturers that feature the Intel Inside sub-brand, while solidifying Intel's dominance as the industry standard for microprocessors.

The Intel Inside sub-brand has also driven technological advancements and innovation in microprocessor technology, with Intel investing in research and development to enhance performance, power efficiency, and capabilities. This continuous innovation has contributed to the sub-brand's reputation and its ability to meet evolving consumer demands.

Furthermore, the Intel Inside sub-brand has fostered collaboration and ecosystem development within the technology industry. A thriving ecosystem has been created through partnerships with computer manufacturers, software developers, and other technology companies, where hardware and software providers align their offerings with Intel microprocessors, leading to optimized performance, compatibility, and innovation.

The influence of the Intel Inside sub-brand on consumer purchasing decisions is substantial. Consumers actively seek computers with Intel Inside due to the sub-brand's association with superior performance, reliability, and compatibility. This, in turn, drives sales and market share for the sub-brand, as consumers trust the Intel brand and its commitment to delivering high-quality microprocessors.

The Intel Inside sub-brand has profoundly impacted the technology industry, including increased brand recognition, sales growth, the establishment of industry standards, technological advancements, ecosystem development, influence on consumer purchasing decisions, and the development of brand loyalty and trust. These outcomes and impacts have solidified Intel's position as a leading provider of microprocessors and have shaped the computing landscape.

In conclusion, developing sub-brands to highlight specific ingredients or components used in products offers several benefits to businesses. By giving prominence to key ingredients, companies can differentiate their products, communicate unique value propositions, and enhance brand image. The process involves identifying key ingredients with unique selling propositions, conducting market research to understand consumer preferences, establishing partnerships with ingredient suppliers, creating distinct brand identities for sub-brands, and developing targeted marketing strategies. Successful implementation of ingredient branding can result in increased consumer engagement, expanded market reach, and enhanced brand equity. It allows companies to showcase the importance of specific ingredients, build trust with consumers, and deliver products that meet their needs and expectations.

* * *

15

Personalization and Customization

Personalization refers to tailoring products, services, or experiences to meet the unique needs and preferences of individual customers. It involves offering personalized options, features, or recommendations based on customer data and insights. Customization, on the other hand, involves giving customers the ability to create or modify products according to their specific requirements or preferences.

Personalization and customization play a crucial role in today's customer-centric market. By offering personalized and customized products or services, sub-brands can cater to the individual preferences, tastes, and needs of customers. This level of customization enhances the overall customer experience by providing tailored solutions that align with their specific requirements.

Personalization and customization also help build stronger relationships with customers, increase customer satisfaction and loyalty, and differentiate the brand from competitors. Additionally, they contribute to higher customer engagement, increased sales, and positive word-of-mouth recommendations, ultimately driving business growth.

Example 01: Nike By You (formerly known as NikeiD)

Nike recognized the growing demand for personalized and customized athletic footwear and apparel, driven by customers seeking products that align with their unique style, preferences, and performance needs. To meet this demand, Nike introduced Nike By You, a sub-brand targeting individuals who desire personalized athletic wear.

Nike By You primarily caters to athletes, sports enthusiasts, and fashion-conscious consumers who want to express their individuality through their athletic wear. The sub-brand offers a wide range of customization options, empowering customers to design products that reflect their personal tastes and preferences.

Customers have the freedom to customize various aspects of their footwear and apparel, including colours, materials, patterns, designs, and even add personalized text or graphics. This level of customization allows customers to create truly unique and tailored products.

Nike By You also allows customers to design their products from scratch or choose from pre-designed templates. This flexibility ensures that customers can create personalized items that meet their specific needs and preferences.

By introducing Nike By You as a sub-brand, Nike aims to differentiate its personalized and customized offerings from its standard product line. This dedicated platform focuses specifically on catering to the customization needs of customers, providing a seamless and personalized experience.

Brand Fit: Nike By You aligns with Nike's overall brand image of empowering athletes and individuals to reach their full potential. It leverages Nike's reputation for innovation, performance, and style to deliver personalized products that meet the diverse preferences of its customers.

Outcomes: Nike By You has been successful in driving customer engagement and loyalty. It has created a community of customers who take pride in their personalized Nike products, sharing their designs on social media and inspiring others. The sub-brand has also contributed to increased sales and revenue for Nike by offering higher-priced customized products.

By launching Nike By You, Nike has effectively tapped into the desire for personalized and customized athletic footwear and apparel. The sub-brand has allowed Nike to cater to the specific needs of customers, enhance brand loyalty, and gain a competitive edge in the market. It showcases the power of sub-brands in offering personalized and customized product/service offerings that meet the demands of today's consumers.

Example 02: Coca-Cola Freestyle

Coca-Cola identified the growing desire among consumers for more customizable beverage options, driven by the need to tailor their drink choices to suit their individual tastes and preferences. This recognition led to the development of Coca-Cola Freestyle, a sub-brand that specifically targets individuals seeking unique and personalized drink experiences.

Coca-Cola Freestyle primarily appeals to beverage enthusiasts, soda lovers, and those who enjoy experimenting with different flavours and combinations. It caters to both young and adult demographics, offering a range of options to satisfy diverse preferences.

Customers can personalize their beverages using Coca-Cola Freestyle's wide selection of flavour options and mix-ins. The sub-brand allows customers to choose from a variety of Coca-Cola's trademarked flavours, including Sprite, Fanta, and Coca-Cola, and blend them to create their own unique drink combinations.

Coca-Cola Freestyle also offers other choices, including traditional options, diet alternatives, and limited-time or regional exclusives. The interactive touch-screen interface enables customers to mix and match flavours, adjust the intensity, and add additional enhancements like fruit flavours or caffeine boosts, resulting in a truly customized beverage experience.

Brand Fit: Coca-Cola Freestyle aligns with Coca-Cola's overarching brand image of enjoyment, refreshment, and individuality. It leverages the brand's legacy and widespread recognition to provide customers with a unique and customizable beverage experience.

Outcomes: Coca-Cola Freestyle has successfully enhanced customer engagement and driven foot traffic to participating locations. It has created a sense of excitement and novelty around the Coca-Cola brand, leading to increased customer loyalty and positive brand perception. The sub-brand has also provided valuable data and insights to Coca-Cola about customer preferences and flavour trends.

The sub-brand has allowed Coca-Cola to offer its customers a unique and interactive experience, resulting in increased customer loyalty and differentiation from competitors. It showcases sub-brands' value in providing personalized product/service offerings that resonate with consumers and enhances the overall brand experience.

Example 03: LEGO's "Pick a Brick"

LEGO's "Pick a Brick" is a sub-brand and service that caters to the desire for personalized and customized LEGO building experiences. Recognizing the need for more control and creative freedom among its customers, LEGO introduced "Pick a Brick" to offer individuals the flexibility to choose specific LEGO bricks and elements to build their own unique creations.

The target segment for "Pick a Brick" includes LEGO enthusiasts and builders of all ages who are passionate about LEGO's building system. This service appeals to individuals who seek to personalize their LEGO sets, customize their creations, and explore their creativity through building unique models.

The "Pick a Brick" service provides customers with a wide selection of individual LEGO bricks and elements to choose from. Through an extensive catalogue of available pieces, customers can browse and select the specific bricks they need or desire. Unlike traditional LEGO sets with predetermined designs, "Pick a Brick" allows for personalized customization, empowering customers to build their own designs and bring their creative ideas to life.

By offering this level of customization, "Pick a Brick" enables LEGO enthusiasts to go beyond the pre-designed models and expand their building options. Whether they need a specific piece to complete an existing set or want to build something entirely new, customers have the freedom to select the exact LEGO elements required for their projects.

Brand Fit: The "Pick a Brick" service aligns with LEGO's core values of creativity, imagination, and building experiences. It reinforces LEGO's commitment to providing customers with the tools and resources to express their creativity and build according to their own preferences.

Outcomes: The "Pick a Brick" service has been successful in enhancing customer engagement and satisfaction within the LEGO community. It has expanded LEGO's product offerings beyond pre-designed sets and allowed customers to unleash their creativity by building their own unique creations. The service has contributed to LEGO's brand reputation as a company that values customer customization and personalization.

LEGO's "Pick a Brick" exemplifies how personalization and customization sub-brands can cater to the specific needs and desires of customers, fostering creativity, and strengthening brand engagement.

Developing sub-brands that offer personalized or customized products or services is a strategic approach that allows businesses to cater to individual customer preferences, enhance customer experience, and differentiate themselves in the market. By offering customization options, businesses can provide unique value propositions, foster deeper customer engagement, and build stronger brand loyalty. The ability to tailor products or services to specific customer needs and desires not only satisfies customers' desire for personalization but also enables businesses to tap into new market segments and drive revenue growth.

* * *

16

Seasonal Branding

S easonal branding refers to the practice of creating sub-brands that are specifically tailored to a particular season or time of the year. It involves designing unique brand identities, messaging, and product offerings that align with the themes and characteristics of a specific season, such as holidays, weather, cultural events, or seasonal trends.

The importance of seasonal branding lies in its ability to generate excitement and drive sales for businesses. By capitalizing on the emotional and psychological associations that consumers have with different seasons, brands can create a sense of urgency, anticipation, and relevance that motivates customers to engage with their products or services.

Seasonal branding offers several benefits, including:

1. Increased customer engagement: Seasonal branding creates a sense of novelty and exclusivity, attracting the attention of consumers and encouraging them to explore new offerings or limited-time promotions. This heightened engagement can lead to increased customer loyalty and repeat purchases.
2. Enhanced brand relevance: Aligning brand messaging, visuals, and product offerings with the characteristics of a specific season helps brands appear timely and relevant to consumers. This can strengthen

the brand's connection with its target audience and increase its overall brand perception.

3. Opportunity for differentiation: Seasonal branding allows brands to stand out from competitors by offering unique and innovative products or experiences that are tailored to the season. It provides a platform for creativity, enabling brands to showcase their distinctiveness and capture the attention of consumers in a crowded marketplace.

4. Sales and revenue growth: Seasonal branding strategies can drive increased sales during peak seasons or holiday periods when consumer spending is typically higher. By capitalizing on seasonal demand and creating a sense of urgency, brands can experience a boost in revenue and profitability.

5. Emotional connection with consumers: Seasonal branding taps into the emotions and nostalgia associated with specific seasons, creating a deeper connection between the brand and its customers. By evoking positive feelings and memories, brands can foster long-term relationships and create brand advocates.

Seasonal branding serves as a powerful tool for businesses to generate excitement, drive sales, differentiate themselves from competitors, and build a strong emotional connection with their target audience.

Creating A Seasonal Sub-brand

Creating sub-brands for seasonal offerings involves the development of dedicated brand identities, product lines, or marketing campaigns that are specifically tailored to a particular season or holiday. Here is a detailed explanation of the process:

1. Understanding seasonal demand: Businesses need to analyze consumer behaviour and preferences during different seasons. This includes identifying popular holidays, festivities, or seasonal trends that drive

consumer spending. By understanding seasonal demand, businesses can determine the appropriate timing and nature of their seasonal offerings.

2. Identifying unique selling points: Once the seasonal opportunities are identified, businesses should determine the unique selling points (USPs) that will set their seasonal sub-brand apart. This can include factors such as exclusive product offerings, limited-time promotions, special packaging, or thematic branding that resonates with the season.

3. Developing brand identity: Creating a distinct brand identity for the seasonal sub-brand is crucial. This includes designing a unique logo, brand name, visual elements, and messaging that align with the season and evoke the desired emotions or associations. The brand identity should reflect the essence of the season and appeal to the target audience.

4. Tailoring products or services: The seasonal sub-brand should offer products or services that align with the specific season or holiday. This may involve developing new products, modifying existing ones, or introducing limited-time variations. The products should be designed to meet the unique needs and preferences of customers during that season.

5. Implementing seasonal marketing campaigns: Effective marketing campaigns are essential to generate excitement and drive sales for seasonal offerings. This may involve creating themed advertisements, leveraging social media platforms, launching targeted promotions, or collaborating with influencers or partners who align with the season. The marketing efforts should communicate the value, exclusivity, and timeliness of the seasonal offerings.

6. Managing inventory and operations: Seasonal sub-brands require careful planning and management of inventory and operations. Businesses need to ensure they have sufficient stock of seasonal products, manage production and distribution timelines, and effectively communicate the availability of seasonal offerings to customers. Efficient operations and supply chain management are crucial to meet the increased demand during the season.

7. Monitoring and adapting: It is important to monitor the performance of the seasonal sub-brand and gather customer feedback. This allows

businesses to evaluate the effectiveness of their strategies, make neces-sary adjustments, and continuously improve their seasonal offerings. By learning from each season's performance, businesses can refine their approach and better cater to customer preferences in subsequent seasons.

The ultimate goal of creating sub-brands for seasonal offerings is to generate excitement, engage customers, and drive sales during specific seasons or holidays. By tailoring products, developing unique brand identities, and implementing targeted marketing campaigns, businesses can effectively leverage seasonal opportunities and enhance customer experiences.

Example 01: Starbucks' Pumpkin Spice Latte

Starbucks recognized that the fall season was a prime opportunity to introduce a seasonal beverage that would capture the essence of autumn and resonate with customers. They conducted market research to understand customer behaviour and needs during this time of year and found that customers had a strong affinity for warm and cosy flavours that embodied the spirit of fall.

Armed with this understanding, Starbucks set out to create a beverage called Pumpkin Spice Latte that would deliver a unique and indulgent coffee experience tailored specifically to the preferences of its target audience. This target segment primarily consisted of young adults and coffee enthusiasts who eagerly embraced the traditions and flavours associated with the fall season.

The Pumpkin Spice Latte was a distinctive combination of rich espresso, warm spices, and creamy sweetness. It perfectly captured the essence of autumn, providing customers with a cosy and indulgent treat. The beverage quickly became synonymous with the fall season, captivating customers and inspiring a seasonal tradition that extended beyond simply enjoying a cup of coffee.

The Pumpkin Spice Latte's popularity and loyal following among young adults and coffee enthusiasts demonstrated Starbucks' ability to understand and cater to the desires of its target audience. By creating a truly indulgent and memorable coffee experience for the autumn months, Starbucks successfully tapped into the desires and preferences of this target segment.

Value Proposition: Starbucks positioned the Pumpkin Spice Latte as a limited-time offering combining their signature espresso with pumpkin spice flavours, topped with whipped cream and a sprinkle of seasoning. The beverage offered a comforting and nostalgic taste that captured the essence of fall.

Brand Fit: The Pumpkin Spice Latte aligned well with Starbucks' brand identity of providing high-quality coffee experiences and catering to customer preferences. The seasonal offering complemented their existing menu while introducing a new and exciting flavour profile.

Outcomes: The Pumpkin Spice Latte became an instant hit and developed a cult following. It created a sense of exclusivity and urgency as customers eagerly awaited its annual return. The seasonal sub-brand contributed significantly to Starbucks' sales during the fall season, driving increased foot traffic to their stores and boosting overall brand loyalty.

The Pumpkin Spice Latte's popularity and sales outcomes demonstrate the effectiveness of seasonal sub-brands in driving customer engagement, sales, and brand loyalty.

Example 02: Hershey's "Holiday Edition" Chocolates

Hershey's, the renowned chocolate brand, introduces a sub-brand called "Holiday Edition" during the festive season. This sub-brand is specifically designed to cater to the holiday-themed market and leverage the seasonal demand for chocolates.

To execute this strategy, Hershey's first identified seasonal opportunities. They recognized the high consumer demand for chocolates during holidays like Christmas, Easter, Halloween, and Valentine's Day. They identified these seasons as key opportunities to introduce special edition chocolates that align with the festive spirit and consumer preferences.

Next, Hershey's conducted market research to understand consumers' specific needs and preferences during each holiday season. They analyzed consumer trends, purchase patterns, and seasonal flavour preferences to create products that resonate with the target audience.

Finally, Hershey's designed unique packaging and flavours for its "Holiday Edition" chocolates. The packaging designs captured the essence of the specific holiday, using vibrant colours, festive illustrations, or holiday-themed shapes to create an attractive and visually appealing product. Additionally, they introduced seasonal flavours such as peppermint, gingerbread, or pumpkin spice to enhance the holiday experience.

Through the execution of their "Holiday Edition" sub-brand strategy, Hershey's successfully leveraged the seasonal demand for chocolates and tapped into the emotional connection consumers have with holiday celebrations.

Brand Fit: The "Holiday Edition" sub-brand aligns with Hershey's brand values of indulgence, celebration, and joy. It allows Hershey's to tap into the emotional connections associated with holidays and position their chocolates as a must-have treat during these special occasions. The sub-brand reinforces the brand's image and builds on its existing reputation for high-quality and delicious chocolates.

Outcomes and Impact: The introduction of Hershey's "Holiday Edition" chocolates generates excitement among consumers during the respective holiday seasons. The unique packaging, seasonal flavours, and limited-time availability create a sense of exclusivity and urgency, driving sales and creating a sense of anticipation among chocolate lovers. The sub-brand helps Hershey's maintain a strong market presence during these key seasons and establishes a connection with consumers that goes beyond their regular product offerings.

By creating the sub-brand "Holiday Edition," Hershey's effectively taps into the seasonal demand for chocolates and maximizes their market potential during holidays. The unique packaging, flavours, and limited-time availability create a sense of novelty and anticipation, attracting consumers and driving sales. The sub-brand reinforces Hershey's brand equity and positions them as a go-to choice for holiday treats.

In conclusion, creating sub-brands for seasonal or limited-time offerings effectively generates excitement and drives sales. By leveraging the power of seasons and tapping into consumer behaviour and preferences during specific times of the year, brands can create a sense of anticipation and exclusivity. Sub-brands allow for targeted marketing and tailored product offerings that align with seasonal themes, flavours, and packaging. This approach helps brands stand out in a competitive market, attract new customers, and strengthen their emotional connection with existing ones. Additionally, the time-bound nature of seasonal sub-brands creates a sense of urgency, encouraging consumers to make a purchase and fostering a perception of limited availability.

* * *

17

Brand Revitalization

B rand revitalization refers to the strategic process of refreshing or repositioning an existing brand that may have lost relevance or market share. It involves making significant changes to the brand's image, messaging, and product offerings to attract and engage customers in a rapidly evolving market.

Brand revitalization is crucial for businesses to stay competitive and adapt to changing consumer preferences. It helps in the following ways:

1. Maintaining brand relevance: In a dynamic marketplace, consumer preferences, trends, and competitive landscapes shift rapidly. Brand revitalization allows businesses to update their brand image, product offerings, and communication strategies to align with current market demands, ensuring continued relevance.

2. Regaining market share: Brands that have lost market share or faced declining sales can revitalize their brand to regain customer attention and loyalty. By refreshing their brand identity, addressing customer pain points, and introducing innovative offerings, businesses can recapture lost market share and attract new customers.

3. Enhancing brand perception: Brand revitalization can positively impact how customers perceive a brand. Businesses can enhance brand reputa-

tion, customer trust, and loyalty by repositioning the brand, improving product quality, or addressing previous shortcomings.

4. Driving growth and profitability: Revitalizing a brand can increase sales, customer engagement, and overall business growth. It allows businesses to tap into new market segments, expand their customer base, and create opportunities for revenue generation.

5. Differentiating from competitors: In competitive industries, brand revitalization can help businesses stand out from competitors. By repositioning the brand, introducing unique offerings, or leveraging innovative marketing strategies, businesses can differentiate themselves and create a distinctive brand identity.

Brand revitalization is essential for businesses to adapt to changing market dynamics, attract and retain customers, and drive long-term growth and profitability. It enables brands to evolve with their target audience, maintain relevance, and secure a competitive edge in the marketplace.

Deciding on Sub-brand

When revitalizing a brand, the decision to develop sub-brands depends on several factors, including the extent of the brand's revitalization, the desired positioning, and the target audience. Here are a few considerations to determine whether a sub-brand is needed:

1. Degree of change: If the revitalization involves significant changes in the brand's image, product offerings, or target market, a sub-brand can help differentiate the new direction from the existing brand. It allows for a clear separation between the revitalized and original brands, signalling to customers that something new and different is being offered.

2. Target audience segmentation: If the revitalization aims to target a specific customer segment or address a distinct market need, a sub-brand can be useful. It allows for tailored messaging and positioning that

resonates with the target audience, creating a more focused and relevant brand experience.

3. Competitive landscape: If the revitalization involves entering a highly competitive market, a sub-brand can provide a fresh start and help the brand stand out. It allows for a differentiated identity, positioning, and messaging that sets the brand apart from existing competitors.

4. Brand architecture considerations: Assess the brand's existing architecture and how the revitalized brand fits within it. If the revitalization represents a significant departure from the original brand's positioning or values, a sub-brand can help maintain the integrity of the original brand while introducing the new direction.

5. Customer perception and expectations: Consider how customers perceive the existing brand and whether a sub-brand is needed to manage their expectations during the revitalization. If customers strongly associate with the original brand, a sub-brand can help communicate the revitalization efforts without disrupting their perceptions.

6. Brand equity preservation: If the existing brand has strong brand equity, developing a sub-brand can help preserve that equity while introducing new elements. It allows for a gradual transition and minimizes the risk of diluting the existing brand's value and customer loyalty.

7. Communication clarity: If the revitalization involves complex changes or multiple facets, a sub-brand can provide clarity in communicating the different elements of the revitalization. It allows for separate messaging and positioning that can be tailored to specific aspects of the revitalized brand, avoiding confusion or mixed signals.

8. Product or service differentiation: If the revitalization includes the introduction of new products or services, a sub-brand can be used to differentiate these offerings from the existing ones. It helps customers understand the specific value proposition of the new products or services and creates a distinct identity for them within the brand portfolio.

9. Test and learn: Introducing a sub-brand during revitalization can also serve as a testing ground to gauge customer response and market acceptance. It allows for experimentation and flexibility, as the sub-

brand can be adjusted or phased out if it doesn't resonate with the intended audience, without affecting the core brand.

10. Relevance and modernization: In some cases, the existing brand may have lost relevance or become outdated. Developing a sub-brand can be a way to modernize the brand's image and appeal to new generations of customers while retaining the core brand's equity and recognition.

Ultimately, the decision to develop a sub-brand during brand revitalization should be based on a thorough analysis of the brand's goals, target audience, competitive landscape, and desired brand architecture. It is important to carefully evaluate the potential benefits and challenges of introducing a sub-brand to ensure it aligns with the revitalization strategy and enhances the overall brand's impact and relevance.

Analyzing the Need for Revitalisation

Assessing the need for brand revitalization involves comprehensively analysing various factors that indicate a declining brand. Here are some key steps to consider:

1. Identifying signs of a declining brand: Look for indicators that suggest the brand's performance is declining. This can include decreasing sales, loss of market share, declining customer loyalty, negative customer feedback, outdated brand image, or lack of relevance in the market.

2. Analyzing market trends and competitive landscape: Assess the industry's broader market dynamics and trends. Identify emerging competitors, changing consumer preferences, technological advancements, and evolving market demands. Analyze how the brand is positioned compared to its competitors and whether it effectively addresses market shifts.

3. Gathering customer feedback and insights: Engage with customers through surveys, interviews, focus groups, and social media listening to understand their perceptions and experiences with the brand. Identify

pain points, areas for improvement, and changes in customer expectations. Customer feedback is crucial in understanding how the brand is currently perceived and what aspects need revitalization.

4. Conducting brand equity assessment: Evaluate the brand's current equity by analyzing brand awareness, brand associations, brand loyalty, and brand differentiation. Assess whether the brand's equity is strong and if it resonates with the target audience. If there are gaps or weaknesses in brand equity, it may indicate the need for revitalization.

5. Assessing internal alignment and capabilities: Evaluate internal factors such as organizational alignment, leadership commitment, brand culture, and operational capabilities. Determine if the internal structure and capabilities are aligned with the brand's objectives and if there is sufficient support to drive the revitalization efforts effectively.

By thoroughly assessing these factors, brands can gain insights into the need for brand revitalization. It helps identify improvement areas, understand the brand's current standing in the market, and set a clear direction for the revitalization strategy.

Example 01: McCafé

McDonald's, a global fast-food chain, successfully implemented a sub-brand called McCafé as part of its brand revitalization efforts. McCafé was introduced to cater to the evolving coffee market, target a broader customer base, and create a distinct brand image within McDonald's portfolio.

McDonald's identified the need for brand revitalization due to declining sales, evolving consumer preferences, and an outdated brand image. Through extensive market research, they identified a growing demand for speciality coffee and a desire for premium, healthier beverage options. They discovered specific segments, including coffee enthusiasts who valued the art of coffee-making and desired an elevated coffee experience, health-conscious consumers seeking alternatives to traditional fast food, and premium beverage seekers craving indulgent experiences.

However, McDonald's faced a challenge: its brand was primarily associated with fast food and not known for high-quality coffee. To address this, McDonald's decided to introduce a sub-brand dedicated to coffee. They believed that a separate brand would challenge existing perceptions and reshape the narrative surrounding their coffee offerings.

McCafé was created to meet the demands of coffee enthusiasts, health-conscious consumers, and those seeking a premium beverage experience. It aimed to provide high-quality and speciality coffee beverages that appealed to the discerning tastes of coffee enthusiasts. Moreover, McCafé offered healthier beverage options to cater to health-conscious consumers and indulgent experiences for those seeking premium beverages.

By introducing McCafé as a distinct sub-brand, McDonald's aimed to challenge the perception that it was solely a fast-food chain and communicate its commitment to providing a premium coffee experience. The sub-brand's range of speciality drinks and sophisticated coffee shop atmosphere helped differentiate McDonald's from its fast-food image, attracting customers seeking an upscale coffee experience and paying a premium for it.

The sub-brand showcased McDonald's dedication to high-quality coffee beans, skilled baristas, and a diverse menu of speciality beverages. By doing so, McDonald's aimed to reshape the perception of being solely a fast-food chain and communicate its commitment to providing a wide range of customizable and high-quality coffee options.

Additionally, the sub-brand strategy positioned McDonald's as a viable alternative to other coffee chains and speciality coffee shops. McCafé offered convenience, affordability, and the trusted brand name of McDonald's, enticing customers who may have been loyal to competitors. McDonald's aimed to expand its customer base, challenge dominant players in the coffee market, and establish itself as a preferred coffee destination by providing an opportunity for customers to reconsider their perceptions.

To promote the McCafé sub-brand and drive brand revitalization, McDonald's implemented various marketing and communication strategies. Extensive advertising campaigns highlighted the quality and variety of McCafé's coffee offerings. The store layouts were redesigned to create a distinct McCafé section, complete with its own branding and signage, enhancing the overall customer experience and reinforcing the sub-brand's positioning as a provider of premium coffee.

Brand Fit: The brand fit between McDonald's and McCafé is evident in several aspects. First, both brands share a commitment to quality and convenience. With its established reputation for providing consistent and reliable food service, McDonald's extends these qualities to the McCafé sub-brand. Customers can expect the same level of quality and efficiency in their coffee experience.

Second, McCafé maintains a visual and experiential connection to McDonald's through its store layout and branding. While McCafé sections within McDonald's restaurants have a distinct design and atmosphere, they still bear a resemblance to the overall McDonald's aesthetic. This connection helps customers feel familiar and comfortable with the McCafé experience, leveraging the trust and recognition associated with the parent brand.

Lastly, the affordability and accessibility associated with McDonald's are also reflected in the McCafé offering. Despite positioning itself as a provider of premium coffee, McCafé maintains competitive pricing, making it an attractive option for a wide range of customers. The convenience of finding McCafé within McDonald's locations further enhances its accessibility.

Brand Architecture: McCafé is positioned as a distinct sub-brand under McDonald's, targeting consumers seeking a premium coffee experience. With a separate identity, McCafé diversifies McDonald's product offerings and captures a larger share of the coffee market. It appeals to coffee enthusiasts and premium beverage seekers with speciality drinks like lattes and cappuccinos. McCafé also caters to health-conscious consumers by offering healthier beverage choices. This brand portfolio strategy showcases McDonald's commitment to quality and elevates the overall coffee experience, positioning the company as an alternative to other coffee chains and speciality coffee shops.

The introduction of the McCafé sub-brand successfully revitalized McDonald's brand image, attracted new customers, and allowed the company to tap into the growing coffee market. McCafé's success translated into increased customer traffic, higher average order values, and improved customer perceptions of McDonald's as a place for quality coffee. The sub-brand significantly addressed changing consumer preferences, expanded McDonald's product offerings, and enhanced the overall customer experience.

Example 02: Cadillac V

Cadillac felt the need to revitalize its brand due to several factors. Firstly, the brand faced declining sales and market share, indicating a disconnect with evolving consumer preferences. Cadillac's traditional image of producing large, comfortable luxury vehicles was not resonating with younger, performance-focused buyers. Additionally, Cadillac recognized the growing competition in the luxury automobile market, particularly from European brands known for their sporty and high-performance offerings.

So, Cadillac wanted to shed its reputation as a brand primarily favoured by older consumers. Instead, the brand aspired to appeal to a younger demographic that valued dynamic driving experiences, cutting-edge technology, and modern design. This required a strategic shift to align with the changing demands of the luxury automobile market and position itself as a more desirable and relevant choice.

Cadillac introduced the Cadillac V sub-brand as part of its revitalisation strategy to make itself a more desirable and relevant choice among luxury car buyers. The V-Series sub-brand positioned Cadillac as a provider of high-performance vehicles, catering to those seeking exhilarating driving experiences and more performance-oriented brand identity.

Cadillac successfully differentiated itself in the competitive luxury automobile market by introducing the V-Series sub-brand. It provided a platform to introduce new models, features, and marketing strategies aligned with the target audience's preferences. This strategic move allowed Cadillac to strengthen its appeal, regain market share, and establish itself as a formidable player in the luxury performance segment.

As a part of revitalizing its brand, Cadillac implemented several other strategies. First, they focused on product development, introducing new models like the Cadillac ATS-V and CTS-V that catered to the preferences of younger, performance-oriented buyers. These vehicles featured powerful engines, sporty handling, and advanced technology.

Simultaneously, Cadillac underwent a significant design transformation, adopting a more aggressive and modern aesthetic. They incorporated bold styling elements such as angular lines, distinctive LED lighting, and a more assertive grille design. This design shift aimed to appeal to a younger audience and differentiate Cadillac from its traditional image.

Cadillac also invested in marketing and advertising campaigns to showcase its revitalized brand. These campaigns highlighted the performance capabilities, advanced technology, and luxurious features of their vehicles. Digital channels and collaborations with influential figures from the worlds of fashion, music, and sports were used to target a younger demographic.

Enhancing the overall customer experience was another crucial aspect of Cadillac's revitalization strategy. They improved dealership facilities, offered personalized services, and introduced exclusive ownership benefits. These efforts aimed to create a premium, engaging experience aligned with Cadillac's new brand identity.

Furthermore, Cadillac forged brand partnerships to reinforce its image and expand its reach. Collaborations with high-end fashion events like New York Fashion Week helped connect with a broader audience and strengthen the association with luxury and style.

Cadillac successfully revitalised its brand by focusing on performance, undergoing a design transformation, investing in marketing and advertising, enhancing the customer experience, and forming strategic partnerships. These cohesive efforts positioned Cadillac as a competitive player in the luxury automobile market and appealed to a younger demographic seeking dynamic and modern luxury vehicles.

Brand Fit: The Cadillac V-Series sub-brand strongly aligns with the parent brand's image and values. Cadillac is renowned for producing luxury vehicles that prioritize comfort, refinement, and sophistication. The V-Series sub-brand complements these characteristics by delivering high-performance vehicles that embody Cadillac's spirit.

Maintaining consistency with the parent brand, the V-Series vehicles incorporate distinctive Cadillac design elements and styling cues, ensuring a cohesive and recognizable brand aesthetic. This seamless integration reinforces the brand's identity and maintains brand equity.

The introduction of the V-Series sub-brand allows Cadillac to expand its product portfolio while staying true to its core essence. Cadillac caters to a specific segment by targeting performance-oriented customers without compromising the overall brand image. This strategic move helps Cadillac tap into the growing demand for high-performance luxury vehicles and attract a new audience.

Furthermore, the V-Series sub-brand reinforces Cadillac's commitment to innovation and technological advancement. These vehicles incorporate cutting-edge technologies, advanced engineering, and track-inspired features, showcasing Cadillac's dedication to pushing the boundaries of performance. This resonates with the brand's promise of delivering state-of-the-art luxury vehicles that combine comfort, style, and exceptional performance.

Brand Architecture: Cadillac's brand portfolio strategy for the V-Series sub-brand involves creating a distinct product line that targets performance-oriented customers while maintaining the core brand image. This strategy allows Cadillac to expand its offerings without compromising its brand identity.

Cadillac diversified its product portfolio and captured a unique market segment by introducing the V-Series sub-brand. This sub-brand allows Cadillac to cater to customers who prioritize performance and seek an elevated driving experience. It allows Cadillac to differentiate itself in the luxury automobile market and compete with other high-performance brands.

Despite being a distinct sub-brand, the V-Series maintains a strong connection to the parent Cadillac brand. It incorporates Cadillac's signature design language and upholds the core brand values, ensuring consistency and enhancing brand recognition among customers. This connection strengthens the overall brand portfolio and reinforces the association of the V-Series with Cadillac's legacy of luxury and quality.

Cadillac successfully revitalized its brand by creating the V-Series sub-brand and connected with a new audience seeking high-performance luxury vehicles. The sub-brand allowed Cadillac to differentiate itself, communicate its commitment to performance, and capture market share in the competitive luxury performance segment.

In conclusion, creating a sub-brand for brand revitalization is a strategic approach used to rejuvenate an existing brand. It involves developing a separate brand identity that aligns with the new direction and targets specific market segments. This process requires assessing the brand's current state, market trends, and customer insights. The sub-brand serves as a vehicle for change, allowing the introduction of new products or experiences that resonate with evolving customer preferences.

$$* * *$$

18

Event or Sponsorship Branding

C reating sub-brands for event or sponsorship branding involves establishing dedicated brand identities associated with specific events or sponsorships. This approach enables companies to enhance their brand visibility and engagement by leveraging the unique opportunities presented by these occasions.

Event or sponsorship branding is of significant importance in enhancing brand visibility and engagement for several reasons. Firstly, it allows brands to reach a targeted audience that is already interested in or aligned with the event or sponsorship. By associating with these events, brands can connect with a specific demographic or interest group, increasing the likelihood of capturing their attention and engagement.

Secondly, event or sponsorship branding provides an opportunity for brands to enhance their brand image and reputation. By aligning with well-regarded events or sponsorships, brands can benefit from the positive associations and perceptions associated with these occasions, effectively elevating their own brand image in the minds of consumers.

Moreover, event or sponsorship branding offers a platform for experiential marketing. Brands can create immersive experiences and activations that allow consumers to engage with the brand in a meaningful way. This not only creates a memorable brand experience but also fosters a deeper connection and engagement with the target audience.

Additionally, event or sponsorship branding facilitates the building of brand associations and partnerships. By aligning with an event or sponsorship, brands can leverage the credibility and reputation of the event or sponsorship to strengthen their own brand positioning. This association helps in creating positive brand associations and can open doors for potential collaborations and partnerships in the future.

In summary, by strategically creating sub-brands for event or sponsorship branding, companies can effectively leverage these opportunities to increase brand visibility and engagement and ultimately drive business success.

Criteria for Creating Sub-brands

The decision to create a sub-brand for event or sponsorship branding should be based on several criteria, which are outlined below:

1. Brand Alignment: The event or sponsorship should align with the brand's values, positioning, and target audience. It is essential to ensure that the event or sponsorship is relevant and resonates with the brand's identity. This alignment ensures that the sub-brand created for the event or sponsorship is consistent with the overall brand image and messaging.
2. Target Audience Relevance: The event or sponsorship should provide access to a target audience that aligns with the brand's target market. By identifying the demographic, interests, and behaviours of the event or sponsorship attendees, brands can determine if there is a significant overlap with their target audience. This relevance ensures that the sub-brand can effectively reach and engage the desired customer segment.
3. Brand Extension Potential: The event or sponsorship should offer opportunities for brand extension and exploration of new markets. It should provide a platform for the brand to expand its reach and connect with potential customers who may not have been previously exposed to the brand. This criterion is particularly relevant when brands aim to enter new geographical regions or target new customer segments.

4. Brand Visibility and Exposure: The event or sponsorship should provide significant visibility and exposure for the brand. It should attract a substantial audience and media attention, ensuring that the sub-brand receives ample exposure. This exposure can significantly enhance brand awareness and recognition.

5. Strategic Partnerships: The event or sponsorship should offer the potential for strategic partnerships and collaborations. By associating with influential individuals, organizations, or brands through the event or sponsorship, the sub-brand can leverage its credibility and expand its network, leading to additional brand opportunities and growth.

6. Return on Investment (ROI): The decision to create a sub-brand for event or sponsorship branding should be based on a thorough assessment of the potential return on investment. Brands should evaluate the anticipated benefits, such as increased brand awareness, customer engagement, sales, and long-term brand equity, against the associated costs and resources required for the sub-brand creation and participation in the event or sponsorship.

Brands can make informed decisions by carefully considering the above criteria and effectively leverage event or sponsorship branding to enhance its visibility, engagement, and overall brand success.

Strategies for Establishing Event or Sponsorship Sub-Brands

When establishing event or sponsorship sub-brands, there are several strategies that brands can employ to maximize their impact and engagement. These strategies include:

1. Clear Brand Messaging: Develop clear and consistent brand messaging that aligns with the event or sponsorship. This ensures that the sub-brand effectively communicates the brand's values, purpose, and offerings to the target audience.

2. Unique Visual Identity: Create a distinct visual identity for the sub-brand that captures the essence of the event or sponsorship while maintaining brand recognition. This includes designing a unique logo, color palette, and visual elements that differentiate the sub-brand from the main brand.

3. Tailored Experiences: Customize the brand experience to suit the event or sponsorship audience. Consider the preferences, needs, and expectations of the attendees and design experiences that resonate with them. This can include interactive activations, exclusive offers, or personalized content.

4. Activation and Engagement: Develop creative activations and engagement strategies to connect with the event or sponsorship attendees. This can involve interactive booths, experiential installations, contests, giveaways, or social media campaigns that encourage participation and foster a sense of excitement and involvement.

5. Collaborative Partnerships: Seek collaborations with event organizers, sponsors, or other brands associated with the event or sponsorship. Partnering with like-minded organizations can amplify the brand's reach, create synergies, and enhance the overall experience for attendees.

6. Integrated Marketing Communications: Develop integrated marketing communications that promote the sub-brand and its association with the event or sponsorship. Utilize various channels such as social media, email marketing, advertising, public relations, and on-site activations to generate awareness, build anticipation, and drive engagement.

7. Post-Event Follow-Up: Maintain the connection with attendees after the event or sponsorship through targeted follow-up communications. This can include personalized thank-you messages, exclusive offers, or post-event content that keeps the brand top-of-mind and nurtures ongoing relationships.

8. Measuring Success: Establish key performance indicators (KPIs) to measure the success of the event or sponsorship sub-branding efforts. This can include metrics such as brand visibility, engagement levels, social media reach, customer feedback, and conversion rates. Analyzing these metrics allows brands to evaluate the effectiveness of their strategies

and make data-driven decisions for future events or sponsorships.

By implementing these strategies, brands can establish event or sponsorship sub-brands that effectively engage the target audience, enhance brand visibility, and drive meaningful connections with consumers during and after the event or sponsorship.

Example 01: Google Cloud Next

Google, a global technology giant, organizes the annual Google Cloud Next conference to showcase its latest advancements and solutions in cloud computing. To give the event a distinct identity and strengthen its branding, Google created the sub-brand "Google Cloud Next."

The purpose of the Google Cloud Next sub-brand was to differentiate the conference from Google's main brand and tailor the messaging, visuals, and overall experience to the specific audience and objectives of the event. By creating a sub-brand, Google aimed to build anticipation, drive engagement, and establish Google Cloud Next as a premier industry event.

One of the key aspects of the sub-branding strategy was the development of a unique and recognizable logo for Google Cloud Next. The logo incorporated the recognizable Google Cloud logo elements but included the word "Next" in a distinct font and design. This visually identified the event as separate from the main Google Cloud brand while maintaining a sense of continuity and connection.

Google Cloud Next also had its own dedicated website, which provided comprehensive information about the conference, including agenda, speakers, sessions, and registration details. The website design aligned with the visual identity of the sub-brand, featuring the distinctive Google Cloud Next logo, vibrant colours, and engaging graphics. This ensured a cohesive and immersive brand experience for visitors.

In terms of marketing and communication, Google used various channels to promote Google Cloud Next. The sub-brand had its own social media presence, including accounts on platforms like Twitter, LinkedIn, and YouTube. These channels allowed Google to share updates, announcements, and engaging content related to the conference, creating a buzz among the target audience and building anticipation.

Additionally, Google leveraged its existing network and partnerships to enhance the sub-brand's reach and impact. The company collaborated with industry leaders, technology experts, and influential figures to participate as speakers and panellists at the event. This not only added credibility to the conference but also helped attract a diverse audience and foster collaboration within the cloud computing community.

The Google Cloud Next sub-brand successfully positioned the conference as a premier industry event and created a distinct identity within the cloud computing landscape. The sub-branding strategy allowed Google to tailor the event experience to the specific needs and interests of attendees, sponsors, and partners. It enabled Google to communicate its cloud computing expertise and innovation in a targeted and impactful manner, reinforcing its position as a leader in the industry.

Brand Fit: Firstly, Google is widely recognized as a global innovator and provider of cutting-edge technology solutions. Google Cloud Next, as a sub-brand, extends this reputation into the realm of cloud computing and demonstrates Google's commitment to advancing the field. The sub-brand leverages Google's expertise in data management, artificial intelligence, and scalable infrastructure, aligning with the parent brand's emphasis on technological innovation and excellence.

Secondly, both Google and Google Cloud Next share a consistent visual identity, maintaining recognizable brand elements. The sub-brand incorporates the familiar Google logo colours and typography, ensuring a visual connection with the parent brand. This consistency reinforces the association between Google Cloud Next and Google, enhancing brand recognition and trust.

Furthermore, the core values of Google, such as user-centricity, accessibility, and collaboration, extend to Google Cloud Next. The sub-brand aims to empower businesses and developers by providing accessible cloud solutions, fostering collaboration within the cloud computing community, and enabling seamless integration with other Google services. This alignment reinforces the parent brand's commitment to delivering value and fostering positive user experiences. Moreover, Google's reputation as a trusted and reliable technology provider enhances the credibility and trustworthiness of the Google Cloud Next sub-brand. Customers and stakeholders perceive Google Cloud Next as a reliable and secure platform backed by Google's extensive resources, expertise, and track record.

Brand Architecture: Google Cloud Next's brand architecture portfolio strategy aligns seamlessly with the overall brand portfolio of Google. Positioned as a sub-brand, Google Cloud Next focuses on the cloud computing market while maintaining a strong association with the parent brand.

By leveraging Google's reputation and expertise in areas such as data management and artificial intelligence, Google Cloud Next reinforces its credibility and market presence. The sub-brand strategy allows for differentiation within the brand portfolio, effectively communicating Google's commitment to innovation and thought leadership in the cloud industry.

Maintaining a consistent visual identity with Google, including logo colors and typography, strengthens the association and brand recognition. This portfolio strategy promotes synergy and coherence among the various sub-brands and products offered by Google.

Additionally, the brand architecture portfolio strategy provides flexibility for future expansion within the cloud computing space. It allows for the introduction of additional sub-brands or product extensions under the Google Cloud umbrella, ensuring a cohesive and well-defined brand portfolio.

Example 02: Red Bull Music

Red Bull, the well-known energy drink company, recognized the influential role of music in shaping culture and decided to establish a strong presence in the music industry through the creation of Red Bull Music. This sub-brand aimed to connect with a broader audience of music enthusiasts and embody a more edgy and creative identity compared to the Red Bull parent brand.

Red Bull Music exemplifies the company's dedication to supporting emerging artists and vibrant music scenes while remaining true to the core brand values of energy, adventure, and pushing boundaries.

Red Bull Music sponsors and organizes a wide range of music events, festivals, and competitions worldwide. These events not only feature established artists but also provide platforms for emerging talents to showcase their skills and gain exposure.

One of the notable events organized by Red Bull Music is the Red Bull Music Academy. This global music institution brings together aspiring musicians, producers, and DJs for a series of workshops, lectures, and collaborative sessions with industry professionals. The academy offers a unique learning experience and networking opportunities for aspiring musicians.

Red Bull Music also sponsors and curates stages at renowned music festivals, such as Primavera Sound and Lollapalooza. These stages showcase a diverse lineup of artists representing various genres and styles and provide a platform for innovative and boundary-pushing performances.

Through event and sponsorship branding, Red Bull Music creates immersive experiences for music fans. These experiences often go beyond the confines of traditional concert settings and take place in unique and unexpected locations. Red Bull Music has organized concerts in abandoned warehouses, rooftops, and even on mountaintops, providing unforgettable experiences for attendees.

The sub-brand's marketing strategy extends beyond events through content creation and distribution. Red Bull Music produces and shares music-related content, including documentaries, interviews, and live recordings, through various digital platforms. This content not only engages music fans but also reinforces the brand's association with music culture.

The success of Red Bull Music can be attributed to its ability to create authentic connections with artists, fans, and the broader music community. By actively supporting and nurturing emerging talents, Red Bull Music has positioned itself as a credible and influential player in the music industry.

Brand Fit: Red Bull Music sub-brand aligns seamlessly with the overarching brand identity and values of Red Bull, reinforcing its position as an innovative and energetic company.

Both Red Bull and Red Bull Music share a common focus on energy and excitement. The parent brand is known for its association with extreme sports and adrenaline-fueled activities, while Red Bull Music taps into the energy and passion of the music industry. This alignment creates a cohesive brand experience and reinforces Red Bull's overall brand proposition of fueling active and adventurous lifestyles.

Red Bull's commitment to supporting emerging talents and pushing boundaries extends to Red Bull Music. The sub-brand provides a platform for up-and-coming artists, music scenes, and unconventional genres, reflecting Red Bull's dedication to promoting creativity and innovation. This synergy enhances the credibility and authenticity of Red Bull Music within the music industry.

Red Bull's reputation as a global lifestyle brand and its extensive marketing efforts contribute to the brand's fit with Red Bull Music. The parent brand's strong presence and sponsorship of various events and athletes create brand visibility and awareness, which spills over to the sub-brand. This association with a well-established and respected brand adds value and trust to Red Bull Music's endeavours.

Moreover, the visual identity of Red Bull Music maintains consistency with the parent brand. The iconic Red Bull logo and the recognizable colour scheme are incorporated into the sub-brand's branding, creating a visual connection and reinforcing the brand association. This visual consistency enhances brand recognition and strengthens the brand fit between Red Bull and Red Bull Music.

In summary, Red Bull Music serves as a compelling example of a sub-brand that leverages event and sponsorship branding to establish a strong presence in the music industry. By aligning with Red Bull's core brand values and embracing unconventional marketing strategies, Red Bull Music has successfully engaged with music fans, supported emerging artists, and solidified its position as a key player in the global music landscape.

In conclusion, creating sub-brands for specific events or sponsorships offers significant benefits in terms of enhancing brand visibility and engagement. By associating with well-known events or sponsorships, brands can tap into the excitement and passion surrounding these occasions, reaching a broader audience and increasing brand exposure. Sub-brands provide a dedicated platform to showcase the brand's alignment with the event or sponsorship, allowing for targeted marketing and communication strategies. Through strategic partnerships, innovative campaigns, and immersive experiences, brands can create memorable connections with consumers, strengthen brand loyalty, and drive sales.

* * *

19

Corporate Branding

C orporate branding is the practice of creating a unified brand identity for a large corporation, encompassing all its business units, divisions, and subsidiaries. It establishes a consistent brand image, values, and messaging that represent the corporation as a whole, ensuring brand coherence across the organization.

In today's business landscape, corporations often face the challenge of managing diverse businesses and product lines under a single corporate umbrella. This complexity can create difficulties in effectively communicating and connecting with target audiences. To overcome this challenge, corporations employ sub-brands as a strategic tool within their corporate branding approach.

Sub-branding involves creating distinct brand identities for individual business units, divisions, or subsidiaries while maintaining a cohesive and overarching corporate brand. This strategy allows companies to tailor their messaging and positioning to specific market segments, effectively communicate the unique offerings of each business entity, and establish a strong presence in different industries.

By leveraging sub-brands, corporations can achieve brand differentiation, ensuring that each business unit stands out and appeals to its specific target audience. This differentiation helps to avoid brand confusion and allows customers to better understand and engage with the offerings of each business unit or subsidiary.

Furthermore, sub-branding supports market positioning by enabling corporations to emphasize the unique value propositions of their different businesses. Each sub-brand can highlight its specific expertise, product or service offerings, and target market, positioning itself as a leader or specialist in its respective field.

Additionally, sub-brands within a corporate branding strategy maximize customer engagement by tailoring messaging and experiences to specific customer segments. This approach allows corporations to build strong connections with their target audience, catering to their unique needs and preferences.

Some key benefits of corporate branding and sub-brands include:

1. Clarity and focus: Sub-brands enable clear positioning and differentiation of different business units, making it easier for customers to understand the specific offerings and benefits of each unit.

2. Brand independence and autonomy: Sub-brands allow business units to have their own distinct identity and decision-making power while benefiting from the overall reputation and resources of the corporate brand.

3. Market positioning and competitive advantage: Sub-brands enable a more targeted approach to specific market segments, catering to the unique needs and preferences of different customer groups. This enhances the corporation's competitive advantage by leveraging specialized expertise and tailored solutions.

4. Managing brand perception and reputation: Corporate branding helps shape the perception and reputation of the corporation as a whole, influencing stakeholders' trust and confidence. Sub-brands contribute to this by delivering consistent brand experiences that align with the overall corporate brand promise.

5. Leveraging economies of scale: Corporate branding allows for shared resources, synergies, and efficiencies across business units, maximizing

the corporation's overall market impact and operational effectiveness.

By implementing corporate branding and using sub-brands, a large corporation can effectively manage its diverse business units, maintain brand coherence, and leverage the strengths of each unit to drive overall brand success.

Criteria for Deciding the Need for a Sub-brand

Deciding on the requirement for sub-brands in corporate branding requires careful consideration and analysis. Here are some key factors to help make this decision:

1. Business Units/Divisions: Assess the number of distinct business units or divisions within the corporation. If there are multiple units that operate independently or offer diverse products/services, it may indicate the need for sub-brands to differentiate and manage them effectively.
2. Target Audience: Understand the target audience for each business unit or division. If there are significant differences in customer preferences, needs, or behaviors across these segments, it may warrant the creation of sub-brands to cater to their specific requirements.
3. Market Differentiation: Evaluate the level of market differentiation required for each business unit or division. If there are distinct value propositions, positioning, or competitive advantages that set them apart from one another, creating sub-brands can help communicate these differences effectively.
4. Brand Architecture: Consider the existing brand architecture of the corporation. Analyze whether the current brand hierarchy and structure adequately represent and manage the various business units. If there is a need to clarify the relationships between the corporate brand and its divisions, sub-brands can serve as a solution.
5. Brand Coherence: Assess the overall brand coherence and consistency

across the corporation. If the diverse products or services offered by different units risk diluting the core brand identity or confusing customers, sub-brands can help maintain brand coherence while allowing for flexibility and customization.

6. Strategic Goals: Align the decision on sub-brands with the strategic goals of the corporation. Evaluate whether creating sub-brands will support the corporation's growth plans, market expansion, or entry into new segments. Sub-brands should align with the strategic direction of the corporation and contribute to its overall success.

7. Resource Allocation: Consider the resources required to develop and manage sub-brands. Assess whether the benefits of creating sub-brands outweigh the costs associated with brand development, marketing, and operational support. Adequate resources should be available to ensure the successful implementation and maintenance of sub-brands.

It is important to note that the decision to create sub-brands should be based on a thorough analysis of these factors and should align with the corporation's overall brand strategy and objectives. Consulting with brand experts, conducting market research, and seeking input from stakeholders can provide valuable insights in making an informed decision.

Example 01: GE

GE is a multinational conglomerate operating in various industries, such as aviation, healthcare, renewable energy, and power generation. To effectively manage its diverse portfolio, GE has employed sub-brands to differentiate its business units and maintain brand coherence.

One prominent sub-brand within GE is GE Aviation. As a leading provider of aircraft engines, GE Aviation focuses on the aerospace industry and serves a distinct customer base. By creating a dedicated sub-brand, GE can leverage its expertise in aviation and establish a strong presence in this specific market segment. The GE Aviation sub-brand signifies a specialized focus on aviation-related products and services, allowing the business unit to communicate its value proposition clearly to customers.

Another example is GE Healthcare, a sub-brand that specializes in providing healthcare technology and solutions. With this sub-brand, GE is able to cater to the unique needs of the healthcare industry and position itself as a trusted provider of innovative medical technologies and services. By differentiating GE Healthcare from its other business units, GE can enhance its visibility and credibility in the healthcare sector, where specific expertise and solutions are required.

These sub-brands within GE serve multiple purposes. Firstly, they allow GE to target specific industries and customer segments effectively. By tailoring their offerings and messaging to the needs of each market, GE can build stronger relationships with customers and establish a competitive advantage within those sectors. Additionally, the sub-brands help maintain brand coherence by ensuring that each business unit operates with its own distinct identity while still being connected to the overarching GE brand.

The use of sub-brands also facilitates internal management and strategic alignment within GE. Each business unit can operate autonomously under its sub-brand, focusing on its specific objectives, market dynamics, and innovation efforts. At the same time, these units can leverage the resources, expertise, and reputation of the broader GE brand to drive growth and achieve strategic goals.

Furthermore, the sub-brands within GE enable effective communication and marketing strategies. Each sub-brand can develop its unique brand positioning, messaging, and visual identity, tailored to the specific target audience and industry. This allows GE to create more relevant and compelling marketing campaigns, building stronger connections with customers and driving brand loyalty.

The outcomes of GE's approach to using sub-brands for differentiation within the corporation have been positive. By clearly delineating its business units through sub-brands, GE has been able to effectively navigate different industries, meet customer needs, and maintain brand relevance. The sub-brands have helped GE establish a strong presence in various markets, build industry-specific expertise, and drive growth within each business unit.

Example 02: IBM

IBM, also known as International Business Machines Corporation, is a global technology and consulting company that specializes in providing hardware, software, and services solutions to businesses and organizations. IBM is an excellent example of a company that has effectively used sub-brands for corporate branding.

IBM has established several sub-brands to cater to different business segments and industries. These sub-brands include IBM Watson, IBM Cloud, IBM Security, IBM Blockchain, and IBM Quantum.

IBM Watson is an AI platform that utilizes advanced analytics, machine learning, and natural language processing capabilities. It helps businesses analyze data, gain insights, and make informed decisions. The creation of IBM Watson as a sub-brand showcases IBM's expertise in AI and cognitive computing technologies.

IBM Cloud provides a range of cloud computing services, including IaaS, PaaS, and SaaS solutions. It offers businesses scalable and flexible cloud-based solutions for storage, computing, and application development. IBM Cloud positions IBM as a trusted provider of enterprise-grade cloud services.

IBM Security is dedicated to providing comprehensive cybersecurity solutions to businesses. It focuses on threat detection, risk management, and data security. Leveraging advanced analytics and AI, IBM Security helps organizations protect their data, networks, and digital assets.

IBM Blockchain focuses on blockchain technology and solutions. It offers businesses a secure and transparent platform for managing transactions in industries like supply chain, finance, and healthcare. IBM Blockchain enables organizations to streamline processes, enhance trust, and improve collaboration within their ecosystems.

IBM Quantum is dedicated to quantum computing, an emerging field that leverages the principles of quantum mechanics. It offers cloud-based access to quantum computers and resources for businesses and researchers. IBM Quantum allows organizations to explore and harness the potential of quantum computing.

IBM's sub-brand strategy for corporate branding enables the company to target specific market segments, establish a strong presence in various industries, and communicate its specialized offerings effectively. Each sub-brand within the IBM portfolio carries its own brand identity, messaging, and value proposition while benefiting from the reputation and resources of IBM as the parent brand.

Furthermore, IBM's sub-brands align with the company's overarching brand values, including innovation, reliability, and expertise. The sub-brands reinforce IBM's position as a technology leader and a trusted partner for businesses worldwide.

In summary, IBM's approach to creating sub-brands for corporate branding allows the company to strategically position itself in different technology domains, target specific market segments, and showcase its expertise and capabilities. The sub-brands strengthen IBM's brand portfolio, extend its reach, and enhance its competitiveness in the ever-evolving technology landscape.

In conclusion, creating sub-brands to differentiate different business units or divisions within a larger corporation is a strategic approach that offers several benefits. It allows the corporation to effectively manage diverse product portfolios, cater to specific customer needs, and maintain brand coherence. By leveraging sub-brands, corporations can focus on specific market segments, tailor their marketing strategies, and establish a strong presence in each respective category. Sub-brands provide flexibility in responding to market trends and allow for targeted product development and marketing efforts.

* * *

20

Licensing and Franchising

L icensing and franchising are powerful strategies employed by businesses to develop sub-brands within their overall brand portfolio. These approaches involve granting rights and permissions to third-party entities, allowing them to use the parent company's brand, trademarks, and intellectual property in exchange for a fee or a share of the revenue. This enables the parent company to expand its brand presence and reach into new markets or customer segments.

In the context of sub-brands, licensing and franchising offer a unique opportunity to create distinct and independent brand identities that operate under the umbrella of the parent company. By leveraging the parent brand's reputation, equity, and market position, these sub-brands can tap into new business opportunities and target specific consumer segments more effectively.

Both licensing and franchising allow the parent company to extend its brand beyond its core offerings while maintaining a level of control and consistency. While licensing involves granting rights to use the brand for the production and distribution of specific products or services, franchising goes a step further by providing a complete business model, operational guidelines, and ongoing support to franchisees.

The use of licensing and franchising as strategies for sub-brand development has become increasingly popular due to their potential for rapid expansion, market penetration, and revenue generation. However, it is crucial for companies to carefully consider their licensing or franchising partners, maintain brand consistency, and ensure a mutually beneficial relationship to successfully leverage these strategies for sub-brand growth.

Licensing and Franchising Benefits

Licensing and franchising play a vital role in expanding brand presence and reach for businesses. Here are some key reasons why these strategies are important:

1. Market Expansion: Licensing and franchising allow a brand to enter new markets and geographical regions more efficiently. By partnering with local licensees or franchisees who have a better understanding of the local market dynamics, cultural nuances, and consumer preferences, the brand can expand its footprint rapidly and tap into previously untapped customer segments.

2. Capitalize on Local Expertise: Licensing and franchising enable brands to leverage the expertise and resources of local partners. Franchisees or licensees bring their knowledge of the local market, customer base, and operational efficiencies, which can contribute to the success of the sub-brand. This localized approach helps the brand tailor its offerings to suit the specific needs and preferences of the target market.

3. Faster Market Penetration: Through licensing and franchising, brands can accelerate their market penetration and overcome entry barriers. By leveraging the established networks, distribution channels, and customer base of licensees or franchisees, the brand can quickly establish its presence and gain traction in new markets.

4. Risk Mitigation: Licensing and franchising allow brands to expand their presence with lower risk and investment compared to opening and operating company-owned outlets. Franchisees and licensees bear a significant portion of the financial burden, including startup costs,

operational expenses, and ongoing fees, reducing the risk exposure for the brand.

5. Brand Extension: Licensing and franchising enable brands to extend their offerings and diversify their product or service portfolio. By partnering with licensees or franchisees who specialize in complementary products or services, the brand can leverage its expertise to create sub-brands that cater to different customer needs and expand its brand's relevance and appeal.

6. Brand Visibility and Awareness: Through licensing and franchising, the brand can benefit from the increased visibility and awareness generated by multiple sub-brands operating under its umbrella. Each sub-brand serves as a touchpoint for engaging with customers, building brand recognition, and reinforcing the overall brand identity.

7. Revenue Generation: Licensing and franchising offer significant revenue-generating opportunities for the brand. The licensing fees, royalties, and ongoing support fees collected from licensees or franchisees contribute to the brand's financial growth. Additionally, the expansion of sub-brands through licensing and franchising can lead to increased sales, market share, and overall brand value.

By leveraging licensing and franchising effectively, brands can strengthen their position in the market, reach a wider customer base, and achieve sustainable growth.

Licensing as a Strategy for Sub-Brand Development

Licensing is a strategy for sub-brand development where a brand grants permission to another company or individual (known as the licensee) to use its brand name, trademarks, logos, and other intellectual property assets in association with specific products, services, or businesses. This allows the licensee to leverage the brand's established reputation, brand equity, and consumer recognition to market and sell their offerings.

Here's how licensing works:

1. Licensing Agreement: The brand owner and the licensee enter into a licensing agreement that outlines the terms and conditions of the licensing arrangement. This agreement specifies the scope of the license, the rights granted to the licensee, and any restrictions or limitations on the use of the brand assets.

2. Brand Assets and Intellectual Property: The brand owner provides the licensee with access to its brand assets, including trademarks, logos, designs, and other intellectual property. The licensee is authorized to use these assets on their products, packaging, marketing materials, and other relevant channels.

3. Quality Control: The brand owner maintains control over the quality and standards associated with the licensed products or services. They ensure that the licensee adheres to the brand's guidelines and maintains the desired level of quality to protect the brand's reputation.

4. Royalties and Fees: In exchange for using the brand assets, the licensee typically pays royalties or licensing fees to the brand owner. These fees may be based on a percentage of sales, a fixed amount, or a combination of both, depending on the terms agreed upon in the licensing agreement.

5. Marketing and Promotion: Both the brand owner and the licensee collaborate on marketing and promotion efforts to maximize the exposure and success of the licensed products or services. They may engage in joint marketing campaigns, co-branding initiatives, or other promotional activities to leverage the strength of the brand and drive consumer awareness and demand.

6. Territory and Duration: The licensing agreement specifies the geographic territory in which the licensee can operate and sell the licensed products or services. It also outlines the duration of the licensing arrangement, including any renewal or termination provisions.

7. Benefits for Both Parties: Licensing offers benefits for both the brand owner and the licensee. The brand owner expands its brand reach without the need for significant capital investment, while the licensee gains

access to a recognized brand, established consumer base, and increased market credibility, which can lead to higher sales and profitability.

Licensing is a mutually beneficial strategy that allows brands to extend their presence, enter new markets, and diversify their product offerings. It provides an opportunity for the brand owner to generate additional revenue through licensing fees and royalties while leveraging the licensee's resources, expertise, and distribution channels. For the licensee, licensing offers a shortcut to market entry, access to a well-known brand, and the potential for accelerated growth.

Example 01: LEGO Star Wars line.

LEGO, a renowned toy brand known for its building blocks, recognized an opportunity to expand its product offering and reach by partnering with popular entertainment franchises. One notable example of sub-brand development through licensing agreements is the collaboration between LEGO and the Star Wars franchise.

Through a licensing agreement with Lucasfilm, the company that owns the Star Wars franchise, LEGO gained the rights to use Star Wars intellectual property in their LEGO sets. This agreement allowed LEGO to create and market LEGO sets based on characters, vehicles, and settings from the Star Wars movies.

LEGO designers and engineers worked closely with Lucasfilm to develop LEGO sets that faithfully represented the Star Wars universe. They created intricate models of spaceships, vehicles, and iconic locations from the movies, providing fans with the opportunity to recreate their favourite scenes and embark on their own imaginative adventures.

LEGO seamlessly integrated the Star Wars branding and imagery into its packaging, marketing materials, and product displays. This cohesive and recognizable sub-brand, known as LEGO Star Wars, stood out on store shelves and attracted the attention of LEGO enthusiasts and Star Wars fans alike.

To generate excitement and awareness for the LEGO Star Wars line, LEGO collaborated with Lucasfilm on joint marketing and promotional campaigns. This included television advertisements, digital marketing initiatives, and special events tied to movie releases or significant milestones in the Star Wars franchise.

The LEGO Star Wars line quickly gained popularity and became a huge success among LEGO enthusiasts, Star Wars fans, and collectors. It captured the essence of both LEGO and Star Wars, offering a unique and engaging play experience that appealed to a broad audience.

Over the years, the LEGO Star Wars line expanded to include more sets, characters, and scenes from different Star Wars movies and TV series. The licensing agreement allowed LEGO to continuously release new products, capitalizing on the enduring popularity of the Star Wars franchise.

The partnership between LEGO and Star Wars through licensing agreements showcased the power of sub-brand development in capturing the imagination and loyalty of consumers. It demonstrated how licensing could enable a brand to tap into an existing fanbase, leverage established intellectual property, and create a successful sub-brand that aligns with the values and essence of both the licensor and licensee.

The LEGO Star Wars sub-brand not only contributed to the growth and success of LEGO but also helped to further expand the Star Wars franchise's reach and influence.

Example 02: Nike NBA

Nike, a leading sportswear brand, recognized the immense popularity and global appeal of basketball as a sport. To capitalize on this opportunity and expand its brand presence in the basketball market, Nike entered into a licensing agreement with the National Basketball Association (NBA), the premier professional basketball league.

Through an exclusive licensing agreement with the NBA, Nike gained the rights to produce and market NBA-branded apparel, footwear, and accessories. This agreement allowed Nike to tap into the NBA's brand equity and association with elite basketball.

Nike leveraged the licensing agreement to develop a range of NBA-inspired products, including basketball shoes, jerseys, shorts, and other apparel. They incorporated team logos, player names, and league branding into the designs, creating a distinctive sub-brand that represented the essence of the NBA.

To further enhance the sub-brand's credibility and appeal, Nike signed endorsement deals with some of the NBA's biggest stars, such as LeBron James, Kevin Durant, and Kobe Bryant. These athletes became the faces of the NBA sub-brand within Nike's product lineup, adding star power and creating a strong connection between the sub-brand and the league's top talent.

Nike strategically distributed the NBA sub-brand products through various channels, including Nike retail stores, authorized resellers, and NBA team stores. This widespread availability and accessibility ensured that basketball fans and consumers worldwide could easily purchase and engage with the NBA-branded products.

Nike launched comprehensive marketing campaigns to promote the NBA sub-brand. This included television and digital advertisements, social media activations, and sponsorship of NBA events and initiatives. Nike capitalized on the global reach of the NBA to engage with fans across different regions and cultures, fueling excitement and driving brand awareness.

To foster a sense of community and brand loyalty among basketball enthusiasts, Nike organized interactive experiences, community events, and fan activations. They organized basketball clinics, fan meet-and-greets, and grassroots initiatives, providing opportunities for fans to connect with the NBA sub-brand and the sport they love.

The collaboration between Nike and the NBA through licensing agreements resulted in the successful development of the NBA sub-brand within Nike's product portfolio. This sub-brand allowed Nike to establish a strong presence in the basketball market, catering to the passionate fan base and capitalizing on the popularity of the NBA.

The NBA sub-brand not only boosted Nike's sales and market share but also enhanced the league's global visibility and fan engagement. It created a synergy between the sport of basketball, the NBA, and Nike as a trusted and aspirational sportswear brand.

Franchising as a Strategy for Sub-Brand Development

Franchising is a strategy for sub-brand development that involves granting the rights to third-party individuals or businesses (franchisees) to operate under an established brand name and business model. The franchisor, which is the parent company or brand owner, grants the franchisee the license to operate a business using its established brand, systems, and support.

Here are key characteristics and how franchising works:

1. Established Brand: Franchising typically involves an established and successful brand that has a proven track record in the market. The franchisor's brand reputation and recognition are key factors that attract potential franchisees.

2. Business Model and Systems: The franchisor provides the franchisee with a comprehensive business model, including operating procedures, marketing strategies, and guidelines for maintaining brand standards. This ensures consistency across all franchise locations and helps maintain the brand's reputation and customer experience.

3. Licensing Agreement: The franchisor and franchisee enter into a legally binding licensing agreement that outlines the terms and conditions of the franchise relationship. This agreement covers aspects such as the use of the brand name, fees, territory rights, training, ongoing support, and quality control.

4. Financial Investment: Franchisees typically pay an initial franchise fee to acquire the rights to operate under the brand name. They also pay ongoing fees, such as royalty fees based on a percentage of their sales, advertising fees, and other costs specified in the agreement. Franchisees are responsible for financing their own franchise location and managing

its day-to-day operations.

5. Training and Support: Franchisors provide initial training programs to ensure that franchisees understand the brand's operations, standards, and best practices. Ongoing support, such as marketing assistance, operational guidance, and regular communication, helps franchisees succeed and maintain brand consistency.

6. Expansion and Growth: Franchising allows the brand to expand its presence rapidly by leveraging the resources, capital, and entrepreneurial spirit of franchisees. Franchisees benefit from the established brand recognition and support system provided by the franchisor, helping them start and operate a business more successfully than if they were starting from scratch.

7. Brand Control: Franchisors maintain control over their brand by enforcing specific standards and guidelines. They have the authority to ensure that all franchise locations adhere to brand consistency, quality control, and customer experience standards.

Franchising offers several advantages, including accelerated brand growth, wider geographic reach, shared investment, and reduced operational risks for both franchisor and franchisee. It allows the brand to leverage the expertise and local knowledge of franchisees while maintaining brand control and standards. Franchisees benefit from a proven business model, brand recognition, and ongoing support, increasing their chances of success.

It is important for both franchisor and franchisee to enter into franchising agreements with a clear understanding of their rights, responsibilities, and expectations to ensure a mutually beneficial and successful relationship.

Example 01: Anytime Fitness

Anytime Fitness, a global chain of 24-hour fitness centers, has demonstrated the successful development of sub-brands through franchising agreements. The brand recognized the need to cater to different customer segments and locations, leading to the creation of the sub-brand Anytime Fitness Express.

Anytime Fitness Express was introduced to target customers in densely populated urban areas and smaller locations where space constraints made it challenging to establish a full-scale fitness center. The sub-brand differentiated itself by providing a streamlined fitness experience with a smaller footprint and limited equipment options, emphasizing efficiency and convenience without compromising on quality.

To expand the reach of the sub-brand, Anytime Fitness adopted a franchising model. Independent franchisees were granted the rights to open and operate Anytime Fitness Express locations under the guidance and support of the parent company. Anytime Fitness provided comprehensive training, operational support, and marketing resources to ensure brand consistency and maintain the high standards associated with the parent brand.

The introduction of Anytime Fitness Express allowed the brand to penetrate new markets that were previously underserved or had limited space availability. It appealed to busy urban dwellers seeking quick and convenient workout options. Despite being a sub-brand, Anytime Fitness Express maintained strong brand cohesion with the parent brand, leveraging its reputation, trust, and recognition to provide customers with a consistent experience across both formats.

The development of Anytime Fitness Express expanded the market presence of Anytime Fitness and contributed to the brand's overall growth. The sub-brand enabled the franchise to adapt to varying customer needs and maximize its market share. The franchising model attracted aspiring entrepreneurs interested in the fitness industry but with limited space or resources to establish a full-scale gym. The success of Anytime Fitness Express relied on the dedication and commitment of its franchisees.

By addressing specific customer needs and capitalizing on franchise opportunities, Anytime Fitness successfully expanded its market reach and solidified its position within the fitness industry. The differentiation of Anytime Fitness Express, coupled with its franchising model and alignment with the parent brand's values and reputation, contributed to its growth and success.

Example 02: Courtyard by Marriott

Courtyard by Marriott, a sub-brand of Marriott International, exemplifies successful sub-brand development in the hospitality industry. Designed specifically for modern business travellers, Courtyard by Marriott offers a balanced combination of productivity, connectivity, and relaxation.

Operating under a franchising model, Courtyard by Marriott allows independent owners to establish and operate their own hotels under the trusted Marriott brand. This approach enables Marriott International to expand its presence rapidly and leverage the expertise and resources of local entrepreneurs.

The target audience for Courtyard by Marriott consists of business travellers who prioritize convenience, technology, and comfort during their stays. The sub-brand caters to professionals on the go, aiming to create a productive and enjoyable travel experience.

Courtyard by Marriott sets itself apart through its contemporary design and amenities. The hotels feature functional and ergonomic spaces, modern technology integration, flexible workspaces, and high-speed internet access, ensuring a conducive environment for business travellers.

With a focus on meeting the unique needs of business travellers, Courtyard by Marriott offers focused services such as 24-hour business centres, meeting rooms, fitness facilities, and on-site dining options. These amenities ensure that guests have everything they need for a seamless and productive stay.

Maintaining brand consistency across its properties, Marriott International ensures that guests receive a consistent experience regardless of the Courtyard by Marriott location. Standardized service, quality, and design elements contribute to building brand recognition and guest loyalty.

Courtyard by Marriott has established a global presence with hotels in major business destinations worldwide. This extensive network allows the sub-brand to serve business travellers in various locations, meeting their needs for reliable and convenient accommodations.

Embracing technology as a key component, Courtyard by Marriott integrates innovative solutions to enhance the guest experience. Mobile check-in and check-out, keyless entry, and in-room connectivity reflect the sub-brand's commitment to meeting the evolving needs of tech-savvy travellers.

Courtyard by Marriott continuously innovates and evolves to remain relevant in the highly competitive hospitality industry. The sub-brand explores new concepts, design elements, and service offerings to meet the changing expectations of business travellers and maintain its position as a preferred choice.

Through the development of Courtyard by Marriott as a sub-brand, Marriott International successfully caters to the specific needs of business travellers. The franchising model enables rapid expansion and market penetration, while brand consistency ensures a reliable and recognizable experience for guests. With its focus on modern design, amenities, and technology integration, Courtyard by Marriott has become a trusted and preferred choice for business travellers worldwide, contributing to the overall success of Marriott International.

In conclusion, sub-brand development through licensing and franchising agreements is a powerful strategy for expanding brand presence, reaching new markets, and diversifying business operations. By leveraging the expertise and resources of local independent partners, companies can create sub-brands that cater to specific customer segments or market niches.

* * *

21

Customer Experience Focus

C ustomer Experience-Focused Sub-Brands refer to the strategic development of sub-brands that prioritize and emphasize unique and exceptional customer experiences. These sub-brands are designed to create memorable interactions, touchpoints, and overall journeys for customers, enhancing their perception and relationship with the brand.

In today's competitive marketplace, customer experience plays a crucial role in brand differentiation and building customer loyalty.

1. Competitive Advantage: Customer experience has become a key differentiating factor as products and services become increasingly similar. Brands that excel in providing exceptional experiences stand out from the competition and gain a competitive advantage in the market.

2. Emotional Connection: Positive customer experiences create emotional connections between customers and brands. When customers feel valued, understood, and cared for, they develop a stronger affinity and loyalty towards the brand.

3. Customer Satisfaction: Satisfying customer needs and expectations is essential for brand success. A seamless and enjoyable customer experience ensures that customers have their needs met, resulting in higher levels of satisfaction and increased likelihood of repeat purchases.

4. Brand Advocacy: Exceptional customer experiences generate positive word-of-mouth recommendations. Satisfied customers are more likely to share their experiences with others, becoming brand advocates who promote the brand organically and attract new customers.

5. Long-Term Relationships: Building customer loyalty through superior experiences leads to long-term relationships. Loyal customers are more likely to continue doing business with the brand, resulting in higher customer lifetime value and reduced customer churn.

6. Brand Reputation: Brands known for delivering exceptional customer experiences develop a positive reputation in the marketplace. A strong brand reputation attracts new customers and enhances the brand's overall image and credibility.

7. Repeat Business and Revenue Growth: When customers have positive experiences, they are more likely to become repeat customers. Increased customer retention and repeat business contribute to revenue growth and profitability for the brand.

Brands that prioritize and excel in delivering exceptional experiences gain a competitive edge, build stronger emotional connections with customers, and ultimately drive long-term success.

Identifying Opportunities for Customer Experience-Focused Sub-Brands

Identifying opportunities for customer experience-focused sub-brands involves a thorough analysis of market trends, customer insights, and the brand's overall strategy. Here are some key steps to identify these opportunities in detail:

1. Market Research and Analysis: Conduct comprehensive market research to understand the current landscape and identify emerging trends related to customer experience. Explore industry reports, competitor

analysis, and consumer behaviour studies to gain insights into customer preferences, expectations, and pain points. This research will help identify gaps in the market where a customer experience-focused sub-brand could thrive.

2. Customer Insights and Feedback: Gather customer feedback through surveys, focus groups, observational research, or social media listening. Pay attention to their experiences, challenges, and suggestions related to your brand or industry. This qualitative data will provide valuable insights into areas where a customer experience-focused sub-brand could address unmet needs or enhance existing experiences.

3. Brand Strategy Alignment: Evaluate your brand's overall strategy and positioning. Identify key brand attributes, values, and promises that can be leveraged to create exceptional customer experiences. Assess how well your current brand strategy aligns with delivering outstanding experiences, and identify any gaps or opportunities for improvement.

4. Customer Journey Mapping: Map out the customer journey across various touchpoints, from pre-purchase to post-purchase interactions. Identify critical touchpoints where customer experience plays a significant role and determine if there are opportunities to enhance those experiences. This could include streamlining processes, personalizing interactions, or introducing innovative features that surprise and delight customers.

5. Competitive Analysis: Analyze the customer experience offerings of your competitors and identify areas where they may be falling short. Look for opportunities to differentiate your brand by delivering superior experiences or filling gaps that competitors have overlooked. This analysis will help identify potential niches or segments where a customer experience-focused sub-brand can thrive.

6. Target Segment Analysis: Identify specific customer segments that highly value exceptional experiences. This could be based on demographics, psychographics, or specific needs and preferences. Understand their pain points, desires, and aspirations to design tailored experiences that resonate with them. By targeting these segments with a customer experience-focused sub-brand, you can capture their attention and build

lasting loyalty.

7. Innovation and Technology Assessment: Evaluate the role of innovation and technology in delivering superior customer experiences. Identify emerging technologies, digital platforms, or data-driven solutions that can be leveraged to create innovative experiences. Consider how these technologies align with your brand's values and capabilities and explore opportunities to integrate them into your customer experience-focused sub-brand.

8. Internal Capabilities and Resources: Assess your organization's internal capabilities and resources to support developing and managing a customer experience-focused sub-brand. Consider factors such as operational infrastructure, employee training, technology systems, and customer service capabilities. Ensure that you have the necessary resources and commitment to deliver exceptional experiences consistently.

By conducting a thorough analysis of market trends, customer insights, brand strategy, competition, target segments, innovation, and internal capabilities, you can identify opportunities to develop customer experience-focused sub-brands. This process allows you to align your brand's strengths with customer needs and differentiate yourself by delivering exceptional experiences that create long-term customer loyalty and advocacy.

Designing Unique Customer Experiences for Sub-Brands

Designing unique customer experiences for sub-brands requires a strategic and creative approach that aligns with the brand's values, target audience, and overall business objectives. Here are key considerations and steps involved in the process:

1. Define Brand Persona: Start by clearly defining the brand persona for the sub-brand. This includes identifying its unique personality, values, and positioning within the market. Understand how the sub-brand differs

from the main brand and the specific customer experience it aims to deliver.

2. Customer Journey Mapping: Map out the customer journey for the sub-brand, identifying all touchpoints and interactions a customer has with the brand. This includes pre-purchase, purchase, and post-purchase stages. Analyze each touchpoint to identify opportunities to enhance the customer experience, whether it's through personalization, convenience, or emotional connection.

3. Customer Research: Conduct in-depth research to gain insights into the target audience's needs, preferences, and pain points. This can be done through surveys, focus groups, interviews, or online listening. Understanding the customer's motivations, expectations, and desires will help design experiences that resonate with them.

4. Set Experience Goals: Define clear goals for the customer experiences you want to create with the sub-brand. These goals should align with the brand's values and positioning. For example, if the sub-brand focuses on luxury, the goal may be to create a personalized and exclusive experience for customers.

5. Develop Brand Touchpoints: Identify and develop specific touchpoints where the sub-brand can differentiate itself and deliver a unique experience. This could include website design, packaging, customer service, social media presence, physical store layout, or product features. Each touchpoint should align with the brand persona and contribute to the desired customer experience.

6. Emphasize Emotional Connection: Create experiences that evoke emotions and foster a strong connection with the customers. This can be achieved through storytelling, personalized messaging, or surprise and delight moments. The sub-brand should strive to create memorable experiences that leave a lasting positive impression on customers.

7. Leverage Technology: Utilize technology to enhance the customer experience. This could involve implementing personalized recommendations, seamless online ordering and delivery processes, augmented reality for product visualization, or chatbots for quick customer support.

Technology should be integrated strategically to streamline processes and provide convenience.

8. Consistency and Training: Ensure consistency in delivering the intended customer experience across all touchpoints. Train employees and stakeholders on the sub-brand's values, voice, and customer service standards. Consistent execution of the customer experience is crucial to build trust and loyalty.

9. Measure and Iterate: Establish metrics to measure the success of the customer experience initiatives. This can include customer satisfaction surveys, net promoter scores, or qualitative feedback. Analyze the results and iterate on the experiences based on customer feedback and evolving market trends.

10. Continuous Improvement: Customer experience is an ongoing process. Continuously gather insights, monitor customer feedback, and make necessary adjustments to improve the sub-brand's customer experiences. Stay informed about industry trends and adopt new strategies and technologies to remain competitive.

By following these steps, brands can design unique customer experiences for their sub-brands that differentiate them from competitors, foster customer loyalty, and drive business growth. The key is to align the experiences with the sub-brand's values and target audience while consistently delivering on the brand promise.

Example 01: Starbucks Reserve Roastery

Starbucks Reserve Roastery is a prime example of a customer experience-focused sub-brand. It is an immersive coffee retail concept that offers customers a unique and elevated experience compared to regular Starbucks stores. Here's an in-depth look at how Starbucks created this sub-brand to deliver exceptional customer experiences:

1. Concept and Design: The Starbucks Reserve Roastery is designed to be a coffee lover's paradise. The sub-brand features large, spacious locations with impressive architectural designs and unique interior layouts. The design elements include an open coffee roasting area, interactive brewing stations, and a variety of seating options that encourage customers to relax and enjoy their coffee.

2. Premium Coffee Offerings: Starbucks Reserve Roastery showcases an exclusive line of premium and rare coffee beans from around the world. These speciality coffees are meticulously sourced and roasted in-house, offering customers a chance to experience unique flavours and coffee profiles that are not available in regular Starbucks stores. The focus on quality and craftsmanship creates a sense of exclusivity and sophistication.

3. Immersive Coffee Experience: The sub-brand aims to provide customers with an immersive and educational coffee experience. Customers can observe the coffee roasting process, interact with knowledgeable baristas, and participate in coffee tastings and brewing demonstrations. The staff at Starbucks Reserve Roastery are highly trained to engage customers, share their expertise, and enhance the overall experience through personalized recommendations.

4. Experiential Retail Spaces: The sub-brand features various experiential retail spaces within the store, such as the Arriviamo Bar, offering handcrafted cocktails with coffee-inspired flavours, a Princi bakery offering freshly baked goods, and a merchandise area with unique and limited-edition coffee-related products. These spaces allow customers to engage with different sensory experiences and further deepen their connection with the brand.

5. Digital Integration: Starbucks has incorporated digital technology to enhance the customer experience at the Reserve Roastery. The Starbucks Reserve mobile app allows customers to explore the various coffee offerings, receive personalized recommendations, and access exclusive content about the coffee-making process. Digital menu boards and interactive screens provide additional information and engage customers

throughout their visit.

6. Global Locations: Starbucks has strategically opened Reserve Roastery locations in major cities worldwide, including Seattle, Shanghai, Tokyo, Milan, and New York. This global expansion has allowed the brand to cater to diverse customer preferences and offers localized experiences while maintaining the overarching Reserve Roastery brand identity.

7. Omnichannel Approach: Starbucks has successfully integrated the Reserve Roastery sub-brand into its larger ecosystem. Customers can access Reserve coffee offerings at select Starbucks stores, online through the Starbucks website, and through the Starbucks Reserve subscription program. This seamless integration ensures that customers can continue to enjoy the Reserve Roastery experience beyond the physical locations.

8. Customer Engagement and Loyalty: Starbucks Reserve Roastery focuses on building strong customer relationships and fostering brand loyalty. The sub-brand offers exclusive benefits to its customers, such as early access to new Reserve coffee releases, special events, and customized rewards. This approach encourages repeat visits, word-of-mouth recommendations, and a sense of community among coffee enthusiasts.

The Starbucks Reserve Roastery sub-brand exemplifies how a customer experience-focused approach can elevate a brand and create a distinct offering within the coffee retail industry. By providing immersive experiences, premium offerings, and engaging spaces, Starbucks has successfully differentiated the Reserve Roastery from its regular stores, attracting coffee aficionados and enthusiasts seeking a unique and memorable coffee experience.

Example 02: Apple Stores

Apple Stores serve as a prime example of a customer experience-focused sub-brand. Apple, known for its innovative technology products, recognized the importance of creating a unique retail experience to engage and delight customers. Here's an in-depth look at how Apple Stores have become a benchmark for exceptional customer experiences:

1. Store Design and Layout: Apple Stores feature a sleek and minimalist design, spacious layouts, and strategically placed product displays. The stores are characterized by open spaces, inviting customers to explore and interact with the products. The design focuses on simplicity and elegance, creating a modern, premium atmosphere that aligns with Apple's brand identity.

2. Product Showcasing: The stores prominently display Apple's full range of products, allowing customers to engage with them hands-on. The products are showcased in a visually appealing manner, with clear signage and informative product descriptions. The interactive displays and demo areas enable customers to test the devices and experience their functionalities firsthand.

3. Knowledgeable and Engaging Staff: Apple Stores are known for their highly trained and knowledgeable staff, called Apple Geniuses. These employees are equipped with in-depth product knowledge and trained to provide personalized customer assistance. They offer guidance, answer questions, and provide recommendations, enhancing the overall customer experience and ensuring customers feel supported in their decision-making process.

4. Customer Support and Service: Apple Stores offer a range of support services, such as technical troubleshooting, device setup assistance, and product repairs. The Genius Bar, a dedicated customer service area within the store, allows customers to seek assistance and resolve any issues they may encounter with their Apple products. This commitment to after-sales support further enhances customer satisfaction and loyalty.

5. Educational Workshops and Events: Apple Stores regularly host educational workshops and events to provide customers with additional value and learning opportunities. These workshops cover various topics, such as photography, coding, and music production, allowing customers to enhance their skills and get the most out of their Apple devices. By offering these educational resources, Apple strengthens its relationship

with customers and positions itself as a trusted source of knowledge and inspiration.

6. Seamless Integration of Online and Offline Channels: Apple Stores seamlessly integrate the online and offline customer experience. Customers can explore products and make purchases both in-store and through Apple's online store. The Apple Store app allows customers to schedule appointments, reserve products for pickup, and access personalized recommendations. This omnichannel approach ensures a consistent and convenient experience across different touchpoints.

7. Community Engagement: Apple Stores serve as community hubs, hosting various events and initiatives to engage with local communities. These activities may include live performances, art exhibitions, coding sessions for kids, and entrepreneurship workshops. By fostering a sense of community and creating a welcoming environment, Apple Stores go beyond retail spaces and become gathering places connecting people with shared interests.

8. Brand Loyalty and Advocacy: Apple has successfully built a loyal customer base and brand advocates through its customer experience-focused approach. Customers who have positive experiences in Apple Stores often become loyal supporters of the brand and recommend Apple products to others. This word-of-mouth advocacy further strengthens Apple's position in the market and drives customer acquisition.

The Apple Stores sub-brand is a testament to the power of customer experience in enhancing brand differentiation and loyalty. By creating immersive retail environments, providing exceptional customer service, and seamlessly integrating online and offline channels, Apple has set a high standard for customer experiences in the technology retail industry.

In conclusion, developing and launching sub-brands that emphasize unique customer experiences is a strategic approach that can profoundly impact a company's success. By prioritizing creating exceptional and memorable experiences, businesses can differentiate themselves from competitors and build strong connections with their target audience.

When executed effectively, sub-brands that emphasize unique customer experiences can increase customer loyalty, advocacy, and business growth. Customers with positive and memorable experiences are more likely to become brand ambassadors, sharing their experiences with others and driving new customer acquisition.

This strategy can drive customer satisfaction, revenue growth, and long-term business success.

* * *

22

Health and Wellness

D
eveloping and introducing sub-brands for health and wellness involves creating distinct brand entities within an organization that focus specifically on catering to the needs and aspirations of conscious consumers in the health and wellness market. These sub-brands are designed to offer products or services that promote physical, mental, and emotional well-being. By emphasizing health, sustainability, and personal development, these sub-brands aim to differentiate themselves in the market and attract a specific target audience seeking holistic wellness solutions. The concept recognizes the growing consumer demand for health and wellness offerings and the need for brands to adapt and align with evolving consumer preferences in this space.

Targeting conscious consumers in the health and wellness market has become increasingly important due to several factors. Firstly, there has been a significant shift in consumer behaviour and preferences towards prioritizing their health and well-being. Consumers are now more aware and informed about the impact of their choices on their physical and mental health, and they actively seek products and services that align with their wellness goals.

Secondly, the rise of social and environmental consciousness has led to a growing concern for sustainable and ethical practices. Conscious consumers are mindful of the environmental impact, animal welfare, and social responsibility associated with the products they purchase. They are more likely to support brands that demonstrate a commitment to these values and actively promote sustainable and responsible practices.

Furthermore, the health and wellness market has witnessed significant growth and innovation driven by increasing consumer demand. This market encompasses various sectors, including fitness, nutrition, mindfulness, natural and organic products, and holistic wellness services. By targeting conscious consumers, brands can tap into this expanding market and capitalize on the opportunities it presents.

Targeting conscious consumers in the health and wellness market also fosters brand loyalty and advocacy. Conscious consumers are often passionate about their well-being and actively engage with brands that align with their values. By meeting their needs and providing meaningful experiences, brands can build strong connections and relationships with these consumers, resulting in repeat business and positive word-of-mouth recommendations.

Factors to be Considered for Creating a Sub-brand

Several factors should be considered when creating a sub-brand for targeting the health and wellness market. These factors include:

1. Consumer Insights: Gain a deep understanding of the target audience within the health and wellness market. Conduct market research to identify their needs, preferences, and motivations. Understand their pain points, aspirations, and behaviours to develop a sub-brand that resonates with them.

2. Market Analysis: Analyze the health and wellness landscape, including trends, competition, and opportunities. Identify gaps in the market where the sub-brand can offer unique value and differentiation. Assess the market's growth potential, target segments, and distribution channels.

3. Brand Strategy Alignment: Ensure that the sub-brand aligns with the

overall brand strategy and values. It should be consistent with the core brand's mission, vision, and positioning. Evaluate if the health and wellness focus complements the brand's existing products or requires a separate identity.

4. Unique Value Proposition: Define a clear and compelling value proposition for the sub-brand. Identify what sets it apart from competitors and why consumers should choose the sub-brand for their health and wellness needs. This could be based on factors such as ingredient quality, ethical sourcing, sustainability, or specific health benefits.

5. Product Development: Develop products or services catering to the target audience's health and wellness needs. Consider factors such as natural or organic ingredients, nutritional benefits, convenience, and eco-friendliness. Ensure that the product offering aligns with the brand's positioning and meets the desired quality standards.

6. Brand Identity and Messaging: Create a distinct brand identity for the sub-brand that reflects its health and wellness focus. This includes the brand name, logo, visual design, and brand voice. Craft messaging that effectively communicates the sub-brand's value proposition and resonates with health-conscious consumers.

7. Distribution Channels: Determine the appropriate distribution channels to reach the target audience effectively. This could include online platforms, health food stores, speciality retailers, or partnering with wellness centres or gyms. Select channels that align with the sub-brand's positioning and provide easy access to the target customers.

8. Marketing and Communication: Develop a comprehensive marketing and communication strategy to promote the sub-brand. This includes creating targeted campaigns, leveraging social media and digital channels, partnering with influencers or health experts, and engaging in content marketing. Tailor the messaging to highlight the sub-brand's health benefits, authenticity, and commitment to consumer well-being.

9. Regulatory Compliance: Ensure that the sub-brand complies with relevant health and wellness regulations and industry standards. This includes adhering to labelling requirements, safety guidelines, and specific

certifications or approvals for health-related products or services.

10. Partnerships and Collaborations: Explore partnerships and collaborations with industry experts, health professionals, influencers, or organizations that align with the sub-brand's values. These collaborations can provide credibility, expertise, and additional marketing opportunities to reach the target audience effectively.

11. Consumer Education: Invest in consumer education initiatives to empower and inform customers about the benefits of the sub-brand's health and wellness offerings. Provide resources, tips, and educational content that help consumers make informed decisions and adopt a healthier lifestyle.

12. Customer Engagement and Support: Create channels for customer engagement, feedback, and support. This can include customer service channels, online communities, or loyalty programs that foster a sense of community and provide ongoing support to consumers on their health and wellness journey.

13. Sustainability and Social Responsibility: Consider integrating sustainability and social responsibility practices into the sub-brand's operations. This can involve using eco-friendly packaging, supporting ethical sourcing practices, or giving back to relevant health or environmental causes. Demonstrating a commitment to sustainability and social responsibility can enhance the sub-brand's appeal to conscious consumers.

14. Continuous Evaluation and Transformation: Regularly evaluate the performance of the sub-brand, including sales, customer feedback, market trends, and competitive landscape. Use this information to make necessary adjustments and improvements to the sub-brand's offerings, marketing strategies, or positioning to ensure its ongoing success in the health and wellness market.

By considering these factors, brands can make informed decisions when creating a sub-brand for targeting the health and wellness market. This ensures that the sub-brand effectively meets consumer needs, stands out in a competitive market, and builds a strong brand-consumer connection.

Example 01: Nestlé and Nestlé Health Science

Nestlé Health Science, a subsidiary of Nestlé, serves as a notable example of a company that successfully developed and introduced a sub-brand focusing on health and wellness. Founded in 2011, Nestlé Health Science aimed to pioneer nutritional science and create innovative solutions to address specific health needs.

Identifying the Opportunity: Nestlé recognized the rising demand for personalized nutrition and the increasing prevalence of health conditions requiring specialized dietary management. Leveraging its expertise in nutrition, the company saw an opportunity to develop a sub-brand catering to consumers with unique health needs.

Developing Nestlé Health Science: Nestlé Health Science prioritized research, development, and innovation to provide targeted nutritional solutions. Collaborating with healthcare professionals, researchers, and scientists, the company formulated products to support the nutritional needs of individuals with conditions like digestive disorders, metabolic conditions, and malnutrition.

Product Portfolio and Innovation: Nestlé Health Science introduced a range of specialized products under its sub-brand, including nutritional supplements, medical foods, and dietary management solutions. These products were carefully formulated with specific nutrients and ingredients to address nutritional gaps and support overall health and well-being.

Notable Sub-Brands:

- Optifast: A weight loss program utilizing meal replacements and shakes to assist individuals in losing weight.
- Peptamen: A nutritional supplement for people with gastrointestinal disorders.
- Alitrem: A liquid food for people with severe malabsorption.

Partnerships and Expertise: Nestlé Health Science forged strategic partnerships with healthcare institutions, research organizations, and universities to advance personalized nutrition understanding and develop evidence-based solutions. This collaborative approach enabled the company to leverage the expertise of healthcare professionals and gain scientific credibility.

Brand Fit: Nestle has a long-standing reputation for quality, taste, and innovation. Nestlé's portfolio includes popular brands in categories such as confectionery, coffee, dairy products, and culinary items.

On the other hand, Nestlé Health Science is a specialized subsidiary of Nestlé that focuses on nutritional therapies and personalized health science solutions. It is dedicated to providing science-based nutritional solutions to support health and well-being across different life stages.

The brand fit between Nestlé and Nestlé Health Science is evident in their shared commitment to nutrition and well-being. Nestlé Health Science leverages Nestlé's expertise and resources to develop innovative products and services that address specific health conditions and nutritional needs.

The collaboration between the two brands allows Nestlé Health Science to tap into Nestlé's extensive distribution network, brand recognition, and research and development capabilities. At the same time, Nestlé benefits from the insights and advancements in personalized nutrition and health science offered by Nestlé Health Science.

Outcomes and Impact: The creation of Nestlé Health Science allowed Nestlé to diversify its product portfolio and tap into the growing health and wellness market. The sub-brand gained recognition and trust within the healthcare community and among consumers with specific health conditions. It contributed to Nestlé's overall brand reputation as a company committed to promoting health and well-being.

By recognizing the opportunity in personalized nutrition and leveraging its expertise in nutrition science, Nestlé created a sub-brand that addresses specific health needs and provides targeted nutritional solutions. The strategic partnerships, research and development efforts, and effective marketing and communication strategies have allowed Nestlé Health Science to establish itself as a trusted player in the health and wellness industry.

Example 02: Herbal Essences Bio:Renew

Herbal Essences, a well-established hair care brand, recognized the growing consumer demand for natural and healthier products in the health and wellness space. To cater to this evolving market, they embarked on a strategic initiative to create a sub-brand called Herbal Essences Bio:Renew. This example explores the journey of Herbal Essences in developing and launching Bio:Renew, a sub-brand that embodies their commitment to providing consumers with more sustainable and nature-inspired hair care solutions.

Identifying the Opportunity: Herbal Essences conducted extensive market research and consumer surveys to identify the emerging trends and demands in the health and wellness industry. They discovered a growing interest among consumers for products with natural ingredients, free from harsh chemicals, and environmentally friendly. Recognizing this opportunity, Herbal Essences saw the potential to leverage its brand equity and expertise in hair care to create a sub-brand that specifically caters to these needs.

Brand Positioning and Purpose: Herbal Essences Bio:Renew was a sub-brand offering hair care products formulated with real botanicals and plant-based ingredients. The purpose of Bio:Renew was to provide consumers with a healthier and more sustainable hair care option that nourishes and revitalizes hair naturally. The brand aimed to create a sensory experience by infusing fragrances inspired by nature into its products, further enhancing the overall wellness experience.

Product Development and Formulation: Herbal Essences invested in research and development to formulate Bio:Renew products that met their stringent natural ingredients and sustainability standards. They partnered with botanists and scientists to identify and extract botanicals known for their hair care benefits. The formulations were carefully crafted to deliver effective results while avoiding harsh chemicals like sulfates, parabens, and colourants.

Packaging and Design: Herbal Essences Bio:Renew adopted packaging designs that reflected freshness and botanical elements to align with the brand's focus on nature-inspired solutions. The packaging featured vibrant colours, imagery of plants and flowers, and clear communication of the natural ingredients used in the products. The design aimed to evoke a sense of purity, eco-friendliness, and connection with nature.

Brand Fit: As a sub-brand of Herbal Essences, Bio:Renew aligns perfectly with the parent brand's core values and positioning. Both brands prioritize the use of natural ingredients and the promotion of sustainable practices.

Bio:Renew focuses specifically on the use of bio-renewable ingredients, which are derived from renewable resources such as plants and minerals. This emphasis on sustainable sourcing and eco-friendly practices resonates with Herbal Essences' commitment to nature-inspired formulas and environmentally conscious production.

By incorporating bio-renewable ingredients, Herbal Essences Bio:Renew further enhances the brand's reputation for delivering products that are not only effective but also in harmony with nature. The use of these ingredients promotes a connection to the natural world and reinforces Herbal Essences' emphasis on botanical-based hair care.

The brand fit between Herbal Essences and Bio:Renew extends beyond their shared commitment to natural ingredients. Both brands embrace a joyful, sensory experience in their products, offering fragrant and indulgent formulations that delight the senses during hair care routines.

Additionally, the packaging design and brand imagery of Bio:Renew seamlessly align with the overall Herbal Essences brand aesthetic, maintaining consistency and recognition among consumers.

Outcomes and Impact: The launch of Herbal Essences Bio:Renew received positive reception from consumers seeking natural and sustainable hair care options. The sub-brand successfully captured a segment of health-conscious consumers who valued the brand's commitment to using botanicals and avoiding harsh chemicals. Sales of Bio:Renew products grew steadily, contributing to the overall success and expansion of Herbal Essences in the health and wellness market.

In conclusion, introducing sub-brands focusing on health and wellness is a strategic approach to cater to the increasing demand from health-conscious consumers. By developing sub-brands that specifically address the needs and preferences of this consumer segment, companies can tap into a growing market and differentiate themselves from competitors.

Introducing sub-brands that focus on health and wellness expands a company's product portfolio and enhances its brand image, demonstrating a commitment to promoting well-being and a healthier lifestyle. As the health and wellness trend continues to grow, companies prioritising this market segment through sub-brands are well-positioned to meet consumer expectations, drive customer loyalty, and capitalize on the opportunities the health-conscious consumer base presents.

* * *

23

Professional or Expertise Branding

Professional or expertise branding is a strategic approach in which a brand positions itself as a knowledgeable and authoritative figure in a specific industry or field. It involves leveraging the brand's expertise, experience, and thought leadership to establish a reputation as a trusted industry leader.

The significance of professional or expertise branding lies in its ability to differentiate a brand from competitors and enhance its credibility among customers. By positioning the brand as an expert, it gains a competitive advantage and becomes the go-to choice for customers seeking specialized knowledge, solutions, or services. It helps build trust, instils confidence, and fosters long-term customer relationships.

Through professional branding, a brand can showcase its deep understanding of the industry, its ability to provide innovative solutions, and its commitment to staying ahead of industry trends. This positioning attracts customers who value expertise and are willing to invest in products or services that offer superior knowledge and insights.

Furthermore, professional branding allows a brand to have a distinct voice and authority within its industry. It opens doors for collaboration, partnerships, and thought leadership opportunities. It enables the brand to shape industry conversations, influence trends, and establish a strong presence in the market.

Overall, professional or expertise branding is a strategic tool for positioning a brand as an industry leader, building credibility, attracting customers seeking specialized knowledge, and gaining a competitive edge in the market.

Importance of Professional or Expertise Branding

Professional or Expertise branding plays a crucial role in establishing a brand's credibility, building trust among customers, and commanding higher prices for products or services. Here are some key reasons why professional branding is important:

1. Establishing Credibility: Professional branding positions the brand as an expert and leader in a specific industry or field. By showcasing the brand's knowledge, experience, and thought leadership, it establishes credibility and enhances the brand's reputation.

2. Building Trust and Loyalty: When a brand is recognized as an expert, customers trust its expertise and rely on its products or services. Professional branding fosters a sense of trust and reliability, leading to long-term customer relationships. Customers are more likely to be loyal to a brand they perceive as knowledgeable and experienced.

3. Commanding Higher Prices: A brand that is positioned as an industry leader can justify higher prices for its offerings. Customers are willing to pay a premium for products or services that are backed by expertise, specialized knowledge, and proven results. Professional branding helps create a perception of higher value, allowing the brand to command premium pricing.

4. Attracting Customers Seeking Expertise: Professional branding appeals to customers who are specifically seeking specialized expertise and solutions. These customers value the insights, knowledge, and guidance provided by industry leaders. By positioning the brand as an expert, it becomes an attractive choice for customers who prioritize expertise and are willing to invest in products or services that offer superior knowledge

and solutions.

5. Gaining a Competitive Advantage: Professional branding gives the brand a competitive edge by differentiating it from competitors. By establishing the brand as a leader in its industry or field, it creates a distinct identity and sets itself apart from others. Customers are more likely to choose a brand that is perceived as a knowledgeable expert, giving the brand a competitive advantage in the market.

By positioning the brand as an industry leader and expert, it creates a strong brand identity that resonates with customers and contributes to long-term success.

Identifying the Industry or Field of expertise

Identifying the industry or field in which the brand aims to establish expertise is a crucial step in developing a sub-brand for professional or expertise branding. Here is an overview of the process:

1. Assess Core Competencies: Start by assessing the brand's core competencies, strengths, and areas of expertise. Look at the brand's existing products, services, and capabilities to identify the areas where the brand excels and has a competitive advantage.

2. Market Research: Conduct thorough market research to identify industries or fields that align with the brand's core competencies and where there is a demand for specialized expertise. Look for market trends, customer needs, and emerging opportunities in different industries or fields.

3. Customer Analysis: Analyze the brand's target audience and customer base to understand their needs, pain points, and aspirations. Identify the industries or fields that directly relate to the target audience's interests and requirements.

4. Competitor Analysis: Study the competitive landscape to identify gaps or

opportunities where the brand can position itself as an industry leader. Assess the competitors' strengths, weaknesses, and market positioning to find a niche where the brand can establish its expertise.

5. Internal Assessment: Evaluate the brand's internal resources, expertise, and capabilities to determine if it has the necessary knowledge, skills, and infrastructure to establish itself as an expert in the identified industry or field. Identify any gaps that need to be filled through hiring, partnerships, or investments.

6. Strategic Fit: Consider the strategic fit between the brand's overall business objectives and the identified industry or field of expertise. Ensure that the chosen industry aligns with the brand's long-term vision, values, and growth aspirations.

7. Feasibility and Market Potential: Assess the feasibility and market potential of entering the identified industry or field. Consider factors such as market size, growth rate, competitive intensity, regulatory environment, and customer demand to determine if it is a viable and profitable opportunity.

8. Decision-making: Based on the analysis and evaluation, make an informed decision about the industry or field in which the brand aims to establish expertise. This decision should align with the brand's overall strategy, core competencies, customer needs, and market dynamics.

By following this process, brands can effectively identify the industry or field in which they can establish expertise and develop a sub-brand that positions them as leaders or experts in that specific domain. It ensures that the brand's expertise is relevant, valuable, and differentiated, ultimately attracting customers seeking specialized solutions and building a strong reputation as an industry authority.

Sub-brand Development Factors

When developing a sub-brand for professional or expertise branding, there are several key points to consider. These include:

1. Clear Brand Positioning: Define the brand's positioning within the industry or field of expertise. Determine the unique value proposition, competitive advantage, and key differentiators that set the brand apart from competitors.
2. Target Audience: Identify the specific target audience within the industry or field. Understand their needs, pain points, aspirations, and preferences to tailor the sub-brand's messaging, offerings, and customer experience to effectively resonate with them.
3. Expertise and Knowledge: Ensure that the brand possesses the necessary expertise, knowledge, and skills to establish credibility and authority in the chosen industry or field. Invest in continuous learning, training, and development to stay ahead of industry trends and advancements.
4. Specialized Offerings: Develop specialized products, services, or solutions that address the unique needs and challenges of the target audience. Create offerings that showcase the brand's expertise, innovation, and ability to provide superior solutions.
5. Thought Leadership: Establish the brand as a thought leader and industry authority by sharing valuable insights, research, and expertise through various channels such as blogs, articles, white papers, webinars, and speaking engagements. Demonstrate a deep understanding of the industry and contribute to its advancement.
6. Brand Identity: Create a sub-brand identity that aligns with the main brand but also reflects the expertise and positioning within the specific industry or field. Design a visual identity, brand messaging, and tone of voice that communicates professionalism, knowledge, and trust.
7. Partnerships and Collaborations: Seek partnerships and collaborations with other industry leaders, experts, or associations to further enhance the sub-brand's credibility and reach. Collaborative efforts can include

joint ventures, co-branded initiatives, or strategic alliances that amplify the brand's expertise.

8. Marketing and Communication Strategy: Develop a comprehensive marketing and communication strategy to effectively promote the sub-brand's expertise and offerings. Utilize targeted channels such as industry publications, digital platforms, social media, events, and industry-specific networks to reach the target audience.

9. Customer Experience: Design a seamless and exceptional customer experience that reflects the brand's expertise and commitment to customer satisfaction. Focus on personalized interactions, efficient service delivery, and ongoing support to build long-term relationships and loyalty.

10. Monitoring and Adaptation: Continuously monitor market trends, customer feedback, and industry advancements to stay relevant and adapt the sub-brand's offerings and strategies accordingly. Regularly evaluate the effectiveness of the sub-brand in establishing expertise and make necessary adjustments as needed.

By considering these key points, brands can successfully develop a sub-brand for professional or expertise branding. This allows them to position themselves as industry leaders, attract a specific target audience seeking specialized solutions, and differentiate themselves in a competitive marketplace.

Example 01: IBM's Watson

IBM is a renowned technology company known for its expertise in various fields, including artificial intelligence (AI) and cognitive computing. In 2011, IBM introduced a sub-brand called Watson, which was developed to position the company as a leader in the AI industry and showcase its expertise in advanced cognitive technologies. Watson is an artificial intelligence (AI) system that combines advanced analytics, natural language processing, and machine learning capabilities to provide cognitive computing solutions.

Identification of Opportunity: IBM recognized the growing demand for advanced AI technologies and the potential they held for transforming industries such as healthcare, finance, and customer service. Seeing an opportunity to leverage its expertise in AI and cognitive computing, IBM embarked on creating a sub-brand that could cater to these emerging needs.

Objective: IBM's objective with the Watson sub-brand was to demonstrate the power and potential of AI technology and position IBM as a thought leader in the field. They aimed to show how AI could revolutionize industries and solve complex problems by leveraging Watson's advanced capabilities.

Implementation: IBM invested substantial resources in research and development to build the Watson platform. The company assembled a team of experts in AI, natural language processing, and machine learning to develop the underlying technology and algorithms that power Watson's cognitive capabilities. To establish the Watson sub-brand and build thought leadership, IBM took several other strategic steps:

1. Jeopardy! Challenge: IBM created significant buzz by showcasing Watson's capabilities in a high-profile event, Jeopardy! Challenge. Watson competed against former champions of the popular quiz show and emerged victorious, demonstrating its ability to understand and answer complex questions in natural language.

2. Thought Leadership Content: IBM invested in thought leadership content to educate the market about AI and Watson's capabilities. They published research papers, case studies, and white papers, highlighting the applications of Watson in different domains. IBM also actively participated in industry conferences, events, and webinars, where their experts shared insights and expertise.

3. Developer Community Engagement: IBM recognized the importance of engaging with developers and fostering a community around Watson. They launched the Watson Developer Community, providing developers with tools, resources, and support to build applications and solutions using Watson's AI technology. This helped in expanding the ecosystem around Watson and attracting innovative use cases.

4. Strategic Partnerships: To enhance the reach and applicability of Watson, IBM formed strategic partnerships with leading organizations and institutions. These partnerships allowed Watson to tap into industry-specific expertise and data, enabling it to provide tailored solutions and insights to professionals in those domains.

5. Application in Different Industries: IBM positioned Watson as a versatile platform that could be applied across various industries. It demonstrated the potential of Watson's cognitive computing by showcasing its ability to analyze vast amounts of data, understand complex language, and provide valuable insights to professionals in fields like healthcare, finance, retail, and more.

6. Industry-Specific Offerings: IBM developed industry-specific solutions and services under the Watson sub-brand. For instance, Watson Health offers AI-powered healthcare solutions that help medical professionals analyze patient data, assist in diagnoses, and provide personalized treatment recommendations. Similarly, Watson Financial Services offers AI solutions for financial institutions to enhance risk assessment, fraud detection, and customer service.

7. Expertise and Reputation: IBM's long-standing reputation as a leader in technology and innovation lent credibility to the Watson sub-brand. The company's deep expertise in AI and its track record of delivering cutting-edge solutions instilled confidence in customers and professionals looking to leverage cognitive computing in their respective fields.

8. Continuous Innovation: IBM continues to invest in the advancement of Watson, continually improving its capabilities and expanding its range of applications. The company encourages collaboration with developers, data scientists, and domain experts to explore new use cases and foster innovation within the Watson ecosystem.

In 2013, IBM launched a sub-brand called IBM Watson Health. The IBM Watson Health sub-brand is focused on using Watson to improve healthcare. The sub-brand offers a variety of products and services, including:

- **Watson for Oncology:** This product uses Watson to help oncologists diagnose and treat cancer.
- **Watson for Genomics:** This product uses Watson to help researchers understand the human genome.
- **Watson for Drug Discovery:** This product uses Watson to help drug developers discover new drugs.

The IBM Watson Health sub-brand has been successful in helping IBM to differentiate its products from the competition. The sub-brand has also helped IBM to attract new customers in the healthcare industry.

Outcomes and Impact: IBM's strategic approach in developing the Watson sub-brand yielded remarkable results. Through the Watson sub-brand, IBM established itself as a thought leader in the AI industry, showcasing its expertise and leadership in cognitive computing through the success of the Jeopardy! challenge and the deployment of Watson in various industries. This led to increased industry adoption of AI technology, as organizations partnered with IBM to leverage Watson's capabilities for a wide range of applications, from healthcare diagnostics to financial analysis. Watson's advanced AI capabilities and deep understanding of industries also helped differentiate IBM from its competitors, positioning the company as a trusted partner for organizations seeking innovative AI-powered solutions. Furthermore, the success of the Watson sub-brand contributed to IBM's revenue growth, as businesses across industries turned to IBM for their expertise and solutions, driving demand and generating revenue.

The development and introduction of the Watson sub-brand enabled IBM to establish thought leadership, drive industry adoption of AI technology, differentiate their brand, and generate substantial business opportunities in the evolving field of cognitive computing.

Example 02: General Electric's GE Aviation

General Electric (GE) is a multinational conglomerate known for its expertise in various industries, including aviation. GE Aviation, a subsidiary of GE, successfully developed and introduced a sub-brand focused on professional or expertise branding within the aviation industry.

Identification of Opportunity: General Electric recognized the significant growth potential in the aviation industry and the need for specialized expertise in aircraft engine manufacturing and services. Leveraging its existing capabilities in engineering and technology, GE identified an opportunity to create a dedicated sub-brand that would cater specifically to the aviation sector.

Objective: GE Aviation aimed to position itself as a leader in the aviation industry by establishing expertise and thought leadership in aircraft engines and related technologies. The sub-brand was developed to showcase GE Aviation's specialized knowledge, innovative solutions, and commitment to advancing the field of aviation.

Implementation: To achieve its objective, GE Aviation implemented several strategies:

1. Research and Development: GE Aviation invested heavily in research and development to drive innovation and advance aviation technology. They focused on developing state-of-the-art aircraft engines and related systems, employing cutting-edge materials, designs, and manufacturing processes. This commitment to R&D showcased their expertise and positioned them as leaders in the field.

2. Innovative Engine Technologies: GE Aviation introduced several groundbreaking engine technologies under its sub-brand. Notable examples include the GE90, the world's most powerful jet engine at the time of its introduction, and the GEnx, an engine that significantly reduced fuel consumption and emissions. These innovative technologies helped establish GE Aviation as a leader in the industry and set new benchmarks for performance and efficiency.

3. Strategic Partnerships: GE Aviation formed strategic partnerships with

major aircraft manufacturers, airlines, and industry stakeholders. These collaborations allowed them to co-create and integrate their advanced technologies into aircraft platforms, demonstrating their expertise and influencing industry standards. The partnerships also provided knowledge-sharing opportunities and showcased GE Aviation's thought leadership.

4. Industry Events and Conferences: GE Aviation actively participated in industry events, conferences, and trade shows. They showcased their latest innovations, presented technical papers, and engaged with industry professionals and stakeholders. These platforms enabled them to share their expertise, build relationships, and establish credibility as an industry leader. It solidified GE Aviation's position as a trusted authority in the field.

5. Customer-Centric Approach: GE Aviation focused on understanding and addressing customer needs. They collaborated closely with airlines and aircraft operators to develop customized solutions that optimized performance, efficiency, and reliability. This customer-centric approach highlighted their expertise in delivering tailored solutions and solidified their reputation as a trusted partner.

6. Comprehensive Service and Support: GE Aviation recognized that the aviation industry required advanced engine technologies and comprehensive service and support solutions. The sub-brand established a global network of maintenance, repair, and overhaul (MRO) facilities to provide ongoing engine support and maintenance. This included services such as engine diagnostics, repairs, spare parts provisioning, and fleet management solutions.

7. Digital Transformation: GE Aviation embraced digital transformation and developed advanced digital solutions under its sub-brand. These included tools and technologies for predictive maintenance, real-time engine monitoring, and data analytics. The integration of digital capabilities enabled GE Aviation to offer enhanced performance monitoring, reduced downtime, and improved customer operational efficiency.

8. Industry Leadership and Reputation: GE Aviation's commitment to

innovation, expertise, and customer satisfaction helped the sub-brand establish a strong leadership position in the aviation industry. Its reputation for reliability, performance, and cutting-edge technologies made GE Aviation a preferred choice for aircraft manufacturers and operators worldwide.

9. Global Presence and Customer Base: GE Aviation expanded its global presence by establishing manufacturing facilities, MRO centres, and customer support locations in key aviation hubs worldwide. This global footprint allowed the sub-brand to serve diverse customers, including commercial airlines, military organizations, and business jet operators.

Outcomes and Impact: GE Aviation's strategic efforts in developing and introducing the sub-brand resulted in significant outcomes. They established themselves as an industry leader in providing aircraft engines and related technologies, positioning GE Aviation as a go-to solution provider in the aviation industry. The sub-brand allowed them to showcase continuous innovation and technological advancements, demonstrating their commitment to pushing the boundaries of aviation technology. This led to global recognition and trust within the industry, as their sub-brand became synonymous with expertise, reliability, and performance, earning the business of major airlines, aircraft manufacturers, and operators worldwide. The success of the sub-brand contributed to GE Aviation's business growth, securing contracts, expanding aftermarket services, and establishing long-term partnerships. Overall, the sub-brand's reputation and expertise drove revenue generation and market expansion for GE Aviation.

Through its expertise branding efforts, GE Aviation solidified its position as an industry leader, fostered innovation and technological advancements, gained global recognition, and achieved substantial business growth within the aviation industry.

In summary, developing and introducing a sub-brand focused on professional or expertise branding provide businesses with significant benefits. By establishing credibility and trust, businesses can position themselves as industry leaders and attract customers seeking specialized knowledge and solutions. The sub-brand's ability to command premium prices reflects the value and expertise it brings to the market. Moreover, by fostering innovation and thought leadership within the chosen industry or field, businesses can stay ahead of the competition and drive continued growth. Through this strategic approach, businesses can differentiate themselves and capitalize on their unique strengths and expertise, ultimately solidifying their position as leaders in their respective industries.

* * *

24

Ethical Sourcing and Fair Trade

E thical sourcing and fair trade are concepts that promote responsible and sustainable business practices. Ethical sourcing involves ensuring that products are obtained or produced in a way that aligns with social and environmental standards. Fair trade, on the other hand, focuses on creating equitable trade relationships and providing fair wages and working conditions for producers, especially in developing countries.

These concepts aim to address concerns such as exploitation, environmental degradation, and economic inequality in global supply chains. Ethical sourcing and fair trade practices prioritize transparency, traceability, and accountability throughout the production process. They seek to minimize harm to the environment, protect workers' rights, and support local communities.

Brands that adopt ethical sourcing and fair trade practices demonstrate their commitment to sustainability, social responsibility, and ethical business conduct. These initiatives not only benefit the environment and communities but also resonate with a growing number of consumers who prioritize conscious consumption and seek products that align with their values.

The importance of ethical consumerism has grown significantly due to several factors. Firstly, there is increased awareness and concern among consumers about the social and environmental impacts of their purchasing decisions. People are becoming more conscious of issues such as climate change, human rights abuses, and unfair labor practices. They want to support brands that align with their values and contribute to positive change.

Secondly, the rise of social media and digital connectivity has empowered consumers to voice their opinions and share information about brands' practices. This increased transparency has made it easier for consumers to hold companies accountable and make informed choices about the products they buy.

Thirdly, there is a shift in consumer demographics, with younger generations like millennials and Gen Z emerging as significant consumer groups. These generations are known for their strong social and environmental consciousness and are willing to pay a premium for products and brands that prioritize sustainability, fairness, and social responsibility.

Moreover, governments and regulatory bodies are increasingly implementing stricter regulations and standards related to ethical sourcing, fair trade, and sustainability. This puts pressure on brands to adopt responsible practices or risk facing reputational damage and legal consequences.

In a nutshell, the demand for ethical and sustainable products and brands is growing rapidly. Companies that prioritize ethical sourcing, fair trade, and social responsibility not only meet the expectations of conscious consumers but also gain a competitive edge, enhance their brand reputation, and contribute to a more sustainable and equitable future.

Example 01: Ben & Jerry's and its Sub-Brand, Fairtrade Ice Cream

Ben & Jerry's, a well-known ice cream brand, has established itself as a leader in ethical sourcing and fair trade practices. One of its successful sub-brands that promotes these values is its line of Fairtrade ice creams.

Commitment to Fair Trade: Ben & Jerry's recognized the importance of promoting fair trade within the ice cream industry and decided to create a dedicated sub-brand that embodies these principles. Fairtrade practices mean ensuring that farmers and workers receive fair compensation for their products.

Fairtrade Sourcing: The Fairtrade sub-brand of Ben & Jerry's focuses on sourcing ingredients, such as cocoa, coffee, and vanilla, from certified fair trade cooperatives around the world. This ensures that farmers receive fair prices for their crops, which helps improve their livelihoods and supports sustainable agriculture practices.

Fairtrade Certification: Fairtrade Ice Cream by Ben & Jerry's is certified by Fairtrade International, an organization that sets rigorous social, economic, and environmental standards. This certification ensures that the ingredients used in the ice cream, such as cocoa, sugar, and vanilla, are sourced from farmers who are paid fair prices and work under ethical labour conditions.

Direct Relationships with Farmers: Ben & Jerry's establishes direct relationships with small-scale farmers and cooperatives in developing countries. These relationships enable the company to understand the challenges faced by farmers and provide them with the necessary support and resources. By working directly with farmers, Ben & Jerry's contributes to the long-term sustainability of their communities.

Fairtrade Premiums: Fairtrade Ice Cream supports farming communities by paying fair trade premiums. These premiums are additional funds that go directly to the farmers and workers, allowing them to invest in community development projects, such as education, healthcare, and infrastructure improvements. The sub-brand actively contributes to improving the well-being of farmers and their families.

Transparency and Traceability: Ben & Jerry's maintains transparency in its sourcing practices by providing information about the origins of its ingredients. The company strives to ensure that consumers can trace the journey of the ingredients from farm to scoop. This transparency builds trust and allows consumers to make informed choices that align with their values.

Advocacy and Campaigns: Ben & Jerry's Fairtrade Ice Cream actively engages in advocacy and awareness campaigns to promote fair trade and ethical sourcing. The sub-brand uses its platform to raise awareness about the importance of fair trade and the impact it has on farmers and communities. Ben & Jerry's advocates for fair trade policies and encourages other companies to adopt similar practices.

Collaboration with Stakeholders: Ben & Jerry's collaborates with various stakeholders, including fair trade organizations, NGOs, and farmers' coopera-tives. These collaborations help strengthen the fair trade movement, share best practices, and drive positive change within the industry. By working together, Ben & Jerry's and its partners amplify their impact and create a more equitable and sustainable supply chain.

Quality and Flavor Innovation: Fairtrade Ice Cream by Ben & Jerry's main-tains the company's commitment to high-quality ice cream and innovative flavours. The sub-brand offers a wide range of delicious flavours, ensuring that consumers can enjoy their favourite treats while supporting fair trade and ethical practices.

Outcomes and Impact: By developing the Fairtrade sub-brand, Ben & Jerry's achieves several objectives. First, it demonstrates its commitment to social justice and responsible business practices. This resonates with consumers who prioritize fairness and sustainability when making purchasing decisions.

Second, the Fairtrade sub-brand differentiates Ben & Jerry's from its competitors in the ice cream market. It positions the brand as a leader in ethical sourcing, giving consumers a reason to choose Ben & Jerry's over other options.

Moreover, the Fairtrade sub-brand enhances Ben & Jerry's brand reputation and strengthens customer loyalty. By supporting fair trade practices, the brand aligns itself with the values and beliefs of its target audience. Customers appreciate knowing that their ice cream purchases contribute to positive social and environmental impact.

The Fairtrade sub-brand also serves as a platform for raising awareness and educating consumers about fair trade issues. Ben & Jerry's actively communicates its commitment to fair trade through packaging, marketing materials, and collaborations with fair trade organizations. This helps to increase consumer understanding and engagement with the brand's values.

In summary, Ben & Jerry's Fairtrade sub-brand exemplifies how a company can successfully develop a sub-brand focused on ethical sourcing and fair trade. By prioritizing fair compensation for farmers and supporting sustainable agriculture, Ben & Jerry's creates a unique selling proposition, builds customer loyalty, and strengthens its brand reputation as a socially responsible company in the highly competitive ice cream market.

Example 02: Nestlé's Nespresso

Nestlé, a multinational food and beverage company, successfully developed a sub-brand called Nespresso, which focuses on providing high-quality coffee and promoting sustainability in the coffee industry.

Nespresso is a premium coffee brand offering a range of coffee machines and capsules. It positions itself as a luxury coffee experience, emphasizing the convenience and quality of its products. Nespresso's unique selling proposition lies in its sustainability and responsible sourcing commitment.

Sustainable Coffee Sourcing: Nespresso is dedicated to sourcing coffee beans through sustainable practices. The company works closely with coffee farmers around the world, particularly in regions such as South America and Africa, to ensure the highest quality beans while promoting sustainable agricultural methods. Nespresso's sub-brand emphasizes the importance of responsible sourcing to support coffee farmers and protect the environment.

AAA Sustainable Quality Program: Nespresso established the AAA Sustainable Quality Program to foster long-term relationships with coffee farmers and improve the sustainability of their practices. The program provides training and technical assistance to farmers, helping them enhance the quality and sustainability of their coffee production. Through this initiative, Nespresso supports farmers in implementing environmentally friendly practices and ensures fair working conditions.

Fairtrade and Farmer Welfare: Nespresso actively participates in fair trade practices by working directly with farmers and providing fair prices for their coffee beans. The sub-brand supports the economic empowerment of farmers, ensuring that they receive a fair share of the value generated throughout the coffee supply chain. Nespresso's commitment to fair trade helps improve the livelihoods of coffee farmers and their communities.

Reviving Coffee Farming Regions: Nespresso recognizes the importance of revitalizing coffee farming regions facing declining productivity and environmental degradation. The sub-brand invests in long-term projects to restore and preserve coffee farming landscapes. Nespresso collaborates with local communities, governments, and nonprofit organizations to implement initiatives that enhance the resilience and sustainability of coffee farming regions.

Aluminum Capsule Recycling: Nespresso promotes sustainable practices beyond sourcing coffee beans. The sub-brand introduced an aluminium capsule recycling program to minimize waste and promote circular economy principles. Nespresso encourages consumers to return used capsules for recycling, ensuring that valuable materials are reused in the production of new capsules.

Transparency and Traceability: Nespresso maintains transparency in its supply chain by providing information about the origins of its coffee beans. The sub-brand enables consumers to trace their coffee back to the specific farms and regions where it was produced. Nespresso's commitment to traceability builds trust and allows consumers to make informed choices that support ethical sourcing and fair trade.

Partnerships and Sustainability Initiatives: Nespresso collaborates with various stakeholders, including coffee farmers, nonprofit organizations, and industry experts, to drive sustainability initiatives. The sub-brand actively engages in partnerships to implement programs that support biodiversity conservation, climate resilience, and social welfare in coffee-producing regions. Nespresso's collaborative approach amplifies its impact and drives positive change within the coffee industry.

Outcomes and Impact: The Nespresso sub-brand has been successful in several ways. First, it has positioned Nestlé as a leader in the premium coffee market. By offering a superior coffee experience and promoting sustainability, Nespresso attracts discerning consumers who value quality and ethical practices.

Second, the sub-brand has created a strong sense of brand loyalty among its customers. Nespresso's Club membership program provides exclusive benefits, such as personalized coffee recommendations, limited-edition coffee releases, and recycling initiatives. These efforts contribute to a community of loyal customers who appreciate the brand's commitment to sustainability and enjoy the unique Nespresso coffee experience.

Lastly, Nespresso's sub-brand strategy has had a positive impact on the coffee industry as a whole. By promoting sustainable practices and fair trade, Nespresso sets an example for other coffee companies, encouraging them to prioritize ethical sourcing and environmental responsibility. The sub-brand's initiatives have raised awareness about the importance of supporting coffee farmers and protecting the environment, driving positive change in the industry.

In summary, Nestlé's Nespresso sub-brand exemplifies the successful development and introduction of a sub-brand focused on ethical sourcing, sustainability, and delivering a premium coffee experience.

In conclusion, establishing sub-brands that promote ethical sourcing, fair trade practices, or support local communities is a strategic approach that allows companies to align their brand values with consumer demands for sustainability, fairness, and social responsibility. These sub-brands contribute to positive social and environmental impacts and create a competitive advantage by appealing to conscious consumers. By prioritizing ethical practices and engaging in fair trade, companies can build trust, enhance their brand reputation, and foster customer loyalty. Additionally, supporting local communities through sub-brands fosters a sense of connection and goodwill, further strengthening the brand-consumer relationship.

* * *

25

Generational Marketing

Generational marketing is an approach that involves tailoring marketing strategies and messages to specific generational cohorts based on their shared experiences, values, behaviours, and preferences. Each generation is influenced by different social, economic, and technological factors during their formative years, which shape their attitudes, beliefs, and consumer behaviors. Understanding these generational differences is crucial for businesses to effectively reach and engage with different age groups.

The significance of generational marketing lies in the fact that each generation has unique characteristics and needs that impact their purchasing decisions. By understanding these nuances, brands can create targeted marketing campaigns, products, and services that resonate with specific generations. This approach allows businesses to connect with their target audience on a deeper level, build stronger brand affinity, and increase customer loyalty.

Generational marketing recognizes that different age groups have distinct values, communication preferences, and consumption habits. For example, Millennials (born between 1981 and 1996) are often characterized as tech-savvy, socially conscious, and seeking authentic experiences. Gen Z (born between 1997 and 2012) is known for its digital nativeness, focus on social justice, and preference for personalized interactions. Baby Boomers (born between 1946 and 1964) may prioritize reliability, convenience, and brand reputation.

By tailoring marketing efforts to specific generations, businesses can effectively communicate their brand message, address the unique needs and aspirations of each generation, and create a more personalized and engaging customer experience. This can lead to increased brand awareness, customer acquisition, and long-term customer loyalty. Moreover, generational marketing allows companies to stay relevant in an ever-changing marketplace by adapting their strategies to the evolving preferences and behaviors of different age groups.

Understanding Different Generations

In today's diverse marketplace, businesses need to have a deep understanding of different generational cohorts to effectively target and engage their desired audience. Let's explore the key generational cohorts and their unique characteristics, values, preferences, and purchasing behaviors:

Baby Boomers (Born 1946-1964):

- Baby Boomers are known for their strong work ethic, financial stability, and traditional values. They are often associated with loyalty and brand trust.
- They prioritize personal relationships, family, and security. They value quality and are willing to spend on products and services that align with their values.
- Baby Boomers tend to prefer in-person shopping experiences and value face-to-face customer service. They are less tech-savvy but are increasingly adapting to digital platforms.
- They are loyal customers who appreciate well-established brands. They are willing to invest in products and services that provide convenience, comfort, and reliability.

Generation X (Born 1965-1980):

- Generation X is often characterized as independent, self-reliant, and adaptable. They are known for being sceptical and value work-life balance.
- They value authenticity, individualism, and flexibility. They seek products and services that cater to their busy lifestyles and offer convenience.
- Generation X is comfortable with both online and offline shopping. They appreciate personalized experiences and value brands that understand their unique needs.
- They conduct extensive research before making a purchase decision. They are price-conscious but are willing to invest in products that offer value and meet their specific needs.

Millennials (Born 1981-1996):

- Millennials are a tech-savvy generation that values experiences, diversity, and social causes. They are known for their digital connectivity and desire for work-life balance.
- They prioritize authenticity, sustainability, and social responsibility. They seek brands that align with their values and actively contribute to a positive impact.
- Millennials heavily rely on digital platforms for information, research, and purchases. They appreciate brands that engage with them through social media and offer seamless online experiences.
- Millennials are influenced by peer recommendations, online reviews, and social media influencers. They are open to trying new brands and are early adopters of new technologies.

Generation Z (Born 1997-Present):

- Generation Z, also known as "Digital Natives," grew up in a highly connected world. They are diverse, socially conscious, and entrepreneurial.
- They value authenticity, inclusivity, and sustainability. They seek brands

that demonstrate transparency, engage with social issues, and provide personalized experiences.

- Generation Z is highly active on social media platforms and relies on them for product discovery and recommendations. They expect seamless omnichannel experiences.
- They are more price-conscious than previous generations and are more likely to compare prices online. They prioritize brands that align with their values and offer unique, innovative products.

The Impact of Each Generation on Consumer Trends and Market Dynamics

Each generational cohort has a significant impact on consumer trends and market dynamics. Their unique characteristics, values, and preferences influence the demand for specific products, services, and experiences. For example:

- Millennials and Generation Z's digital fluency and preference for online shopping have driven the growth of e-commerce and the need for seamless digital experiences.
- Baby Boomers' strong purchasing power and preference for personalized customer service have influenced the focus on quality, reliability, and customer-centric approaches.
- Generation X's need for work-life balance and convenience has led to the rise of flexible service models and products that cater to their busy lifestyles.

Understanding the impact of each generation helps businesses tailor their marketing strategies, product offerings, and customer experiences to effectively engage and cater to their target audience. By aligning with the values, preferences, and behaviors of different generations, businesses can adapt to changing market dynamics, stay relevant, and capture the loyalty and trust of their desired customer base.

Importance of Targeting Different Generations

Targeting specific generations is crucial for brands due to several reasons:

Size, Purchasing Power, and Influence: Each generational group represents a significant portion of the consumer population, with their own distinct purchasing power and influence. By targeting specific generations, brands can tap into large consumer segments and leverage their buying potential to drive business growth.

- Baby Boomers: As one of the largest generations, Baby Boomers possess substantial purchasing power and are still active consumers. Ignoring this demographic means missing out on a sizable market.
- Generation X: Though smaller in size than Baby Boomers and Millennials, Generation X holds considerable purchasing power and often occupies influential positions in their careers. They can drive trends and influence the buying decisions of other generations.
- Millennials: The largest generational cohort, Millennials have a significant impact on consumer trends and possess substantial purchasing power. They are known for their brand loyalty and willingness to spend on products aligned with their values.
- Generation Z: With the oldest members entering adulthood, Generation Z represents an emerging market segment. They may have lower purchasing power individually but have a strong influence over family spending and are early adopters of new products and trends.

Evolving Consumer Expectations and Demands: Each generation has its own set of expectations and demands, shaped by their unique experiences, values, and technological advancements during their formative years. To effectively engage and retain customers, brands must understand and cater to these evolving expectations.

By targeting specific generations, brands can tailor their marketing messages, product offerings, and customer experiences to meet the unique needs and expectations of each group. This enables them to establish stronger connections, foster brand loyalty, and gain a competitive edge in the market.

Example 01: Coca-Cola

Coca-Cola is a globally recognized brand that has successfully launched subbrands targeting different generations. The company recognized the importance of catering to various age groups' unique preferences and demands, allowing them to maintain their relevance and connect with consumers across generations.

1. Coca-Cola Classic for Baby Boomers: Coca-Cola Classic has been a longstanding flagship product of the company, appealing to the nostalgic sentiments of Baby Boomers who grew up with the brand. Coca-Cola Classic's timeless taste and iconic branding resonate with this generation, invoking a sense of familiarity and fond memories.
2. Diet Coke for Generation X: As Generation X placed greater emphasis on health and wellness, Coca-Cola introduced Diet Coke to cater to their preferences. Diet Coke provided a low-calorie option for health-conscious consumers while still delivering the distinct taste and experience associated with Coca-Cola.
3. Coca-Cola Zero Sugar for Millennials: Coca-Cola Zero Sugar was developed to capture the attention and loyalty of Millennials. This sub-brand aimed to provide a sugar-free alternative that aligned with Millennials' desire for healthier choices without compromising on taste. Coca-Cola Zero Sugar utilized modern marketing strategies, such as digital campaigns and influencer partnerships, to engage with this tech-savvy generation.

4. Coca-Cola Energy for Generation Z: Recognizing the energy drink trend and the emerging influence of Generation Z, Coca-Cola introduced Coca-Cola Energy. This sub-brand combined the familiar Coca-Cola taste with added caffeine and energy-boosting ingredients to cater to the needs of younger consumers seeking functional beverages.

By launching these sub-brands, Coca-Cola effectively targeted different generations and tapped into their unique preferences, lifestyles, and purchasing behaviours. Each sub-brand was carefully positioned to address the specific needs and values of the respective generation, allowing Coca-Cola to expand its consumer base and maintain relevance in an evolving market.

Example 02: American Eagle Outfitters, Sub-brand: Aerie

American Eagle Outfitters, a popular apparel retailer, successfully launched the sub-brand Aerie to target a different generation of consumers. Aerie is a lingerie and loungewear brand that focuses on body positivity, inclusivity, and promoting natural beauty. It caters specifically to the Millennial and Gen Z demographics, positioning itself as a brand that celebrates real women and encourages self-acceptance.

Facing increasing competition from other clothing retailers and challenges in attracting and retaining Millennial customers, American Eagle Outfitters recognized the need to address younger consumers' unique preferences and values. In 2014, they launched Aerie as a sub-brand, providing a solution that would resonate with the target demographic.

Aerie differentiates itself through its body-positive marketing campaigns, featuring unretouched photos of models of different sizes, shapes, and ethnicities. By challenging traditional beauty standards and embracing diversity, Aerie aligns with the values of authenticity, inclusivity, and positive body image that Millennials and Gen Z consumers prioritize.

With its empowering messaging, comfortable products, and inclusive sizing options, Aerie offers a distinct shopping experience. The sub-brand operates standalone stores and maintains a separate online presence, allowing it to cultivate its own brand identity while leveraging American Eagle's established reputation and resources.

Aerie's success can be attributed to its ability to connect with younger consumers on a deeper level. Through active engagement on social media platforms and initiatives like the #AerieREAL campaign, Aerie fosters a community of followers who resonate with its message. Influencer marketing and partnerships with body-positive advocates further strengthen its connection with the target audience.

The launch of Aerie has allowed American Eagle Outfitters to tap into the evolving consumer mindset and preferences of younger generations. By creating a sub-brand that aligns with the values and aspirations of Millennials and Gen Z, Aerie has carved out a distinct market segment and established a loyal customer base. Its success not only contributes to American Eagle Outfitters' overall growth but also serves as a testament to the power of targeting different generations with a sub-brand that resonates with their values and aspirations.

In conclusion, launching sub-brands that specifically target different generations is a powerful strategy for brands to effectively engage with diverse consumer groups. By understanding the unique characteristics, preferences, and purchasing behaviours of each generation, brands can tailor their offerings and experiences to meet their needs and preferences. This targeted approach enables brands to establish stronger connections, build brand loyalty, and capitalize on the immense market potential presented by each generation. By embracing generational marketing, brands can position themselves as relevant and influential players in the ever-changing consumer landscape.

* * *

26

Cultural or Regional Branding

C reating sub-brands that align with specific cultural or regional identities is a strategic approach in brand-building that emphasizes the importance of fostering a deep sense of connection and authenticity with target audiences. By tailoring sub-brands to resonate with the unique values, traditions, customs, and aspirations of specific cultural or regional groups, companies can establish a genuine bond with consumers and build long-lasting relationships. This approach recognizes that consumers are seeking brands that not only understand their cultural context but also celebrate and respect their identity. By embracing diversity and localizing their offerings, companies can effectively connect with diverse markets, enhance brand loyalty, and differentiate themselves in a competitive landscape. The significance of creating sub-brands that align with cultural or regional identities lies in the ability to establish an emotional connection, build trust, and showcase an authentic understanding of the unique needs and aspirations of specific consumer segments.

Understanding Cultural and Regional Identities

Understanding the cultural and regional nuances of target markets is crucial for successful brand expansion. Each culture and region has its own set of values, traditions, customs, and unique identities that shape consumer behaviours and preferences. By gaining a deep understanding of these aspects, companies can tailor their brand messages, products, and experiences to resonate with the specific needs and aspirations of local consumers.

Cultural sensitivity plays a pivotal role in brand expansion as it demonstrates respect for the cultural values and traditions of the target market. It involves adapting marketing strategies, communication styles, and visual elements to align with the cultural norms and preferences of the local audience. By showing sensitivity and cultural awareness, brands can avoid cultural missteps and establish trust and credibility with consumers.

Localization is another essential aspect of successful brand expansion. It involves customizing products, services, and marketing efforts to suit the specific preferences and requirements of the target market. This can include adapting packaging, flavours, sizing, pricing, and distribution channels to align with local norms and consumer expectations. By localizing their offerings, brands demonstrate their commitment to meeting the market's unique needs and enhancing their relevance and appeal to consumers.

Understanding the cultural and regional nuances of target markets and incorporating cultural sensitivity and localization in brand expansion strategies is vital for building strong connections, driving customer loyalty, and achieving sustainable growth in diverse markets.

Building Connection and Authenticity

Creating sub-brands that resonate with specific cultural or regional identities is a powerful way to establish a genuine connection with consumers. When brands align themselves with their target audience's cultural values, traditions, and identities, it creates a sense of authenticity that consumers can relate to and identify with.

Authenticity is vital in building trust, loyalty, and long-term consumer relationships. In today's saturated market, consumers are increasingly seeking brands that are transparent, genuine, and aligned with their own values. By developing sub-brands authentically representing their target market's cultural or regional identities, brands can establish a deep emotional connection and build trust with consumers.

When a sub-brand reflects and celebrates specific cultural or regional identities, it signals consumers that the brand understands and respects their unique experiences, aspirations, and perspectives. This cultural resonance creates an emotional bond and a sense of belonging, fostering consumer loyalty and advocacy.

Authenticity also helps brands differentiate themselves in a crowded marketplace. By showcasing a genuine commitment to their target audience's cultural values and identities, brands can stand out and attract like-minded consumers seeking products and experiences that align with their own cultural or regional identity.

Moreover, an authentic connection with consumers can lead to long-term relationships and brand loyalty. When consumers feel that a brand truly understands and values their cultural or regional identity, they are more likely to become loyal customers and brand ambassadors, advocating for the brand within their communities.

In summary, creating sub-brands that resonate with specific cultural or regional identities helps establish a genuine connection with consumers by showcasing authenticity. By aligning with consumers' cultural values and identities, brands can build trust, foster loyalty, and develop long-term relationships, ultimately driving business growth and success.

Geographic vs Regional or Cultural Sub-brand

Creating a sub-brand for geographic positioning involves targeting specific geographic regions or locations with tailored products or marketing strategies. It focuses on adapting the brand to meet a particular geographic market's unique needs, preferences, and characteristics. This could involve factors such as language, culture, climate, or local regulations. The goal is to establish a strong presence and resonate with consumers in specific geographic areas.

On the other hand, creating a sub-brand for cultural and regional branding involves emphasizing a specific market's cultural identity, heritage, or regional characteristics. It aims to connect with consumers on a cultural or regional level by incorporating elements that reflect their values, traditions, or lifestyles. This approach recognizes that their cultural background and regional affiliations influence consumers' preferences and behaviours.

Geographic positioning focuses more on adapting to the geographic context, while cultural and regional branding emphasises connecting with consumers at a cultural or regional level. Geographic positioning may involve adjusting product features, marketing messages, or distribution channels to suit the unique characteristics of a particular location. Cultural and regional branding, on the other hand, may involve incorporating symbols, themes, or narratives that resonate with a specific market's cultural identity or regional pride.

Cultural and regional sub-branding emphasizes authenticity and seeks to establish an emotional connection with customers by recognizing and respecting their unique cultural identities. By tailoring products, messaging, and branding to specific cultural or regional preferences, companies show their commitment to understanding and appreciating their target audience's local customs, traditions, and values. This approach helps create a sense of familiarity, relatability, and trust, fostering a deeper emotional connection with customers who feel that the brand genuinely understands and respects their cultural or regional background.

To illustrate the difference, consider a global beverage company that creates a sub-brand for geographic positioning. In one region, they may adapt the flavour profile of their product to cater to local tastes and preferences. They may also create packaging designs incorporating elements specific to that geographic area, such as landmarks or language translations.

In contrast, if the company creates a sub-brand for cultural and regional branding, it may focus on celebrating the cultural heritage of different regions. They may introduce limited-edition flavours inspired by traditional local ingredients or partner with local artists to create unique packaging designs that showcase the region's art and craftsmanship.

Example 01: Nashville Hot Chicken

"Nashville Hot Chicken" is an excellent example of a sub-brand that emphasizes regional pride and cultural identity. Nashville Hot Chicken is a specific style of fried chicken that originated in Nashville, Tennessee. It is known for its spicy seasoning and unique flavour profile.

Nashville Hot Chicken has evolved beyond a mere spicy fried chicken dish; it has become a sub-brand that showcases the influence of cultural and regional identity within the culinary world.

The roots of Nashville Hot Chicken trace back to the African American community in Nashville, where it originated as a distinctive twist on traditional fried chicken. This culinary creation holds immense cultural significance, representing the convergence of flavours, traditions, and community.

To resonate with consumers, Nashville Hot Chicken embraced its cultural origins by highlighting its historical narrative and celebrating the African American heritage through branding. By showcasing the traditions and the people behind this iconic dish, the sub-brand established a genuine connection with customers seeking an authentic and immersive experience.

Its fiery flavour profile is at the core of Nashville Hot Chicken's appeal. The sub-brand carefully balances the intense spiciness with a unique blend of seasonings, resulting in a taste that cannot be replicated elsewhere. Perfecting the signature heat levels allows Nashville Hot Chicken sub-brands to deliver an immersive sensory experience that lingers in the minds and palates of customers.

Regional pride plays a pivotal role in the success of Nashville Hot Chicken sub-brands. They embody the spirit of Nashville by showcasing the city's vibrant culture, renowned music scene, and warm Southern hospitality. From the branding elements to the ambience of the restaurants, these sub-brands create an immersive environment that transports customers to the heart of Nashville, forging a powerful emotional connection.

While deeply rooted in Nashville, Nashville Hot Chicken sub-brands have expanded their reach beyond the city's borders. By maintaining authenticity and preserving the cultural essence, these sub-brands have successfully introduced Nashville's culinary gem to a global audience. Enthusiasts seeking genuine flavors and cultural experiences are drawn to the sub-brands, resulting in an expanded influence and recognition for Nashville Hot Chicken.

In summary, Nashville Hot Chicken serves as a prime example of a sub-brand that authentically represents cultural and regional identity. By embracing its roots, refining its flavors, cultivating a sense of place, and expanding its reach, Nashville Hot Chicken has become more than just a dish—it has become a symbol of Nashville's cultural legacy and an embodiment of its culinary heritage.

Example 02: Levi's "501 Original"

Levi's, a renowned denim brand, successfully created a sub-brand called "501 Original" that exemplifies cultural and regional branding. The "501 Original" sub-brand is an iconic product line that pays homage to Levi's classic and timeless jeans, particularly the original 501 model.

The Levi's 501 jeans hold a significant place in American fashion history and have become a symbol of American style and culture. The brand recognized the enduring appeal and cultural significance of the 501 jeans and decided to leverage this heritage by creating a sub-brand that specifically focuses on the original design and its connection to American culture.

The "501 Original" sub-brand emphasizes the brand's cultural heritage and celebrates its deep roots in American denim history. Levi's has successfully positioned the 501 jeans as a symbol of authenticity, ruggedness, and individuality that resonate with consumers seeking a sense of American nostalgia and style.

Levi's has used various strategies to promote the "501 Original" sub-brand and connect with consumers on a cultural and regional level. The brand has collaborated with influential artists, musicians, and cultural icons who embody the spirit of American culture, such as Bruce Springsteen and James Dean. These collaborations reinforce the sub-brand's connection to American heritage and contribute to its cultural appeal.

In addition to celebrity endorsements, Levi's has implemented marketing campaigns that evoke a sense of nostalgia and celebrate American culture. The brand often features images and videos showcasing the historical significance of the 501 jeans and their association with American icons, events, and lifestyles. This approach helps Levi's establish an emotional connection with consumers and reinforces the cultural and regional branding of the "501 Original" sub-brand.

Furthermore, Levi's has leveraged the customization and personalization trend in the fashion industry to strengthen the cultural branding of the "501 Original" sub-brand. The brand offers customization options that allow consumers to personalize their 501 jeans with patches, embroidery, and other unique elements. This customization aspect not only reflects the individuality of the American style but also allows consumers to express their own cultural and regional identities.

By creating the "501 Original" sub-brand, Levi's has successfully tapped into the cultural and regional significance of its iconic 501 jeans. The sub-brand's emphasis on American heritage, authenticity, and individuality has resonated with consumers who appreciate Levi's denim's cultural symbolism and timeless appeal.

In conclusion, creating sub-brands that resonate with specific cultural or regional identities is a powerful strategy to foster a sense of connection and authenticity. By understanding and embracing a target market's unique values, traditions, and preferences, brands can establish a deep connection with consumers. This connection builds trust, loyalty, and long-term relationships, ultimately driving business success. Sub-brands that authentically reflect cultural or regional identities differentiate themselves in the market and create a strong emotional bond with consumers. By celebrating and respecting local cultures, brands can foster a sense of belonging and relevance, resulting in a meaningful and lasting impact on their target audience.

* * *

Conclusion

Sub-branding is a powerful brand strategy that allows companies to diversify their offerings, reach new audiences, and strengthen their overall brand presence. By developing sub-brands, companies can create targeted and focused identities that cater to specific market segments, industries, or consumer preferences.

The various sub-branding strategies discussed in this book offer valuable insights into how companies can effectively implement sub-brands to achieve their business objectives. Whether it's targeting health and wellness, establishing expertise, promoting ethical sourcing, resonating with specific generations, or aligning with cultural or regional identities, each strategy brings unique benefits and opportunities.

Successful sub-branding requires careful consideration of factors such as market research, brand coherence, differentiation, marketing and communication, and leveraging brand equity. Maintaining a strong connection between the sub-brands and the core brand is crucial while ensuring that each sub-brand has its own distinct positioning and value proposition.

By implementing effective sub-branding strategies, companies can enhance their brand positioning, expand their customer base, build customer loyalty, and drive innovation within their brand portfolio. Sub-brands have the potential to unlock new growth opportunities, increase market share, and create a meaningful and authentic connection with consumers.

We hope that this playbook has not only expanded your knowledge of sub-branding but also sparked your imagination and inspired you to take bold steps towards targeted growth. Armed with the strategies presented within these pages, you now possess the ability to create sub-brands that captivate your audience, differentiate your offerings, and drive long-term business success.

Remember, the journey does not end here. As the business landscape continues to evolve, sub-branding will remain a vital tool in navigating the ever-changing tides of consumer preferences and market dynamics. Embrace this dynamic discipline, experiment, and adapt to the needs of your target audience. Your brand's growth potential knows no bounds.

Thank you for accompanying us on this enlightening journey through the world of sub-branding. Now, it's time to unleash your creativity, apply the knowledge you have gained, and embark on your own sub-branding adventure. May your brand's success be targeted, your growth exponential, and your impact profound.

Wishing you every success on your sub-branding journey,

Shah Mohammed

* * *

About the Author

Shah Mohammed is an accomplished Business Strategy and design-thinking consultant with a passion for innovation and user-centred design. He is the founder of D-Cube Designs, a leading design consultancy based in Chennai, India. With a Master's degree in Design from IIT Kanpur, India, which he obtained in 2004, Shah brings a strong academic background and a wealth of practical experience to his work.

As an Industrial Designer, Shah has played a pivotal role in successfully developing and launching over 300 products across various industries over the past decade. His expertise spans the entire product lifecycle, from conducting in-depth user research to designing intuitive and aesthetically pleasing solutions. Shah's keen understanding of customer needs and his ability to translate them into innovative product designs have earned him a reputation for excellence in the industry.

In addition to his contributions to the field of design, Shah has also established himself as a sought-after Business Strategy consultant. Leveraging his customer-centric approach, he has provided valuable insights and guidance to businesses of all sizes, helping them identify market opportunities, develop effective strategies, and drive growth. His expertise in areas such as branding, emotional branding, creativity techniques, leadership, and building competitive advantages has made him a trusted advisor to CEOs, startup founders, and aspiring entrepreneurs.

Shah is an avid blogger and has been sharing his knowledge and insights through his blog for the past six years. With over three hundred articles covering a wide range of topics, including Branding lessons, Design Thinking, Business Strategy, and Psychology in Business, his blog has become a valuable resource for professionals seeking practical advice and inspiration. The case studies featured in this book are a curated selection of some of his most impactful blogs, offering readers timeless lessons and actionable strategies.

You can connect with me on:

- https://shahmm.medium.com
- https://twitter.com/shahbaba
- https://www.linkedin.com/in/shahmm

Also by Shah Mohammed

Books on Business Strategy

Boil The Ocean: The Story of World's Amazing Brands
Embark on a captivating journey through the world of iconic brands with "Boil The Ocean: The Story of World's Amazing Brands." This thought-provoking book offers a collection of insightful case studies that delve into the successes, failures, and transformative moments of some of the most renowned brands in history.

With meticulous research and captivating storytelling, "Boil The Ocean" offers valuable insights, timeless lessons, and inspiring narratives that will engage both business enthusiasts and casual readers. Whether you are an entrepreneur, marketer, designer, brand strategist, startup owner, CEO, brand consultant, or simply intrigued by the stories behind the brands we know and love, this book will leave you inspired, informed, and eager to explore the dynamic world of branding and business.

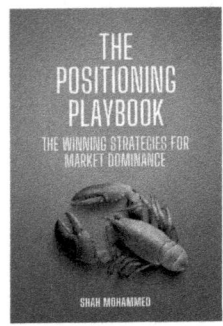

The Positioning Playbook: The Winning Strategies for Market Dominance

Unlock the secrets to market supremacy with "The Positioning Playbook: The Winning Strategies for Market Dominance." This comprehensive guide dives into the art and science of strategic positioning, revealing the proven strategies that will set your business apart from the competition and propel you to the top of your industry.

Discover the power of positioning, going beyond superficial branding and slogans, to create a deep and lasting impact on your target audience. Learn how to carve out a distinct space in consumers' minds, forging emotional connections and delivering unique value that resonates with their needs and desires.

Throughout the book, readers are introduced to thirteen effective positioning strategies, each serving as a pathway to achieving market dominance and sustainable success.